THE **COMPLETE**
HANDBOOK OF
novel
writing

THE **COMPLETE** HANDBOOK OF novel writing

Everything you need to know
about creating & selling your work

MEG LEDER, JACK HEFFRON, AND THE EDITORS OF WRITER'S DIGEST

WRITER'S DIGEST BOOKS
Cincinnati, Ohio
http://www.writersdigest.com

The Complete Handbook of Novel Writing Copyright © 2002 by Writer's Digest Books. Manufactured in the United States of America. All rights reserved. No part of this book may be reproduced in any form or by any electronic or mechanical means including information storage and retrieval systems without permission in writing from the publisher, except by a reviewer, who may quote brief passages in a review. Published by Writer's Digest Books, an imprint of F&W Publication, Inc., 4700 East Galbraith Road, Cincinnati, OH 45236. (800) 289-0963. First edition.

Visit our Web site at www.writersdigest.com for information on more resources for writers.

To receive a free weekly e-mail newsletter delivering tips and updates about writing and about Writer's Digest products, register directly at our Web site at http://newsletters.fwpublications.com.

06   05   04   03   5   4   3   2

Library of Congress Cataloging-in-Publication Data

  The complete handbook of novel writing / edited by Meg Leder, Jack Heffron, and the editors of Writer's Digest.
      p.   cm.
  Includes index.
  ISBN 1-58297-160-9 (hc : alk. paper)—ISBN 1-58297-159-5 (pbk : alk. paper)
  1. Fiction—Authorship—Handbooks, manuals, etc. I. Leder, Meg. II. Heffron, Jack. III. Writer's Digest Books (Firm)

PN3365.C65   2002
808.3—dc21   2002024969
                                                                        CIP

Designed by Mary Barnes Clark
Cover by Brian Roeth

Permissions

"The Philosophy of Plot" copyright © by James N. Frey. Originally appeared in *Writer's Digest*, February 1996. Used with permission of the author.

"The Plot Thickens" copyright © by Monica Wood. Originally appeared in *Writer's Digest*, January 1999. Used with permission of the author.

"What I Stole From the Movies" copyright © by Les Standiford. Originally appeared in *Writer's Digest*, August 1998. Used with permission of the author.

"The Fifty-Page Dash" copyright © by David King. Originally appeared in *Writer's Digest*, February 1999. Used with permission of the author.

"Find Your Novel's Missing Links" copyright © by Elizabeth Lyon. Originally appeared in *Writer's Digest*, July 1996. Used with permission of the author.

"Don't Conclude the Plot . . . Nail the Landing" copyright © by Michael Orlofsky. Originally appeared in *Fiction Writer*, Spring 1997. Used with permission of the author.

"Who's Afraid of Point of View?" copyright © 2001 by Sherri Szeman. Excerpted from *Mastering Point of View*, Writer's Digest Books.

"Creating Four-Dimensional Characters" copyright © by Stephanie Kay Bendel. Originally appeared in *Novel & Short Story Writer's Market 1995*. Used with permission of the author.

"Seven Tools for Talk" copyright © by James Scott Bell. Originally appeared in *Guide to Writing Fiction Today*, 2001. Used with permission of the author.

"Mastering Fiction's First Rule" copyright © by Jack M. Bickham. From *Getting Started in Writing*. Used with permission of the author's estate.

"What Your Story *Says*" copyright © by Nancy Kress. Originally appeared in *Fiction Writer*, Spring 1997. Used with permission of the author.

"Killer-Diller Details Bring Fiction to Life" copyright © by Donna Levin. Excerpted from *Get That Novel Written*, Writer's Digest Books.

"Sense and Sensuality" copyright © by Janet Fitch. Originally appeared in *Fiction Writer*, April 2000. Used with permission of the author.

"Why True-Life Stories Often Don't Make Good Fiction" copyright © by Alyce Miller. Originally appeared in *Novel & Short Story Writer's Market 1995*. Used with permission of the author.

"Fiction's Connecting Link: Emotion" copyright © by Kathy Jacobson. Originally appeared in *Novel & Short Story Writer's Market 1997*. Used with permission of the author.

"Location, Location, Location: Depicting Character Through Place" copyright © by Richard Russo. Excerpted from *Creating Fiction, Inspiration and Insight From Members of the Associated Writing Programs*, Story Press. Used with permission of the author.

"The More and Less of Writing Humorous Fiction" copyright © by Connie Willis. Originally appeared in *Writer's Digest* March 1996. Used with permission of the author.

"How to Start" copyright © by Ann Collette. Originally appeared in *Fiction Writer*, October 1999. Used with permission of the author.

"The Use of the Journal in Writing a Novel" copyright © by Sue Grafton. Ex-

Table of Contents

Introduction

The benefits of attending a writing group, creative writing class, or writers conference are numerous and tangible: You learn about the craft, receive helpful feedback on your novel, hear words that inspire, and make professional contacts. But perhaps one of the best things about participating in one of these groups is, quite simply, being around people who *like* to talk about writing.

The woman sitting next to you relates how she was surprised (and delighted) when, mid-story, her character's personality developed in ways she didn't expect. Another person tells you about the town of Boone, North Carolina, and how, after vacationing there, he knew he found the perfect locale for his novel. Your writing group is quick to share solutions for writers block: washing dishes, journaling, pottery, rewriting the scene from a different point of view. And then there are your teachers or mentors who share their love of the books that shaped their writing style.

As you encounter these voices, you start to think about your own writing. (We writers are, after all, inherently selfish—everything comes back to our *own* words.) You wonder about your protagonist—will he do something surprising? You imagine how changing the setting for your novel might jumpstart it out of its current staleness. You think about books that fell into your path when you needed them, how their stories rang true with you, and how you want to give that feeling to readers of your own.

Listening to people talk about writing gives you ways to grow your own writing. We've collected the best of these voices for you in the pages of *The Complete Handbook of Novel Writing*. Inside, you'll hear from a spectrum of bestsellers, teachers, editors, and agents talking about writing. Through their words, you'll discover the momentum to create and grow your own novels.

In Part One: The Craft, you'll find articles about developing the basics of fiction and improving your technique, on topics ranging from creating a plot that moves to selecting the right point of view for your novel. In Part Two: The Art, you'll read pieces from authors who look beyond the elements of craft in order to help you create a voice and sensibility that's all your own. Part Three: The Process examines the practical aspects of the writing process: getting started, using a journal to help develop your novel, dealing with writers block, and revising successfully. Part Four: The Genres contains sound writing advice for those of you who want to write (or already do write) romance, science fiction, fantasy, mystery, thriller, or inspirational novels. In Part Five: The Marketplace, you'll find practical instruction on the business of getting published, with information on topics such as finding an agent and marketing your novel. And in Part Six: The Interviews, you'll be immersed in the words of some of today's finest writers, who can serve as your personal mentors, as they talk about their books and the challenges and joys of the writing life.

As you're reading *The Complete Handbook of Novel Writing,* listen to the words of these amazing writers. Let them sink in, and let them inspire your *own* writing.

—Meg Leder

The Craft

The Philosophy of Plot

By James N. Frey

Fiction writers come up with some interesting metaphors when speaking of plot. Some say the plot is the highway and the characters are the automobiles. Others talk about stories that are "plot-driven," as if the plot were neither the highway nor the automobile, but the chauffeur. Others seem to have plot phobia and say they *never* plot. Still others turn up their noses at the very notion, as if there's something artificial, fraudulent, contrived.

Metaphors aside, readers and critics also say strange things about plot. They'll say a work of fiction is "*tightly* plotted," or "*strongly or weakly* plotted," or that a story "has too much plot," as if plot were the sort of spice that requires just the right amount. How much is too much?

It's said that some plots stink, and that others are tortured, feeble, confused, boring, or trite.

Fiction writers sometimes speak of character and plot as if they were in opposition to each other. They'll say that they think of their stories as being "70 percent character and 30 percent plot." But how can that be, when a plot is really nothing more than a recap of what the characters do? If the characters do nothing, if they're just sitting there being characters, there isn't a plot at all.

Talking about plot in the abstract, separated from character, is rather like talking about the *pretty* separated from the *maid*. A plot, of course, is not *only* a recap of what characters do. If it were, then a recap of my day thus far would be a plot:

> I got up. I read the *San Francisco Chronicle* while the water boiled for coffee. I kissed my wife good-bye as she hurried off to work. I ate a bowl of bran cereal. I did twenty minutes on my exercise bike while I watched part of a tape of *Damn the Defiant*! I took a shower. I wrote a little on "The Philosophy of Plot." I met a friend for lunch. We both had vegetarian lasagna.

This isn't a plot because the actions of the characters have no significance. What gives significance to actions is taking them toward the resolution of some kind of predicament the character is facing. The predicaments fictional characters might face are infinite in their variety, from trying to light a lifesaving fire with just a few matches, to finding who killed Roger Axelrod, to coming to terms with some inner devil such as self-hatred, loneliness, or the silence of the gods.

All plotted works of fiction are not born equal. Some are intended to be more entertainments, and others are intended to be serious works of art that attempt to shed some light on the insanity of the human condition—or to point out that there is no light to shed and we might as well stop whining about it. But, in all of these stories, the plot is what the characters do in overcoming obstacles in a progression toward a resolution.

Entertaining Plots

In entertainments, the characters tend to face problems that most flesh-and-blood people would never encounter. In an entertainment, a character might find a dead body in the trunk of his car, or be caught in an intergalactic war on Zorgon, or be skewered with Cupid's arrow.

Entertainment plots are largely determined by the conventions of the genre. A detective must unmask a killer. A detective must care who killed Roger Axelrod. In a Western, the heroic marshal can't decide to retire to the Bahamas. In a romance, the heroine doesn't decide to give up on the guy and become a nun.

Furthermore, the characters are engaged in accomplishing specific and concrete goals. The intrepid detective pursues the goal of unmasking the murderer, no matter how many knocks on the head he or she receives. What the characters do—those actions that constitute the plot—are somewhat predictable. The surprises, the originality, the creativity, come in the way in which the goals are accomplished. When James Bond sets out to stop Dr. No from incinerating all the major metropolitan centers of the world with his diamond laser in the sky, the reader knows what the outcome will be; it's the clever and inventive way the demise of Dr. No is accomplished that matters.

A fiction writer plotting entertainments, then, is charged with finding a *mission* for each of the major characters, both heroes and villains, making their motives believable, and seeing to it that they carry out their mission in clever, determined, and resourceful ways. The mission might be to fall in love, to commit a murder, to steal some jewels—virtually anything that'll result in the appropriate actions.

The opposing missions of the various characters create the plot. The best writers of entertainments think of fresh and original ways for these missions to be carried out. Plot, then, for the author of an entertainment, is a matter of playing a game of chess with an alter ego, always asking what clever and resourceful, surprising, yet believable thing this character will do next. And then asking how the character's antagonists will react. In the end there's often a climactic duel—James Bond dumps

Dr. No in a fish tank full of sharks, or the like. Something deliciously, poetically just.

Plotting the Serious Work

Melodramatic derring-do is not remotely related to the plot of a serious work of fiction. In serious fiction, what matters is character development. Take, for example, *Zorba the Greek*, the story of the free-spirited Zorba, who lives for wine, women, and song, and converts his "Boss," the narrator of the story, a rather uptight bookworm, to a life of passion. In *Zorba the Greek*, the Boss's bookworminess is the predicament he's in—he's so trapped he cannot give free rein to his passions. The plot of *Zorba the Greek* is the progress toward the resolution of that predicament, which is the Boss's development.

In *The Red Badge of Courage*, the hero, Henry Fleming, is at first a coward in battle. That is his predicament. He must find his courage. That's *his* development.

It has been eighty-four days since he caught a fish, and the other fishermen have started thinking Santiago, the hero of Hemingway's *The Old Man and the Sea*, is finished. On the eighty-fifth day, Santiago rows out into the deepest part of the Gulf Stream. He's not only after a fish, he's after the reclaiming of his manhood. He succeeds, and that's his development.

In a detective story, the hero often has no development. Hercule Poirot is pretty much the same from beginning to end of a particular novel; he merely changes in the way he perceives things. Popular action heroes such as James Bond, Dirk Pitt, or Captain Kirk don't develop much either; they're pretty much the same beginning to end, from book to book. But in a more serious work of dramatic fiction, the characters do change, often profoundly.

Scrooge in *A Christmas Carol* turns from unrepentant miser to generous celebrant; Charlie Allnut in *The African Queen* changes from a drunken sot to a responsible husband. Fred C.

Dobbs in B. Traven's *The Treasure of the Sierra Madre* is changed from a rather likable, down-and-out tramp to a greedy paranoiac by his lust for gold.

Well-plotted, serious dramatic fiction is transformational by its very nature. The vicarious experience of this transformation is the most important reason people read serious fiction. A plot isn't just a matter of one thing happening after another; it's the progress toward the resolution of a predicament that transforms the character.

Plotting is further complicated by the problem of time.

Say we invent a protagonist, Fred Fix, for a story called "Guess What Happened at the 7-Eleven?" Here's the plot:

> Fred goes to work late one morning and his boss fires him. Because he's fired, he falls into despair. He drinks. He drags himself home at 3:30 the next morning. His wife is frantic. What will they do without money? She weeps bitterly, threatens to leave him. Fred decides to rob a 7-Eleven. . . .

This story follows a *plot line*. In a plot line, everything that happens leads directly to the next. Such plots are often considered to be *tightly woven*. This is a very powerful way to tell a story because, as the story gains momentum, the tensions are not dissipated through gaps in time. Each event folds into the next.

Most entertainments—romances, thrillers, detective stories, Hollywood films—as well as many classics (*The Red Badge of Courage, The Old Man and the Sea, Native Son, Of Mice and Men*, and hundreds more) are plot line stories.

But others are not, such as *Moby Dick*, which covers many months and has a *story line*. In a story line, the events of the story are not causally related to one another but, rather, are part of the same chain of events that are progressing toward resolution.

Les Miserables is told in a story line covering decades. So are

Gone With the Wind, The Autobiography of Miss Jane Pittman, and *Moll Flanders*. In a story line, the character development may be greater because the characters are not only changing as a result of the actions they're taking, but they're growing older as well. A story line is more difficult to handle because the emotions of the characters tend to evaporate over time between the events of the plot. It's difficult to believe, for example, that the flames of passion can still burn after twenty years.

It is possible to combine a story line and plot line in the same work. Usually the story line comes first, serving as a background to the plot line, but not always. In *Zorba the Greek*, for example, the first 90 percent or so of the story that takes place on Crete has a tightly woven plot line. The last chapter, the remaining 10 percent or so, relates Zorba's life of many years after he leaves Crete. The plot line becomes a story line.

Overcoming Plot Problems

At one time or another, all writers—beginners and seasoned professionals, big talents and bad hacks—seem to have problems plotting. The most common problem is that the characters refuse to do what the author has planned for them. Whatever the author does to straighten this out, whatever action she pushes the characters to take, just doesn't seem right. The old sheriff won't strap on his gun as he's supposed to. The heroine won't go up to the hero's loft to see his etchings. The knight in shining armor won't enter the cave and do battle with the dragon.

This problem occurs because the author often identifies too strongly with the protagonist. The author is thinking of how the author would handle this problem, not how the character would handle the problem. The author is plotting her own story, not the character's story.

Frequently, however, characters lie dead on the page not because the author is pushing them to do what is not in them, but because they aren't well orchestrated. Plot arises out of opposing forces—forces that come out of the characters. One of the reasons *Leave It to Beaver* is the butt of so many jokes is that the characters, especially Mr. and Mrs. Cleaver, are badly orchestrated. Mr. and Mrs. Cleaver share the same values, opinions, hopes, and dreams. They're both perfect embodiments of their sterile, suburban, middle-class background. Since they're identical in every way, they're never in conflict with one another. Their bland sameness is stultifying. It's only the obnoxious sociopathic Eddie Haskell who rescues the TV series from the pit of total boredom.

All good plots come from well-orchestrated characters pitted against one another in a conflict of wills. The "Boss" and Zorba, Santiago and the marlin, Scrooge and Bob Cratchit are all well-orchestrated pairs, which by their natures will push the plot forward toward resolution.

If *The African Queen* had focused on *two* old sots in that

Six Tips for Plotting

All good plots, whether for serious fiction or for entertainments, result from dramatic characters who are on fire to obtain goals and who work like hell to achieve them. Avoid at all costs creating a major character who will not or can not act. As you write, keep in mind the following:

• **Chart each major character's development through the actions.** Naturally, the development is not set in concrete. As you draft your story, the development of a character may change, but it helps if you have a broad idea of what the character's transformation will be, say, from a morally rigid old matron to a fevered gambling addict (such as Tarasevitcheva in Dostoevsky's *The Gambler*).

continued

• **In a work of entertainment, chart each major character's actions and indicate his or her motivations.** Make sure each is being as clever and resourceful as possible.

• **Spend some time brainstorming.** Make lists of what the character *might* do. Allow yourself to be outrageous: Don't judge the ideas; just write them down as fast as they come to you. Some will be gold, the rest you toss.

• **Conduct interviews with your characters or write diaries in their voices.** This will help you avoid trying to make characters act in a situation the way you, the author, would act. Probe their feelings and motives, and you will soon know what they would do, not what you would have them do.

• **Follow the "Would he really?" test for believability.** Nothing stops readers faster than a character taking actions that are out of character. Often, if a character's actions seem to fail this test, you can remedy the situation by giving the reader clues as to all the facets of the character. A small brash act early in the story, for example, will establish that a character could act brashly in a large way later.

• **Make sure your characters are well orchestrated.** Avoid pairing up a grizzled old cowhand with another grizzled old cowhand. Better to pair him up with a pregnant young woman or a cocky young gunfighter or a one thousand-year-old space alien. Coldly look at your characters and make sure they are in sharp contrast to one another. Pair a refined, sweet, naive, young ballerina with an older, bookish Talmudic scholar or, perhaps, a vulgar male construction worker or a crafty, preteen pool shark or an aging, thrill-seeking race car driver. If you're confining your story to the world of ballet, you might still achieve good orchestration by pairing your sweet, naive, refined young ballet dancer with an old, sour, burned-out, cynical, former prima donna.

rickety old boat, it would have been nothing more than a bug-infested adventure yarn. But when the uptight, straitlaced, Bible-thumping Rose is pitted against the old sot Charlie All-nut, you have fireworks in every line.

If, at the earliest stages of a work, the author creates the characters as strikingly different from one another as possible, plotting problems will be minimized. Say you're writing about a streetwise kid. Why not have him hide out from the law in a retirement home? Maybe you want to write about a high-powered woman lawyer in her forties. Why not have her fall in love with a twenty-six-year-old ski bum? That's good orchestration.

When you start with well-orchestrated characters, the plot often begins to unfold automatically. Once the characters are pitted against one another, the author needs only to present the predicament to send the characters on their mission. It is in working through the mission that the plot comes alive.

If what the characters do is true to their motivations and personalities and in keeping with their mission, the plot that emerges will not be artificial, fraudulent, or contrived, tortured, feeble, or weak. It will be tight and true to the characters and will have no falsity in it. Creating the plot from a set of well-orchestrated characters is one of the truly creative aspects of the fiction writer's craft. It is an art in itself, the practice of which is one of the great joys of writing.

JAMES N. FREY is an Edgar Award nominee and novelist. His nonfiction works include *How to Write a Damn Good Novel, How to Write a Damn Good Novel II: Advanced Techniques,* and *The Key: How to Write Damn Good Fiction Using the Power of Myth.*

Chapter 2

The Plot Thickens

By Monica Wood

Every good story needs a complication. We learn this fiction-writing fundamental in courses and workshops, by reading a lot or, most painfully, through our own abandoned story drafts. After writing twenty pages about a harmonious family picnic, say, or a well-received rock concert, we discover that a story without a complication flounders, no matter how lovely the prose. A story needs a point of departure, a place from which the character can discover something, transform himself, realize a truth, reject a truth, right a wrong, make a mistake, come to terms.

This point of departure is the story's complication. The dog must get lost. The father must have a heart attack. The sound equipment must break down. The rock star's boyfriend must show up in a rage. A good complication engages the reader, gets the story going, and forms the beginning of a dramatic arc that will lead eventually to the story's conclusion.

Despite being a story's most critical structural element, the complication is often misunderstood, even by writers versed in the fundamentals of storytelling. Armed with the knowledge that a complication is necessary to good fiction, many of us make the mistake of thinking that if an event is exciting enough—an earthquake, a hurricane, a nine-car pileup on the interstate—it constitutes a good complication. This assumption is reasonable enough, but not necessarily true.

Complication Versus Situation

Let's say you're writing a story about a lowly clerk laboring at a nine-to-five job at the Internal Revenue Service. All you have so far is a vague idea of this character: You picture his rumpled shirt, his dirty eyeglasses, his old shoes. You place him in a second-hand Pontiac driving home from work. In other words, you have created a setup: A regular Joe in a dull job heading home. Now what? Something must happen. Enter the nine-car pileup on the interstate. The lowly IRS clerk pulls his car over and gets out. People are screaming, a baby is crying, doors are slamming, engine fires are breaking out; every few minutes our clerk cringes at the squealing brakes of other cars trying to avoid collision.

This is a pretty exciting predicament, filled with sounds and textures and high drama. The story is cooking on all four burners now. The nine-car pileup is a stroke of genius, a textbook complication, right? Wrong. You have made the very common early-draft error of mistaking a situation for a complication.

It's often hard to determine, especially in early drafts, whether or not a story has a bona fide complication. Remember this: A complication must either illuminate, thwart, or alter what the character wants. A good complication puts emotional pressure on a character, prompting that character not only to act, but to *act with purpose*. If the circumstance does none of these things, then it's not a complication at all—it's a situation. This situation, or setup, might be interesting or even astonishing, but it gives the story no point of departure. The character has no compelling motivation to act any differently from anyone else in the same circumstances. We learn nothing about him that we don't already know in general. Putting a character in a situation without adding a complication is like putting him on a hamster wheel—he might run fast, but he gets nowhere, and neither does your story.

Let's go back to the IRS clerk. As the story stands, he can respond in one of two ways to the so-called complication you have put in his way. He can sit in his car and wait till the cops clear the accident scene, or he can get out and start helping people. If he sits in his car feeling bad about himself, there isn't much more you can do with him. If he starts saving people and feels good about himself, the story might be a tad more interesting, but still won't go far. We won't learn much about him because he's not acting—he's reacting. He has nothing at stake, nothing to make this terrible accident anything more than a terrible accident. He might pull some people from a burning back seat or give CPR to a kid on the road, but he's still on the hamster wheel.

Good complications are connected to character—they usually stir some kind of desire or regret, conscious or unconscious, in the character. How can you complicate this situation—a clerk coming upon a pileup—by connecting it to desire or regret within the character? What if the clerk had lost a son in an accidental drowning on a father-son fishing trip? Suddenly this new accident becomes more personal, and the clerk must act with purpose. He has a motivation that's bigger than that of an ordinary bystander helping at the scene. He tries to save as many people as he can, seeking to make up for not having saved his son. The drowning, not the interstate accident, is the complication in this story. The clerk now has something at stake. He must act upon that stake, and his actions illuminate both his desire (to resurrect his son) and his regret (that he could not save his son from drowning).

Now the story has a point of departure: We can learn all about the clerk's inner life by watching him act out the scenario he wishes he could have acted out when his son was in jeopardy. Certain sounds, voices, and faces can recall to him all the tragic aspects of that fateful fishing trip. Upon the stage of this traffic accident, this character can replay the most important event of his life and reveal to us who he is.

Let's apply a different complication to the same situation.

What if the clerk recognizes one of the burning cars as belonging to his worst enemy, a supervisor who cooked the books and then blamed him, resulting in his demotion? When he gets to the car, he finds his enemy's wife and kids trapped inside. The wife and kids, not the accident itself, are the story's complication. Again, the complication personalizes the situation: The clerk can save the wife and kids and use the rescue as his trump card, perhaps a way to get his old job back. It illuminates the character's desire for one-upmanship.

Or maybe you decide on a complication that offers the clerk an opportunity for personal redemption. The wife and kids force him to admit that his enemy is a human being with human connections. In this case, the complication thwarts the character's desire to make his enemy suffer.

In both the drowning example and the wife-and-kids example, the complication provides the story with a point of departure —a way to discover what makes this character tick. Paradoxically, it's often the more subtle, internal elements that complicate a story. The larger predicaments become the stage on which these internal complications are played out.

Telling the Difference

How do you tell the difference between a true complication and a mere situation? Experience helps. Try the following examples, asking yourself if each contains a complication that offers a point of departure, or merely a situation that places the character on a hamster wheel. In each example, I have included what the character wants.

> 1. Ralph's beloved wife is terminally ill. The complication is that she asks him to write her will. (What Ralph wants is to avoid facing the rest of his life alone.)

2. After eight years, a runaway teenager, now a young woman, returns to her parents' house. The complication is that her parents have moved and another family now lives there. (What the runaway wants is to be part of her family again.)

Of these examples, only the second meets the requirements of a complication. In the first, Ralph can write the will, feel sad about it, have a quiet moment with his wife, and that's about it. It's a situation fraught with sadness and maybe even a bit of tension, but it contains no point of departure. But what if the wife includes instructions for her funeral, which she envisions as a block party with a rock band playing "Stairway to Heaven"? This leaves shy Ralph with quite a burden—to contact his neighbors, find a band, and so on—and a vibrant, comical stage on which to play out his impending grief. If what Ralph wants is to avoid facing his life alone, then the complication has the potential to illuminate this desire, or alter it, by forcing him into contact with other people.

In the second example, the new homeowners create an instant dilemma for the runaway. She can either search for her parents or try to insinuate herself into the family that's living in her parents' house. The new family is indeed a complication, for it forces the character to act. If what she wants is to be part of a family, this complication can either thwart (her parents have moved away), alter (she decides against finding them, preferring the new family), or illuminate (she'll take any family, not necessarily the one she lost) her desire.

Raising the Stakes

Now that we have two examples that contain complications, let's determine whether they are good complications. As we saw in the opening example of the IRS clerk, a good complication should raise the stakes for the character. Do the preceding examples meet that criterion?

1. If Ralph is asked to write his wife's will, he has a stake in the sense that the will reminds him of his wife's imminent death. But a story about a man writing his wife's will provides no opportunity for the stakes to change. By adding a good complication (the eccentric terms of the will), we raise the stakes for Ralph. Suddenly he has to face not only death, but also life (hiring a band, meeting the neighbors), which he is even more frightened of.

2. The runaway teen who finds a new family in her old house is a good example of a complication. The stakes rise instantly for this character because the complication reverses her position. Instead of playing the prodigal daughter, she has been thrust into the position of searcher, which is the very position she put her parents in eight years ago.

Thickening the Plot

So far, so good. Both complications raise the stakes for the character. But a good complication should also open pathways to a further complication. Let's test our examples:

1. The eccentric terms of the will open not only one path to Ralph, but several. He could find a band to hire and discover a whole new world of music and youth; he could meet a neighbor on the block who turns out to be an acquaintance from high school; he could discover unknown facts about his wife through the neighbors.

2. The missing parents is a complication that also opens up several paths. The runaway could sit down with the new homeowners and work her way in, trying to turn strangers into substitute parents; she could discover things about her parents by conducting a search—maybe they went broke trying to find her or had another baby to replace her.

A well-chosen complication should give you choices. Juggling choices for your characters is what makes writing fun, after all. If you discover that you're struggling more than you ought to with a draft, perhaps you've run out of interesting choices, or have given yourself too few choices to begin with. Go back to the complication, fatten it up, and start over.

Sustaining Dramatic Tension

Besides raising the stakes and thickening the plot, a complication should create and sustain dramatic tension throughout the story. Do our examples pass the "dramatic tension" test?

1. The eccentric terms of the will could create conflict between Ralph and his wife. As Ralph tries to complete the tasks before him, each offers Ralph new drama and new possibilities for discovering something (either good or bad) about his wife or himself—in short, more tension.

2. A runaway returning to a set of strangers is dramatic all by itself. The tension can be sustained or increased depending on the reaction of the new homeowners. Perhaps they try to help the runaway more than she wants; maybe the runaway realizes that the new homeowners have themselves lost a child and

see her as a miraculous replacement; or the tension could increase as the runaway conducts her search and discovers unwanted or shocking information about her parents.

The Story's Weight

As you can see, your story's complication serves a variety of functions. Even if it fulfills these functions adequately, however, the complication still may not be strong enough to hold up the weight of the story. You have to take a hard look at the complication and decide whether it can carry the number of pages you're planning.

For example, a simple complication—a man loses his job—might carry a very short story of four to eight pages. For a longer story—up to twelve pages—the complication should be more complex: A man loses his job, so his wife kicks him out of the house. For a still longer story, we need a complication that can lead further: A man loses his job, gets kicked out of the house, and, in a fit of despair and nostalgia, goes searching for his long-lost high school sweetheart. This kind of complication can hold up twenty-five or thirty pages for it can lead almost anywhere: The sweetheart can turn out to be dead, or a prostitute, or a CEO in a company owned by the one that just fired him. The wife can chase after her husband once she sees what he's up to, or she can serve him with divorce papers. The choices are many—and the more choices, the more pages the story can credibly sustain.

Internal and External Complications

Complications can spring from internal factors, from things within your character, or from external developments. The IRS clerk, for example, has an internal complication—the memory of his son. The runaway's complication—the parents having moved away—is an external one, an event that has happened outside of her, something she discovers.

Internal complications usually lead to reflection rather than action. Reflective stories are usually short, partly because internal change goes more quickly on the page and partly because reflective stories can try the reader's patience after about ten pages.

External complications typically require more room to play themselves out. The runaway's complication, for instance, demands a lot of action on the part of the character—she must undergo a search, moving from scene to scene as she comes closer to a resolution about her parents' disappearance.

Sometimes it pays to hedge your bets, balancing an internal complication (or a very simple one) with an exciting or unusual situation. In the case of the IRS clerk, the complication is deeply internal, but the situation in which the complication appears—the interstate pileup—is full of action.

Experience will show you how far to take a complication, and how to use it to advance the story, explore character, and engage the reader. The trick is making sure that the complication you have created is a real one in the first place, and provides the hinge on which your story swings open. That's when fiction takes off and when complication turns into fascination for your readers.

MONICA WOOD is the author of two novels, *My Only Story* and *Secret Language*, and a book of connected short stories entitled *Ernie's Ark*. She is also the author of *Pocket Muse: Ideas and Inspirations for Writing*, *Description*, from the Writer's Digest Elements of Fiction series, and several guides to contemporary literature in the high school classroom.

Chapter 3

What I Stole From the Movies

By Les Standiford

Every genre of writing has its essential structural element: poems accrete line by line; nonfiction moves paragraph by paragraph; stories and novels grow scene by scene. That last idea is an important realization for fiction writers, but not necessarily an easy one to make.

For me, the discovery was something of an accident, born of a midlife career detour that took me out of the classroom, where I'd been teaching writing for more than a decade, to Los Angeles, where I became a student again—specifically, a screenwriting fellow at the American Film Institute. I learned plenty about writing for film at AFI, but, as I like to tell my own students nowadays, the most valuable lessons I learned there had to do with the writing of fiction. And particularly the kind of fiction intended to engage the attention of an audience. I was still trying to place my first novel when I began to study screenwriting; a dozen years later, I've published seven, and I credit a large part of this success to techniques I stole from Hollywood.

A Scenic Discovery

The fiction I wrote before my foray westward was typical. Like most other novelists, I made use of the five basic modes of fictional discourse when writing a story: dialogue (*"I love you,"* *she said softly*), action (*She reached across the rumpled sheets to touch the back of his neck*), description (*The motel's clanky air conditioning unit coughed and throbbed in response*), thought (*She wondered for a moment if he'd even heard her*), and exposition (*She'd been in Key Largo for a year now, drawn to the tropics from Detroit by the prospect of meeting a more exciting type of man*).

One of the sad truths I faced as I began writing for the screen was that I could no longer take refuge in exposition or thought, there being no opportunity to use those modes in dramatic writing (with the possible exception of the soliloquy or the voice-over, neither technique being much in filmic vogue these days). Difficult as it was to be deprived of 40 percent of the fiction writer's bag of tricks, I accepted soon enough that anything I wanted to convey about my film characters and story would have to be conveyed dramatically, through description, dialogue, and action alone.

Ultimately, the process brought me to a new appreciation of scene—that dramatic unit of action that features a character or characters speaking/acting/interacting and is delineated by a shift in time or place, or the entrance or exit of a character. The more scenes I wrote for film, the more that style began to creep into my fiction as well. Yet I discovered that far from losing power as a fiction writer, I seemed to be gaining it instead. And I was discovering an entirely new way of propelling my stories forward.

Dirty Harry Meets McDonald's

Let me show you what I discovered.

Assume that as scriptwriters, we've already established a MAN in his thirties pulling into the parking lot of a fast-food restaurant late at night and parking his jalopy toward the back.

In the next scene, we see the employee's entrance door swinging inward with a BANG, our less-than-enthusiastic guy from the jalopy now slogging down the hallway past a locker room, snatching a white coat and paper hat from a hook and moving on into the bowels of the place until he reaches the nook where the take-out station is housed. Our guy notes the time on a wall clock—midnight straight up. He shoos a pimply KID off the stool there, sits down with a sigh. He shrugs his way into the coat, dons the ridiculous hat, adjusts the microphone used to communicate with the customers outside. He notes the pimply kid is watching him. He gives the kid an appraising glance, but there's not much to see. He turns away, closes his eyes for a moment, a pianist about to begin, a diver about to dive. He lets out his breath, opens his eyes, reaches into his coat, withdraws a Dirty-Harry-sized revolver that he clunks down on a shelf just beneath the take-out window. He reaches into another pocket, withdraws a half pint of something, takes a healthy swig. "They didn't say the new security man was gonna be a boozer," the kid says, as our guy slips his bottle back. Our guy thinks about it. "It steadies one's nerves under such tense circumstances," he says mildly, and bangs the flashing red intercom button with the flat of his hand. When we cut outside to a sleek low-rider with heavily smoked windows idling throatily, ominously, by the ordering station, we've moved on to the next scene.

Our scene is a short one, about a page long, amounting to about 1 percent of the typical, one hundred-minute-long contemporary film. If this scene were to stick in our hypothetical film—and said film were to actually be produced and end up costing, let's say, $30 million to make (and that's on the conservative side for a major studio production these days)—then that one-page scene proposed by the writer could be conceived of— in a strange way, admittedly—as a suggestion that someone actually spend about $300,000 to bring that figment of imagination into filmic life.

Let's put it another way: The writer would in fact be suggesting that this one-page scene is worth a cool three hundred grand.

Now, even though it costs a fiction writer virtually nothing to stage a scene on the page, it's my contention that there would be a heck of a lot more effective fiction being written if we all approached the work as if it did. We've all heard the advice: "Use every word you need, but not a single word more." The analogy to the film writer's world gives that principle of economy a brand new shade of meaning. And while dollars have little to do with it, the fiction writer should be asking the same question any capable film producer would ask: "Is this scene truly necessary?" It is the kind of thinking that, put into practice, results in a story with a sense of energy and direction, no handicap so far as editors and readers are concerned.

Making It Worth $300,000

Even without much context, the hypothetical scene above suggests its own reason for being. We are presented with a "security man" whose job it is to protect a burger franchise from the threat of late-night robbers. He's something of a burnout case, but not so far gone that he can't appreciate the tawdriness of his condition. And while he may not be a superhero on the face of it, he clearly poses more of a barrier to thieves than anyone else around. Finally, his very appearance sets up something of an experiment in anticipation for the audience. What would happen if this character had to use that formidable-looking weapon he's just plunked down?

A good scene will do at least one of three things just alluded to:
- enrich character
- provide necessary information to the audience
- move the plot forward

The best scenes do all three. Then there are those scenes that have wormed their way into the story because they have some sweet-sounding sentences (loving description of how those fast-food burgers sizzle and pop on the grill), or provide a glimpse of compelling but extraneous character (the pimply kid's girl-friend who has dropped by to show off her newly pierced tongue, only to leave as our security man enters), or repeat what we have already seen (our security man stops off to buy his half pint on the way to work, making a show of buying a cheap brand of whiskey). These scenes do none of the above and will simply have to go.

Such decisions are easily made in the world where pages are valued at $300,000 and up.

But the priceless principle of economy in fiction should be applied just as rigorously. Long gone are the days when editors had time to pare down mountainous manuscripts to expose the lean, mean stories embedded therein. Modern readers, bombarded by a million requests for their attention, have been conditioned to expect fiction that embeds the Bard's injunction: "More matter, less art."

Thinking in terms of a dramatic scene also makes it more likely that the writer will avoid that age-old bugaboo of the "passive protagonist," that sad sack of a main character who doesn't do much of anything but think or remember or sometimes—kicking and screaming all the way—react to circumstances. While it may be true that most of us, especially us writers, spend our real lives observing, reacting, mulling, and remembering, the most interesting fictional characters are those who get themselves into real jams by doing things.

Never open your story with a character thinking, I advise my students. As a further precaution, don't put a character in a room alone—create a friend, a bystander, a genie, for God's sake, *any* sentient creature with whom your main character can converse, perhaps argue or, better yet, engage in some action. If a person is out and doing, it's more likely that something interesting might happen to her or him. Shut up in a room with only his thoughts for company . . . well, that way lies fictional disaster.

One All-Beef Scene—Hold the Expo

As I've suggested, all scenes can enrich the characters, provide information, and advance the plot without calling on the least dramatic of the five fictional modes: thought and exposition. Were I to convert our Burgerama scene to fiction, I would surely expand it, noting details of our security's man's dress (nothing remarkable, except for the surprisingly good shoes, or maybe a dinged-up but once-expensive watch), his specific brand of whiskey (Early Times? Jack Black? Wild Turkey?), the sights and sounds and smells of the backside of this burger emporium (ah, the grease, the disinfectant, the doomsday clang of that Dumpster). I might possibly extend the moment of meeting and conversation between the security man and pimply kid, but I doubt that I would change the scene's essentially dramatic nature. There's an inherent suspense in revealing our security man's mission in stages. He is transformed bit by bit from just another shzlub piling out of his jalopy to an unlikely employee of the restaurant to a potential agent of justice in one short page.

Were I to allow my readers access to our guy's thoughts as he pulled in the lot (*Exley groaned inwardly as he contemplated the long night of surveillance ahead*), or allude to it directly through exposition as he walks down the hall toward his post at the take-out window (*Exley hadn't wanted this evening's assignment, but his superiors at Acme Security had been adamant*), I would lose something of the suspense I refer to and further vitiate the proceeding by "giving" readers information as opposed to allowing readers to participate in the process of discovery. (This is one of the principal reasons for that time-honored plea of the writing teacher: "Show me, don't tell me.")

Maybe it's because we as writers are alone so often, are so attuned to listening to the run of our thoughts, that we find it more natural to write down the thoughts rather than the deeds of our characters. But speaking as a teacher who has spent some twenty years slogging through manuscripts where thoughts and exposition pile up as thick as the aftermath of a California mudslide, I can attest to the power of the evocative detail, gesture, or fragment of speech. There's much that's implied in our security man's glance, or in his simple response to the kid's criticism of his drinking: "It steadies one's nerves under such tense circumstances."

Just One Scene After Another

By structuring the Burgerama scene in the way that we have, we mirror the way stories as a whole are most profitably structured —with a beginning, middle, and end, each scene or event linked and leading into the next. This linking reminds readers (as well as the writer) that this enterprise is going somewhere. "Ending" the scene decisively also guards against the tendency to drift along, and requires some hard thought about what will happen next.

This naturally prods the writer to imagine a subsequent event that will be in some way more interesting than what has been experienced to date. Who is in that mysterious, rumbling low-rider outside? And what will our security man do if it's who we think it might be? (By the way, Aristotle referred to this phenomenon as "rising action" and promulgated its value for literature long before the advent of wide screens and Dolby surround sound.)

Working scene by scene, the writer finds it easier to move the story along and to jump over extraneous material. If an angry husband throws up his hands in the midst of an argument with his wife and stomps toward the door of his apartment, announcing that he's going out for a drink, there's no need to follow him out the door and down the hall, into the stairwell, down to the street, into his car, and so on. We can simply end the first scene with the slamming of the apartment door and begin the next as our husband signals Charley the bartender for another beer. Readers can easily follow the jump and, once again, be grateful for the author's sense of economy.

Just how much can be skipped? That question gets into larger issues of plot, but let's leave it at this: Skip as much as possible. Get into a scene as late as possible and get out as quickly as you can. Most of today's readers have had considerable exposure to film and are accustomed to making significant jumps. Were we to cut from our security man's post in the bowels of Burgerama to a basement room somewhere and close in on the image of gloved hands jacking a round into the chamber of a shotgun, most viewers—and readers—would understand the connection.

All that's necessary is for readers to see or sense an inexorable flow, a linkage of events, one to the next. The classic illustration is given by E.M. Forster in *Aspects of the Novel*, where he distinguishes between the discontinuous events of a story. (The king died. And then the queen died) and the interconnected events of a plot (The king died. And then the queen died of grief).

There are vast differences between scripts and stories, of course. Few fiction writers would want to give up the opportunity to explore how the minds of their characters work, or to set aside the opportunity to provide necessary background exposition in a succinct fashion.

But even those modes can be enlivened by considering the lessons of artful scene writing: Make those thoughts vivid (*Exley tried to imagine the pimply kid kissing his girlfriend—would her tongue stud get hung up in his braces?*) and be sure any exposition is equally engaging (*Exley had worked the Burgerama stakeout for*

Going Deep

Whether film writers or fiction writers, we're naturally going to be most concerned with what's at the forefront of our attention in any given scene. In the Burgerama scene, if it's the conversation between our security man and the pimply kid that's of prime importance at that moment, then most of our energies as writers will go into making that encounter lively and memorable. But take another scene-enriching tip from Hollywood: Try applying the cinematic practice sometimes referred to as "deep focus."

In our hypothetical film, as the security man and pimply kid spar, the more gifted director or cinematographer might well present something in the background to serve as a subtle counterpoint to the foreground drama. We might see a drunk out in the seating area, trying to get the patty from his burger off the floor and back between the slices of his bun, underscoring the general ennui of the job and our hero's apparent prospects. Or there might be a young girl waiting impatiently for her pimply boyfriend to get off work, checking her newly pierced tongue in a compact mirror.

Anything might work, so long as it is interesting enough to draw us deeper into the scene and is somehow connected to the foreground drama.

a month last year, downing all the burgers, fries, and shakes he wanted. He'd gone from a 33 waist to a 36 and used up two week's salary changing his wardrobe).

Scene Setters

"Steal from everybody," one of my early writing teachers told me. "Take help wherever you can find it." I'm not sure he had Hollywood in mind, but the advice stayed with me anyway.

To help it stay with you, get in the habit of asking yourself a few questions about your scene:

- Is this scene necessary, or am I keeping it around simply because I spent all that time and effort writing it?
- What exactly does it add in terms of character development, necessary information, or plot movement?
- How much of the scene's work can be done by the most dramatic modes of fiction: dialogue, action, and description?
- Have I given my scene its own beginning, middle, and end?
- Is there a place for a background element that might enrich the proceedings?
- Have I gotten in quickly and gotten out as soon as possible?
- What should or would happen next?

Asking yourself these questions at the end, or the beginning, of a day's work will inevitably result in more vivid, energetic, and compelling fiction. I stole the idea from the movies. You can, too.

LES STANDIFORD is director of the Creative Writing Program at Florida International University in Miami. The recipient of the Frank O'Connor Award for Short Fiction and fellowships in fiction from the NEA and the Florida Arts Council, he has published numerous articles and stories. His novels include *Black Mountain* and *Deal With the Dead*.

Chapter 4

The Fifty-Page Dash

By David King

When I asked an agent recently how she decided whether or not to take on a manuscript, she told me she asked for the first fifty pages and read the first sentence. If she liked the first sentence, she read the second. If she liked that one, she read the third, and so on. If she reached the end of the first fifty pages without putting the manuscript down, she signed it up.

Granted, most readers are willing to read your second sentence even if the first one isn't brilliant, but the agent's answer shows the importance of "hook." If you don't grab your readers within, say, your first fifty pages, you won't have them at all. So if you've been gleaning compliments from your writers group and getting good responses to your query letters, but your first fifty pages keep coming back with polite rejections, then you may have a good story that doesn't get started soon enough. If so, it's time to go back to the beginning and start looking for trouble.

Starting the Real Story

Since at least the time of Shakespeare, storytellers have known that leading with a good noisy fight or a ghost was a great way to get the attention of the guys in the cheap seats. Many of my clients open their manuscripts with loud, attention-grabbing scenes. But many of them *became* clients partly because they failed to follow their attention grabber with the actual story. Sometimes that tense, exciting scene at the beginning of chapter one doesn't connect to the real plot until chapter ten.

One recent client opened her story with an army nurse's first day in the blood and mayhem of a field hospital in Vietnam. Unfortunately, the novel was less about the nurse's Vietnam experiences than how those experiences affected her later marriage and motherhood, and we didn't even meet her future husband for another 150 pages. The author solved the problem by opening the next draft with the ex-nurse going into labor for the first time and experiencing a flashback that leaves her huddled under her hospital bed. The maternity ward is less exciting than the field hospital, but the new opening focused less on Vietnam itself and more on how Vietnam affected the nurse, which is where the true story was.

Remember, you want to do more than get your readers' attention in your first fifty pages—you want to draw readers into the story. These opening pages are where you first create the tension that will drive your readers through to the climax. So if you've already opened with an attention-grabbing scene, check back to make sure it also raises the questions that your ending resolves and that the next few scenes enlarge on these questions. If you simply get your readers' attention without doing anything with it, they're bound to resent you and are unlikely to keep reading.

Also, make sure you've made things tough for your main character by the end of your first fifty pages. Your opening scenes may eventually have an impact on the main character, but until the character is actually in trouble, your story hasn't really started.

I recently worked on a medical thriller that opened with a "code"—a team of doctors battling to save a patient, with arcane medications administered in a rush and, ultimately, the shock paddles to the chest. The problem? More than one hundred pages passed before the main character first suspected that another doctor, his old mentor, had practiced euthanasia on the coded patient. So the opening didn't mean anything about this to the readers. I suggested that the author have the doctor feel some doubts about the code immediately after it happened, so readers would realize that the code was actually the beginning of the story.

Finessing the Opening

Of course, some novels are impossible to open with a pertinent attention-grabbing scene. Some murder mysteries have to introduce a number of different suspects before the first body drops. Some romances have to show the couple meeting and getting to know one another before the real tension in the relationship starts. How do you get your readers involved in your story if they need to know a lot of background before the story makes sense?

First, make sure that your readers do, in fact, need to know all the background you're giving them. In the Vietnam novel, readers didn't need to know the nurse's whole story before they saw how it affected her. In fact, discovering what drove her to give birth under her hospital bed rather than on it gave the story an air of mystery that actually increased the tension.

So maybe your readers don't need to know all the details of the con man's real-estate scam before they see his body floating facedown in the pool. They just need to know the scam cost people a lot of money, and you can fill that in during the investigation. Perhaps they don't need to see your lovers meet to understand how things are between them, and you can start the story where each begins to realize the other isn't as perfect as they thought. In short, if your story has a slow beginning, try starting in the middle.

If this won't work, you might want to consider a prologue, where you move part of the middle to the beginning. If you open with a prologue of one of your young lovers attempting suicide, for instance, then your readers will know that the happy relationship they see in chapter one will turn tragic at some point. And if your prologue doesn't make it clear whether or not the suicide succeeds, you give your readers a reason to keep reading.

I once worked on a mystery in which the victim moved into a small town and started throwing money around irresponsibly, creating a lot of anger and greed and making enemies. Since the various motives were pretty intricate (and the detective was also caught up in the victim's financial machinations), it would have been awkward to bring all the details out through flashbacks or during the investigation. The author was essentially saddled with giving the readers 150 pages of story before the detective found a body. A prologue in which the detective found the body solved the problem. To add to the tension, the author didn't identify *whose* body was found—before he dies, the victim drives one or two characters, including the detective's oldest friend, to the point of suicide. Readers were left trying to guess who the body in the woods would turn out to be, and that uncertainty kept them reading until the story caught up with the prologue.

Character and Tension

As with any other plot problem, the best solution to a late-starting story may lie in your characters. An opening that presents sharply drawn and engaging characters may lure readers into the story more quickly than an anonymous bit of adventure. "Call me Ishmael" became a legendary opening line because those three words tell you volumes about who the narrator is and how he feels about his life; you want to find out what kind of story this man has to tell. Sue Grafton's Kinsey Millhone mysteries simply open with Millhone talking to her readers in her charmingly irreverent voice. By the second page of *"G" Is for Gumshoe*, we learn that Millhone cuts her own hair with a nail scissors and, if asked to rate her looks on a scale of one to ten, wouldn't. A character that intriguing leads most readers to keep reading.

Dick Francis is another master of this technique. *Whip Hand*, for instance, opens with a prologue in which the only thing that happens is that an ex-jockey dreams about a race. We don't even learn the man's name, yet the dream shows his deep passion for racing; when he wakes to the realization that he'll never race again, readers share his crushing sense of loss and resignation. The main story starts quickly after that—he is involved in the investigation that is the center of the plot by the end of the first chapter—but readers are hooked from that dream alone.

Of course, most authors get to know their characters as they write them, which means characters are at their most flat and uninteresting in chapter one. But there are a few easy solutions to this problem: One is to simply scrap your first-draft opening and rewrite it once you know who your characters are. Or you could add a prologue that, like the prologue in *Whip Hand*, showcases your main character's personality. Or you could write out the events that happened during the two weeks before your first chapter, so you already know in detail who your characters are before your readers meet them. In any case, you can draw your readers into your story by giving them characters to love from the very beginning.

Laying the Ground Rules

As you rewrite your first fifty pages to start your story with a strong hook and introduce your characters, remember that you're also establishing the ground rules for how you will tell your story. By the end of those fifty pages, your readers should know what genre you're writing in (if any) and what stylistic techniques you'll use, and even have some idea of the metaphysics behind the world you've created. You need to give them a comfortable set of expectations about your mechanics and worldview so they can concentrate on your characters and events. If you later shift those expectations without reason, you run the risk of driving your readers back out of the story.

So if you write from several different points of view, make sure you switch POV at least once early on to let your readers know what to expect. If your world includes occasional magic and miracles, let your readers know such things are possible from the beginning. If the resolution of your story hinges on one particular character, make sure your readers meet that character quickly.

A client once had one of her characters come back as a ghost at the end of the manuscript. Unfortunately, up until that point, her story didn't hint that ghosts were a possibility, so the ghost's appearance shifted her readers into a different sort of universe without any warning. I suggested that the author give the future ghost a mystical bent from the beginning, with occasional premonitions and glimpses of the spirit world. These hints were enough to alert readers that they were in the kind of universe where magic happened.

Of course, there are cases, most often with mysteries, where you can't alert your readers that a given character or plot element is important without giving away your plot twists. One client's manuscript opened with her main character, a corporate lawyer who had just joined the legal team of a major oil company, mourning the apparent suicide of her lover, a researcher for the same company. But because the first few chapters introduced various company managers and showed details of the company's organization, readers knew the company was going to play a role in the plot. It came as no surprise, then, when the

Off to a Fast Start

Study these fast-starting novels to learn how to get your own stories going strong in the first fifty pages:

Nearly anything by Sue Grafton: Her Kinsey Millhone is a wonderfully readable character from word one.

Nearly any by Rex Stout: Archie is a wonderful character, too.

Peter Hoeg's *Smilla's Sense of Snow*: Smilla's reasons for suspecting murder unfold slowly, but they're all out by page fifty and she's interesting long before then.

Stephen King's *Misery*: We're hooked from "I'm in trouble."

Nearly anything by Dick Francis: Always quick out of the gate, with both the story and character well established by the end of chapter one.

Susan Howatch's *Scandalous Risks*: Good use of a frame story to set up what would otherwise be a slow-building tension.

C.J. Cherryh's *The Pride of Chanur*: A human stranded and bleeding in an alien spaceport, and that's just the first scene.

The History of Herodotus: Not strictly fiction, but it's hard to argue with an opening line like, "Those Persians best informed in history say the Phoenicians began the quarrel."

Charles William's *War in Heaven*: Again, a classic opening sentence—"The telephone bell was ringing wildly, but without result, since there was no one in the room but the corpse."

Len Deighton's *Violent Ward*: He doesn't waste any time getting into the story.

E.L. Doctorow's *Billy Bathgate*: Doctorow opens by bringing the cliché of cement overshoes to horrifying life.

Mary Willis Walker's *Under the Beetle's Cellar*: The first sentence gives us Walter Demming; the first two pages give us the horror he's suffering through.

lawyer discovered that her lover was actually murdered because he'd uncovered a conspiracy within the company.

The author had to introduce her readers to the company before she hit them with the truth—plot twists are always more satisfying when there's a sense of the familiar about them. But the company had to have some reason for being in the first fifty pages. She could, for instance, give the lawyer some close friends in the oil company hierarchy, friends who would comfort her over her lover's death. Or the lawyer could deal with her lover's death by throwing herself into her work, which would let the author show the company's organization while readers are watching the lawyer's emotional state. Or the lawyer could suspect that the lover's apparent suicide had something to do with the company—excess tension from overwork, say—and delve into it, only to discover the conspiracy. In any case, the author had to give the company a false reason for appearing so early in the story so readers wouldn't suspect the real reason.

Your readers are willing to take you on faith at the beginning, to invest some effort in learning who your characters are, what your story is about, what your world is like. Pay back their effort quickly. Let them know as early as possible that you're giving them a story, characters, and a world that are worth reading about. If you can do that, then they'll stick around for more than just fifty pages.

DAVID KING is an independent editor who has worked with such authors as Sol Stein, Susan Loesser, and Fran Dorf. He's the co-author of *Self-Editing for Fiction Writers*.

Chapter 5

Find Your Novel's Missing Links

By Elizabeth Lyon

Your novel has all the right ingredients—great characters, an original plot, scintillating imagery. It even has a grabber beginning. But after that, says your critique group or your agent or your significant other, it's about as interesting as the fine print in an insurance policy.

Or perhaps you haven't even finished your manuscript. The first five chapters poured from your fingertips like a fast-flowing river, and you made extensive notes on the ending. Then your inspiration dried up. What went wrong? The middle, that's what. It sits between the beginning and the end, more menacing than a sea of orange highway construction barrels, challenging you to create enough stuff to both advance the plot *and* entertain readers. But how do you get through the middle?

By strategically positioning your novel's plot points to carry readers from start to finish. Every good novel uses obstacles and various small crises to build conflict and suspense. But plot points are bigger than these lesser crises; they are the scenes after which the plot pivots and moves in a different and more suspenseful direction. While any novel will have some form or lesser crisis in nearly every scene, it may have only three to six big scenes that lead up to the biggest scene of all—the climax.

After you've mapped out the essential story, use the five steps described here to make sure your novel moves, from minor crisis to big scene, connecting beginning to end. Together these steps allow you to continually foreshadow ever greater conflict, playing one big scene to the next, stepping up the suspense until you release your readers at the climax, satisfied and eager to read your next book.

Name the Big Scene

Whether your big scene is as sweeping as the destruction of a village by molten lava or as sweet as a first kiss, readers will look forward to it with dread or anticipation only if you alert them to the event's impending arrival. Let your narrative, character conversations, or internal thought speak of the coming big scene—and even name it. In Larry McMurtry's *Lonesome Dove*, Gus, Call, and other characters talk about the first river crossing near the beginning of their cattle drive from Texas to Montana. At first, this coming event sounds as though it won't be very major at all:

> "I want to cross the river as soon as possible." [said Call]
> "It ain't much of a river," Dish said, "I could near jump across it if I had a long-legged horse."

Once you name it, embellish it. This increases the suspense. McMurtry does this a page or two later when he foreshadows some crisis by expressing the men's uneasiness and excitement before the first river crossing:

> "There ain't no point in gettin' too dry," [Pea Eye] pointed out. "We got to cross the river after a while."
> "I'd just as soon go around it," Needle said.
> "I've crossed it many times but I've been lucky."
> "I'll be glad to cross it—maybe I'll get a wash,"

Lippy said. "I can't do much under all this mud."

"Why, that ain't a river, it's just a creek," Dish said. "The last time I crossed it I didn't even notice it. . . ."

"It's just the first of many," Bert said.

"How many rivers is it between here and the Yellowstone?"

Here's another example of naming a coming big scene and embellishing on it to build tension, this time from Orson Scott Card's *Abyss*:

> On that day, it happened that Hurricane Frederick was moving across the Caribbean out of the east-southeast, due to pass over that region of the sea within twenty-four hours.

The hero, Bud Brigman, has a crew working twenty-two miles away, conducting a deep-sea trial from an underwater drilling platform. After Card takes readers through a major crisis of a nuclear-armed submarine sinking, the coming hurricane is talked about in a way that foreshadows trouble. Notice how Card, like McMurtry, signals to readers that this will probably be a major dramatic event:

> "Nothing can stand still in the water during a hurricane," said the President. He had served on a carrier in his youth. . . .
>
> "Right," said the Navy chief.
>
> . . . "The designer allowed for that. If it gets really bad, *Deepcore* [the underwater drilling platform] can cut loose from the umbilical and survive on its own for four days."

Whether the big scene is a river crossing or a hurricane, once the readers can name it, the author has nabbed their curiosity. Will the cowboys get the cattle across the river without a hitch? Will *Deepcore* weather the hurricane, even if it cuts loose?

Often the first meetings of characters become major events worth naming and developing into plot points, such as the first time Dean R. Koontz's characters Travis and Nora meet the beast in *Watchers,* or the first time Michael and Rowan meet in Anne Rice's *The Witching Hour.* Naming the first meeting allows anticipation of it, the same way that everyone anticipates— or dreads—the big scenes of real life (turning-point events such as weddings, reunions, job interviews, or confrontations).

However you do it, don't keep your readers in the dark—this is surprise, not suspense. How different it would be if Little Red Riding Hood arrived at Granny's house without mention of the wolf! His arrival would surprise us, but we'd feel cheated. No chance to savor the anticipation. The only way your readers can salivate over the tasty dish you've planned is if they can visualize it ahead of time and revel in their expectation of how it's going to eventually taste.

Provide a Preview Scene

The movie industry certainly understands the value of sneak previews. Drawing coming attractions from the plot points allows viewers to label them and to want to see the movie. In novels, we can be more subtle in creating previews that mirror big scenes or reflect their essence, signaling readers of what lies ahead.

In *Lonesome Dove,* McMurtry shows the heroes rustling cattle across the Texas border as a preview to the first river crossing. During the drive, a minor character, Sean, falls off his horse and is imperiled by the stampeding herd. This foreshadows his death during the river crossing when he is thrown from his horse and attacked by poisonous snakes.

A preview scene also offers the author a chance to develop

explanations, details, or technicalities that would bog down the heightened drama and pace of a big scene. This preview scene from *Abyss* is dramatic in itself, but it's also packed with background to serve—but not interfere—with a later big scene.

In this scene, a Navy Seal called Monk is sorting through and preparing his specialized equipment when he draws the interest of the crew:

> Hippy made sure he understood every piece of equipment he ever saw.
>
> "What is all this stuff?" [Hippy asked.]
>
> "Fluid breathing system. We just got them. We use it if we need to go really deep."
>
> "How deep?" asked Hippy. . . .
>
> [Monk] couldn't tell him the details, but he could tell him the stuff that was in the library at Duke University. "Anyway, you breathe liquid so you can't be compressed. Pressure doesn't get you as bad. . . . [It's called] Oxygenated fluorocarbon emulsion."
>
> "Bullshit!" said Hippy.

The interaction with Monk and Hippy spans several pages as it fully develops with a goal, conflict, and an unexpected resolution. Readers see Monk grab Hippy's pet rat off his shoulder, put it in a wire box, turn it upside down, and force it into the fluid. While Hippy protests, Monk tries to reassure him:

> "It's okay, I've done this myself." No need to mention that it was probably the most terrifying experience of his life, even though they doped him up a little to help stifle his gag reflex and keep him from thrashing around so much from raw, naked panic as he felt the liquid burn its way into his lungs.

In the rest of the preview scene, readers watch the rat go through its own panic, Hippy's frantic response, and Monk pulling the rat from the liquid. Why all the detail? Astute readers—or a novelist who understands this must be a preview scene—will know that later in the novel, one of the characters will undergo this terror.

Create a Contrasting Scene

You might consider this step in negative/positive or positive/negative terms. If your big scene adds negativity to your characters' lives, then make the scene that precedes it positive, or vice versa. Usually this contrasting scene is short because the author begins to pick up the pace for the plot point that lurks just around the corner.

In *Watchers*, for instance, a big scene has been named in earlier development as the beast is coming. Koontz gives readers horrific previews of the beast's capabilities as it sweeps through a neighborhood and selects one family as its target. We know that somehow, somewhere, the beast and wonder dog Einstein (and his caretakers Travis and Nora) must meet again. So, now it's time for a contrasting scene to the beast's arrival.

Koontz gives several short two-page scenes where the main characters, Travis and Nora, drive to Las Vegas—dog Einstein with them—to get married. In itself, this happy contrasting scene is a big scene for prior subplot development. Here's a touch of the contrasting tone, just before the beast's arrival:

> Sometimes in the morning, sometimes in the late afternoon, more often at night, Nora and Travis made love. She was surprised by her carnal appetite. She could not get enough of him.
>
> "I love your mind and your heart," she told him, "but, God help me, I love your body almost as much! Am I depraved?"

"Good heavens, no. You're just a young, healthy woman."

A few paragraphs later Koontz begins his transition from this joyful consummation of love to the big negative scene:

> Throughout their trip, the joy of matrimony was so all-consuming that the miracle of Einstein's human-like intelligence did not occupy their thoughts as much as previously. But Einstein reminded them of his unique nature when they drew near to Santa Barbara late that afternoon. Forty or fifty miles from home, he grew restless. . . . By the time they were ten miles from home, he was shivering.
>
> "What's wrong with you, fur face?" she asked.
>
> With his expressive brown eyes, Einstein tried hard to convey a complex and important message, but she could not understand him.
>
> Half an hour before dusk, when they reached the city and departed the freeway for surface streets, Einstein began alternately to whine and growl low in his throat.

In contrasting scenes, readers feel the pressure building because something is going to happen. The contrasting scene is the calm before the storm, or the storm before the calm. (Romance novels, for instance, frequently show an argument before a kiss, or a break up before the big love scene.) You may think that your readers might lose interest by knowing exactly what's coming, but attentive readers know the big scene is just a page turn away. Reading the present, contrasting scene builds suspense and is nearly intolerable—it's the moment in the old-time monster movies when an audience member yells, "Don't open that door!"

The Big Scene

When the much-anticipated scene arrives, you must execute your promise in full detail, which means you let your readers share the thoughts and feelings of the point-of-view character, and everything that character smells, tastes, hears, touches, and sees. Make your readers feel what your character feels, whether that event involves saving a child, consummating love, grieving a death, or suffering an attack. In the life of your characters, each crisis is of monumental importance. Remember, no matter what kind of big scene you create, you must not deprive readers of its significance by glossing over it.

When Michael and Rowan finally meet in *The Witching Hour*, readers can hear, feel, and practically taste destiny tumbling into place. This meeting and mating was meant to be. In classic Anne Rice exuberance, she spends the next forty pages letting us bond with this couple, satisfying our thirst with theirs, becoming invested in their passionate need to reach the story goal.

While taking forty pages might be excessive even for a big scene, many inexperienced writers wimp out when this looked-for and longed-for event occurs, glossing over details instead of reveling in them. Overwrite these major scenes; you can always edit them later if necessary. Read novels similar to yours, and study how much development these authors give to their big scenes.

Like chain links, each big scene increases the suspense for the next one, finally leading to the climax. Play with your plotting, looking for ways to keep your readers constantly caught in the web of suspense.

Here's an excerpt from the beast's arrival scene in Koontz's *Watchers*; it follows the contrasting happy honeymoon scene excerpted earlier. After four pages of detail full of emotions, sensory data, and nerve-racking suspense—including Travis's discovery of an eyeless, eviscerated corpse—we pick up the story in Travis's "gloomy dining room":

> Einstein's barking resounded through the house un-
> til it seemed as if a whole pack of dogs must be
> loose in the place.
>
> Travis took one more step, then saw something
> move in the shadowy dining room.
>
> He froze.
>
> Nothing. Nothing moved. Had it been a phantom
> of the mind?
>
> Beyond the arch, layered shadows hung like gray
> and black crepe.
>
> He wasn't sure if he had seen movement or merely
> imagined it.
>
> Back off, get out, now! the inner voice said.
>
> In defiance, Travis raised one foot, intending to step
> into the archway.
>
> The thing in the dining room moved again. This
> time there was no doubt of its presence, because
> it rushed out of the deepest darkness at the far side
> of the chamber, vaulted onto the dining-room ta-
> ble, and came straight at Travis, emitting a blood-
> frenzied shriek. He saw lantern eyes in the gloom,
> and a nearly man-sized figure that—in spite of the
> poor light—gave an impression of deformity.
> Then the thing was coming off the table, straight
> at him.

Koontz takes six more pages to complete the big scene and fully satisfy readers' interest, which began with his character's first encounter with the beast three hundred pages earlier. In all, Koontz spends twelve pages playing out this major scene, which doesn't include the final step.

Disaster and Revelation

All minor and major crises in a novel should end with a disaster and a revelation. Whether the disaster is implied or explicit, it does need to be clear so readers don't flounder along with your protagonist, not knowing which direction the plot is headed. In *Lonesome Dove*, the disaster in the first river crossing scene occurs when Sean dies from the water moccasin's venom; the revelation is the cowboys' becoming aware of the true gravity of the journey:

> "Well, Deets, life is short," Augustus said. "Shorter for some than for others. This is a bad way to start a trip."

Call also reflects on the disaster:

> It only went to show what he already knew, which was that there were more dangers in life than even the sharpest training could anticipate.

Finally, when Sean is buried, Gus offers a final word of revelation:

> "This was a good, brave boy, for we all saw that he conquered his fear of riding. He had a fine tenor voice, and we'll all miss that. But he wasn't used to this part of the world. There's accidents in life and he met with a bad one. We may all do the same if we ain't careful."

This may be the theme of the whole novel. It certainly changes the cowboys' outlook on this journey from one of a hard-working lark to a life-and-death venture. It also shows readers that the rest of this book is likely to be filled with danger. At the same time, McMurtry's careful words of wisdom through the mouthpiece of his two main characters, Call and Gus, give us a nugget of wisdom to carry on our journey.

The revelation that follows each plot point won't change your overall story goal. That must remain the same from the inciting incident to the climax. What changes is the strategy pursued by the protagonist, which is what creates the plot pivot I mentioned in the opening. You can distinguish these bigger scenes from a smaller moment of crisis by checking to see if there's a revelation that changes the direction of the novel.

And if you leave out the revelation that delivers the meaning of the event to the protagonist, then you've left out characterization and you're asking readers to continue reading based on plot alone.

Linking It All Together

By taking time to craft all five steps in each of your book's big scenes and positioning your big scenes throughout the plot line, you ensure reader suspense throughout your novel. Of course, you'll still have calm scenes, tender scenes, scenes of minor crisis and partial resolution. But beneath even these should be the drumbeat of tension and conflict, because readers will know that coming soon is the confrontation with Dad or the taking of the driving test or the breaking of the engagement or whatever scene you've casually named. They'll savor lesser crises and wonder how these foreshadow the bigger ones.

Of course, the structure of these scenes is flexible, and even overlapping. The revelation of one might include the naming of the next. Your big scene might also be a preview or contrasting scene to another big scene yet to come. In *Watchers*, the final showdown with the beast supplants the arrival of the beast. In *Lonesome Dove*, after the first river crossing, readers anticipate future river crossings and wonder who will die next.

Play with your plotting, looking for ways to keep your readers constantly caught in the web of suspense. Get as much work out of each step in a big scene as possible. But *never* skip a step. A story's sagging middle often comes from omitting the preview, the contrasting scene, or even the big scene itself! The first three steps work in concert to build a crescendo aimed at getting readers to the crisis with maximum dramatic impact. Omit any one of them and your story will weaken.

Go ahead, dig out your almost-made-it-novel or the one that flowed right up to chapter five and then stopped. Create conflict. Create plot points.

Create a page-turner.

ELIZABETH LYON is the author of *Nonfiction Book Proposals Anybody Can Write: How to Get a Contract and Advance Before Writing Your Book.*

Chapter 6

Don't Just Conclude the Plot . . .
Nail the Landing

By Michael Orlofsky

There is a paradox about the beginnings of short stories that is
helpful when writing their endings: The opening of a story is both
its strongest and weakest place. Strongest because it must hook
reader interest; weakest because every following line enriches or
deepens the narrative.

There is no such paradox about endings: Each of these must be
the strongest point in its story. In its subtlety, the ending will give
reason for pause and reflection; in its magnificence, the ending will
prompt cheering readers to splinter the author's door from its hinges,
to lay hands on him and carry him through the streets on their
shoulders.

Because of stakes such as these, I find that many beginning writers become unnerved by endings. More than once I've written
Don't bail out! on one of my student's manuscript when the ending
seemed too easy, vague, matter of fact, bombastic, or, ironically,
conclusive.

When beginning writers fail to grasp their *story's sense of ending*,
it's often because they haven't fully grasped the *sense of story*. The
old chestnut remains true: In the end, the protagonist should be
changed by the plot or have been faced with the opportunity to
change.

A Rhetoric of Endings

What is an ending supposed to do? On a basic level, of course, it simply concludes the plot. Homer said it all, and he's a good place to start. For all the richness of *The Iliad*, Homer finishes the epic quite plainly with the line: "So they performed the funeral rites of Hektor, tamer of horses." The burial of the Trojan hero is handled simply yet powerfully, but the function of the scene is to bring the plot to a close. Period. The end.

The end is just the beginning, on the other hand, for characters in the contemporary story, and *this* paradox is responsible for the often-criticized blandness or ambiguity of many modern endings.

As the sense of helplessness, desperation, and cynicism in our century has evolved—and as the Act of the Hero has devolved from crossing the Rubicon to waking up one morning as a cockroach—acts of individuality have become mute and tentative.

In light of this modern condition, the so-called "resolution" at the end of the modern short story often resolves little. Novels need resolutions because of the reader's need to tie up loose ends. A story, on the other hand, *is* a loose end, which often simply *exposes* the subtle and sometimes enigmatic shifts in a character's attitude or outlook. The old-fashioned Aristotelian terms for these shifts in attitude and outlook are *reversal* and *recognition*, and they are as valid today as ever.

Reversal is a change of situation—Aristotle would have identified it as a 180-degree change in fortune, as when Oedipus falls from king of Thebes to blind beggar. In modern fiction, however, the concept of reversal is more important than the *degree* of reversal. For example, at the end of a story, a couple can be shown falling from love to not quite love.

Recognition goes hand in hand with reversal. It happens when the protagonist *realizes* his reversal, realizes the consequences of his choice, or at least lingers on the cusp of realization. Aristotle stresses that reversal and recognition must satisfy the moral sense.

Moral sense is not synonymous with a happy or even righteous ending, however; many endings are unhappy, and life is often unjust. Rather, it is the sense that something humanly important has been at stake in the story: integrity, love, hope, humility, courage, or their opposites.

One of my professors at the Iowa Writers Workshop, Jim McPherson, says one of the major problems of much modern fiction is the lack of a sense of ending. He observes that these endings tend to be static—displaying neither choice nor the struggle of the soul.

Yet, choice and struggle are important, McPherson says, "*if* you believe in fiction as serving a moral purpose." Serious stuff, and the Pulitzer Prize winner was a serious teacher.

Endings should suggest this seriousness. Serious fiction has *always* served a moral purpose because, after all, what is character except a collection of values?

Types of Endings

Every ending should be unique and, ideally, the author should say things that have never been said before. There are several types of endings that are enduring, however, and their sheer popularity over the centuries shows that they are, somehow, inherently satisfying to readers. Here are six of them.

• **Dead men tell no tales.** Death is how all our personal stories will end. But the first *don't* I tell my writing classes is this: Don't kill off characters. Death at the end of a story is valid for two effects—shock or sentimentality—and neither makes for a satisfying ending (except, *maybe*, in thrillers or romances). Killing off characters is a cheap way to achieve closure, and perhaps what bothers me most when students resort to this tactic is my sense of their casualness about violence and death.

Several years ago, a student turned in a story about a couple who responds to a newspaper ad for a crossbow. They drive to the home of another couple selling the weapon. After nine pages of development, in which the foursome are seen in a kind of story of manners, the visiting husband suddenly shoots the seller in the head with one of the crossbow bolts. The visitors leave, deciding they don't want the crossbow after all—because the draw weight was too low.

Whoa! The ending wasn't supported by the plot or character-izations. There was no argument, no suggestion that the visi-tors were homicidal, no motivation. I told the student to rewrite the end. Well, the rascal revised the story, but in addition to killing the seller, the husband now went into the kitchen and killed the seller's wife. Nice and neat shock value, but the student invalidated his nine pages of character development.

The struggle is life, not death. No student has yet persuaded me that a character killed in a story deserves a point of view. Dead men tell no tales.

At the end of *For Whom the Bell Tolls*, Hemingway shows Robert Jordan alive, alone, badly injured, and facing a troop of Franco's cavalry. Hemingway's ending? "He could feel his heart beating against the pine needle floor of the forest." The resonance of the line—kinesthetically and emotionally—is great.

• **Recognition.** Little turns off a mature and sensitive reader more quickly and more intransigently than being told what to think. Yet, beginning fiction writers do this all the time. This is what I mean by endings that are too conclusive. In all likelihood, this is a symptom of a story told more for its message than its drama.

These stories are about an *idea* rather than about a *character* struggling with an idea. The dialogue sounds like philosophi-cal debate; the exposition reads like a set of instructions.

A student once submitted a story about a college student who works her way through four years of school dancing in a strip joint. The woman has been grinding away at the club to the tune of five hundred dollars a night, but as graduation nears, she's faced with the dilemma of staying with the fast money or teaching junior high.

The author provided this ending: "A tough decision lay ahead, but [she] knew she would make the right choice. She had achieved her goals and surpassed them, and even though she had compromised herself with her job, she had every reason to be proud of herself."

There's not much room for reflection here, is there? I understand students' interest in idea and theme because they come to my writing class primed with two, three, or four years of university training in text analysis. I constantly remind them to think like writers, not like literary critics: It's not what an ending means that's important, but how it means. *How* has the author achieved suspense, irony, or empathy?

The best endings never conclude or close; they open. They always keep the synapses firing between the story's pages and the reader's imagination.

The ending of James Joyce's "Araby" is an example of an author's skillful use of theme in combination with a character's dilemma. In the story, the young protagonist finally arrives late at a bazaar he has been waiting anxiously to attend. Many of the stalls already have closed, and the lights in the hall are dimming: "Gazing up into the darkness I saw myself as a creature driven and derided by vanity; and my eyes burned with anguish and anger."

• **Framing with repetition.** One of the most effective ways to produce closure is by framing the narrative. In fiction, well-handled repetition creates richness and resonance—like two parallel mirrors reflecting endlessly.

Imagery often is repeated during periods of emotional crisis;

an example would be that of the rain in Hemingway's *A Fare-well to Arms*. But any element of writing—dialogue, setting, characterization, even a word—can be repeated for reso-nance. Dante ends *Inferno*, *Purgatorio*, and *Paradiso* with the same word: *stars*. Carson McCullers introduces and ends "The Ballad of the Sad Café" with the same sentence: "You might as well go down to the Forks Falls highway and listen to the chain gang."

In addition to providing thematic or tonal completeness, fram-ing also serves the structural function of physically closing the narrative. It satisfies the reader's esthetic need for pattern.

• **Surprise or revelation.** Unveiling a surprise—an unexpected twist in plot or character behavior—may be the oldest tactic for ending a story. It plays on the reader's natural penchant for suspense and delight in revelation.

In contemporary fiction, however, the surprise ending has fallen out of favor. For the highly literate and informed reader, there are few surprises left. Assassinations, drive-by shootings, and other cruel twists of fate are in the headlines every day.

Writers sometimes slap a surprise ending on a story for shock value. For instance, a husband trying to talk his wife into fellatio while driving along the Lake Pontchartrain Causeway when their pickup suddenly swerves into the guardrail and catapults over the water. The end. "But it happens in real life," students say, rallying to defend the story. But real life doesn't always make good fiction.

Surprise endings work best when they evoke irony, anguish, pity, or wonder at human capacity.

• **Journeys.** Another traditional tactic for ending a story is showing the character setting out, or deciding to set out, on a journey. Leave-takings are emotionally charged situations, and the writer can use this built-in emotion to his advantage.

Leave-taking also satisfies one of the basic requirements of the ending: Things can never be the same. A character can escape the plot by embarking on a journey, but the author should never bail out of a difficult story through an "escape" route.

Journeys abound in fiction. Remember the end of *Huckleberry Finn* in which Huck wraps up the plot and then decides to light out for the Territory because he doesn't want Aunt Sally to "sivilize" him?

Lighting out for the Territory—whether it's a physical place on a map or a metaphysical place in the soul—is an American archetype.

In "Barn Burning," for example, William Faulkner describes a boy's escaping a mean and vicious home life:

> He got up. He was a little stiff, but walking would
> cure that. . . . He went on down the hill, toward
> the dark woods within which the liquid silver voices
> of the birds called unceasing—the rapid and urgent
> beating . . . heart of the late spring night. He did not
> look back.

Another advantage of a journey is that it leaves the narrative open for a sequel.

• **Responding to the theme.** All endings respond to the story's theme to one extent or another: sometimes as a whisper, sometimes as a roar. The tactic works best, however, when emotional and intellectual power are balanced.

Of the many ways to end a story, responding to the theme takes the most skill. Too little emphasis, and the ending will seem flat or vague; too much, and it will sound contrived, with the added consequence that the story may appear told for the sake of meaning rather than for drama.

The tradition goes back (at least) to the Greek tragedies of the fifth century B.C., when the chorus's final speech would reveal the play's moral. In a modern story that ends with a response to theme, the author also steps forward to comment on matters in the narrative.

Either the authorial voice makes the declaration, or the thoughts or words of a character do. At the end of D.H. Lawrence's "Odour of Chrysanthemums," a wife has just finished washing and shrouding her husband, who was killed in a mine accident:

> Then with peace sunk heavy on her heart, she went about making tidy the kitchen. She knew she submitted to life, which was her immediate master. But from death, her ultimate master, she winced with fear and shame.

Sometimes the author addresses theme by asking questions about a character or situation—but as often as not, the questions go unanswered. At the end of "Goodbye, My Brother," John Cheever asks, "Oh, what can you do with a man like that?" He responds with lovely imagery and this final line: "Diana and Helen. . . . I saw that they were naked, unshy, beautiful, and full of grace, and I watched the naked women walk out of the sea."

Methods for Writing Endings

You've got the idea, the opening, the characters, the plot, even the climax. But you don't know how to end the story. Here are a few tactics to discover the meaningful ending hidden in every good story.

- **Freewriting.** Perhaps the most basic approach to finding an ending is to discover it through writing. The author just writes until his intuition tells him that *this* ganglia of sentences is right.

The advantage to this approach is that it frees the author to explore plot and character. The disadvantage is that the author may write *ad infinitum* without discovering a satisfying climax.

In such a case, the author may have to go through a process of elimination to get to the heart of the matter. These are the questions to ask: Who is the story really about? What is really at stake?

Remembering the average length of a short story—twenty double-spaced typed pages—while writing is a good check and balance. With that built-in limit, the subconscious will often act as a natural editor.

In her hard but truthful way, Flannery O'Connor writes in *Mystery and Manners:* "[If you] start with a real personality, a real character, then something is bound to happen; and you don't have to know *what* before you begin. In fact, it may be better if you don't know what before you begin. You ought to be able to discover something from your stories. If you don't, probably *nobody* else will [my italics]."

• **Writing back from the climax.** An opposite approach to fast-and-loose freewriting is deciding on the climax first and then developing a plot to reach it.

The disadvantage of writing to a preconceived ending is that plots and characters are notorious for having wills of their own—and they often want to take the story in directions other than the ones planned by the author. These directions may, in fact, be the better alternative, but the writer may be resistant to following them.

John Gardner writes that most well-made stories are built by working backward from the climax "since in the final draft, we can be sure, the writer will have introduced whatever preparation his ending needs."

The key element Gardner introduces is *revision*. I suspect many students believe that a story should drop whole from their heads through some sort of parthenogenesis, like Athena dropping from Zeus's brow—in full armor, beautiful, immortal. Gardner tells young writers to reread their drafts critically at least a hundred times. In the process, they can add passages that will help readers understand the endings.

- **Save the best for last.** Every writer has had the experience of creating exquisite prose, rich imagery, or snappy dialogue. Often the experience extends to sketches or scene-length material. Many writers call these passages "gifts" because they come almost effortlessly and invariably are *right*.

Sometimes the material is so strong that it should be saved for an ending. That's how Richard Bausch explains the ending of his story, "The Fireman's Wife," collected in *The Best American Short Stories 1990*: "During the writing of it, I came upon the last line somewhere just after the middle. I circled the line and went on writing, knowing it was the end, and that I hadn't earned it yet."

Here's the line Bausch saved for his ending:

> As she closes the door, something in the flow of her
> own mind appalls her, and she stops, stands in the dim
> hallway, frozen in a kind of wonder: she had been
> thinking in an abstract way, almost idly, as though
> it had nothing at all to do with her, about how people
> will go to such lengths leaving a room—wishing
> not to disturb, not to awaken, a loved one.

It's helpful to remember those notes that drift across your consciousness while writing. I jot them down at the bottom of the

Recommended Reading

Though all great stories have a great endings, the following are some of my favorites.

For a book-length study of successful endings dating back to Chaucer (but focusing on thirty-five American stories), see John Gerlach's *Toward the End: Closure and Structure in the American Short Story*. Also valuable, for short story and novel writers alike, is John Gardner's *The Art of Fiction*.

Endings notable for their "recognition," when the main character realizes the consequences of his or her choice:
"The Lady With the [Pet] Dog," *by Anton Chekhov*
"Emperor of the Air," *by Ethan Canin*
"Cathedral," *by Raymond Carver*
"Guests of the Nation," *by Frank O'Connor*
"Testimony of Pilot," *by Barry Hannah*
"A & P," *by John Updike*
"A Loaf of Bread," *by James Alan McPherson*

Stories that end with a death:
"Death in Venice," (novella), *by Thomas Mann*
"The Prussian Officer," *by D.H. Lawrence*
"Deaths of Distant Friends," *by Updike*
"The Snows of Kilimanjaro," *by Ernest Hemingway*
"Wash" and "Carcassonne," *by William Faulkner*

Stories framed with repetition:
"The Ballad of the Sad Café," (novella), *by Carson McCullers*
"Indian Camp," *by Hemingway*
"Heart of Darkness," (novella), *by Joseph Conrad*
"What We Talk About When We Talk About Love," *by Carver*
continued

Surprise endings:
"The Necklace," *by Guy de Maupassant*
"A Rose for Emily," *by Faulkner*
"The Bet," *by Chekhov*
"The Pit and the Pendulum," *by Edgar Allan Poe*
"The Lottery," *by Shirley Jackson*
"Roman Fever," *by Edith Wharton*

Stories that end with journeys:
"The Things They Carried," *by Tim O'Brien*
"The Battler," *by Hemingway*
"The Management of Grief," *by Bharati Mukherjee*
"A Very Old Man With Enormous Wings," *by Gabriel Garcia Márquez*
"The Dead," *by James Joyce*

Endings that respond to the theme:
"Odour of Chrysanthemums," *by Lawrence*
"The Bear" (the story, not the novella), *by Faulkner*
"Goodbye, My Brother," *by John Cheever*
"Meneseteung," *by Alice Munro*
"Bartleby the Scrivener," *by Herman Melville*
"Araby," *by James Joyce*

page I'm on. Too often I've postponed noting an image or snatch of dialogue, and it vanished before I could think twice about it.

Choosing the Right Ending

How do you know which ending is right? An experienced author knows just as a bird knows when it's time to head south for the winter: There's a certain slant of light, a certain tingling in the spine. Inexperienced writers will learn, too, but it takes time.

Broadly speaking, there are three types of stories: those told for plot (action, adventure, mystery), those exploring an idea (religious, romance, historical, experimental), and those concerned with character (slice-of-life, psychological profile, autobiographical fiction, "literary" stories).

Decide on your story's most important quality: plot, idea, or character. All stories will be a mixture, of course, but one of these elements always outweighs the others.

A story leaning heavily on plotting, a murder mystery for example, has to end with a surprise or revelation—some element of the plot. The reader's anticipation and excitement must be satisfied—the culprit must make a fatal mistake, or the missing clue must surface, exposing the killer.

A story exploring an idea should ultimately come to terms with that idea by addressing the theme. Readers want to feel in the company of an author who has thought deeply about his subject. Readers hate to be left hanging and, in the end, their natural impulse is to applaud, so make it easy for them to do that. In a story about love triumphing over adversity, for example, readers should be shown (not told) the triumph.

Stories focusing on character are really focusing on personality, the psyche, the soul. Endings that work best for examinations of character often come right out of life: *dialogue* that gives the character pause to reflect; a repeated *image* that has assumed significance for the protagonist; a *journey* of escape or—better yet—a journey of challenge.

Once you know what you're creating, start freewriting or, if you already have a climax in mind, building the plot around the epiphany. If you're confident of your sense of story—if your character has changed as a result of a difficult decision, choice, or moral struggle—then the perfect ending should flow naturally from the events that have preceded it.

Just one final word of advice: Don't bump your head on the door frame as cheering crowds carry you from the house.

MICHAEL ORLOFSKY is a professor at Troy State University in Alabama where he teaches writing and literature. He's a graduate of the Iowa Writers Workshop and has taught short fiction at the Iowa Summer Writing Festival.

Who's Afraid of Point of View?

By Sherri Szeman

Wanna see something scary? Take a look at a few of the terms floating around in creative writing handbooks to explain point of view:
viewpoint character, focus character, referential and nonreferential
narrative, psycho-narration, subjective narration, overt or covert
narration, anonymous narration from multiple character point of
view, zero focalization, implied or self-effaced author. It's enough
to make you shudder. It's no wonder that many creative writers are
confused about point of view in fiction.

It doesn't help to turn to literary criticism either. Some critics
argue, for example, that every story is told by a narrator, even fairy
tales and folktales, which start with "once upon a time." Though
it's true that the technical definition of the term *narrator* is "one
who tells a story" and the author is, indeed, the one telling the story,
popular and traditional usage limits the term *narrator* to an "I" or
"we" in the story, whether as an active participant, like Huck in
Mark Twain's *The Adventures of Huckleberry Finn*, or as an observer, like Nick in F. Scott Fitzgerald's *The Great Gatsby*.

Literary critics claim that "third-person narrators" stand completely outside the story they're telling, speaking of the participants
within the story in the grammatical third person, using he, she, it,
they. As if that weren't confusing enough to someone trying to understand literary point of view, some critics complicate the situation

even further by presenting terms like *heterodiegetic narrator* and *homodiegetic narrator*, as Gérard Genette did in *Narrative Discourse: An Essay in Method* and *Narrative Discourse Revisited*. Knowing that those terms were based on Plato's terms for *authorial discourse* (diegesis), which is differentiated from the *imitated speech of a character* (mimesis), doesn't make the terms any easier to understand or remember. And it certainly doesn't help creative writers learn how to master point of view.

So, despite rhetorician and critic Wayne C. Booth's complaint in *Rhetoric of Fiction* that there are not enough divisions or distinctions to point of view, most writers still understand the more limited terms with which many of us grew up:

- first-person point of view, with an "I" or a "we" telling the story
- third-person unlimited, also known as the omniscient point of view since the author is considered godlike, written in grammatical third person: he, she, it, they
- third-person limited, one version of which is also called the fly-on-the-wall or the camera point of view, also in grammatical third person
- second-person point of view, addressing a "you," which is sometimes the reader

Why Point of View Is Important to Novelists

Most nonfiction writing does not trouble itself with point of view. Mostly, these works are written in the voices of their authors or in unlimited point of view, where the author provides all the information her readers may need. Poetry concerns itself with point of view (and voice) most often in dramatic monologues, like T.S. Eliot's "The Love Song of J. Alfred Prufrock" and "The Journey of the Magi" or like Robert Browning's "My Last Duchess," in which the voice of the first-person narrator is so distinctive that it develops his character. In fiction, however, point of view is vitally important. It can completely alter the reader's experience of the characters and events that take place. Examine these classic opening lines:

- "All happy families resemble one another, but each unhappy family is unhappy in its own way." (*Anna Karenina*, by Leo Tolstoy)
- "You don't know about me, without you have read a book by the name of 'The Adventures of Tom Sawyer,' but that ain't no matter." (*The Adventures of Huckleberry Finn*, by Mark Twain)
- "Dear Father and Mother: I have great trouble, and some comfort, to acquaint you with." (*Pamela: Or Virtue Rewarded*, by Samuel Richardson)
- "Miss Brooke had that kind of beauty which seems to be thrown into relief by poor dress." (*Middlemarch*, by George Eliot).
- "Alexey Fyodorovitch Karamazov was the third son of Fyodor Pavlovitch Karamazov, a landowner well known in our district in his own day, and still remembered among us owing to his gloomy and tragic death, which happened thirteen years ago, and which I shall describe in its proper place." (*The Brothers Karamazov*, by Fyodor Dostoevsky).
- "I had the story, bit by bit, from various people, and, as generally happens in such cases, each time it was a different story." (*Ethan Frome*, by Edith Wharton)

Imagine, for a moment, these lines written from a different point of view. Change the opening of Eliot's *Middlemarch* from unlimited to first person: "I have that kind of beauty which seems to be thrown into relief by poor dress." What a different opinion we have of Miss Dorothea Brooke if it is her voice rather than an omniscient author's that describes her beauty. Likewise, changing Twain's *The Adventures of Huckleberry Finn* from first person completely eliminates the distinct and unique voice of his narrator-protagonist. Change the point of view of Dostoevsky's *The Brothers Karamazov* or Wharton's *Ethan Frome,* and we lose the delicious thrill and intimacy of hearing a neighbor, friend, or family member relate someone else's secret and tragic history.

It is not an exaggeration to say that a novel *is* its point of view, for point of view determines the readers' responses, controls the readers' sympathies or empathies for the characters, and engages or distances the readers' emotional involvement in the fictional world. Without point of view, we lose the rich texture and sheen of fiction's fabric. Without point of view, we do not have engaging, disturbing, or memorable fiction. In novels, point of view is even more important than it is in short stories and novellas, if only because of the more extensive world the author is creating. Point of view can help you create your fictional world more realistically and make your characters more alive for your audience, so it is essential to understand and master point of view.

What Point of View Is *Not*

Point of view is not determined by the main character, whether you call him protagonist, antagonist, viewpoint character, focal character, or implied author. Point of view is not determined by any characters, no matter which of them the novel focuses on. Point of view is not determined by setting, time period, or atmosphere, nor is it determined by whether or not the author's personal beliefs in any way correspond with those expressed in the novel (by characters in thoughts, monologues or dialogue, or by an omniscient voice in unlimited point of view).

Point of view is not regulated by whether the characters are speaking to themselves, to some specific listener, or to a more nebulous and distant audience. It is not based on a narrator's reliability or unreliability, participation in or observation of the events related. Point of view is not themes, symbolism, or political agendas disguised as fiction. Point of view is not determined by whether the author shows or tells, by whether the characters are round, flat, evolving, or static. Point of view is not determined by the novel's genre, be it fantasy, science fiction, mystery, suspense, romance, Western, or literary fiction. All genres have examples of novels written in each of the various points of view.

What Is Point of View?

So what is point of view? Most simply stated, it's how the novel is written.

That's all there is to it. How the book is written.

How Many Points of View Are There?

So just how many points of view are there? For simplicity's sake, we are going to concentrate on the traditional divisions with a few distinctions for clarification: first, second, unlimited, outer limited, inner limited, and combo.

• First person: If there's an "I" or a "we" telling the story, then a narrator is present, and the book is written in first-person point of view. The narrator may be reliable or unreliable, but in either case, the events in the novel are limited to what the narrator can observe and to the narrator's psychological and emotional life.

• Second person: If someone is directly addressed as "you" (and not in dialogue), then second-person point of view is being used. This directly addressed "you" may be the readers themselves; humanity in general; other actual or implied characters in the novel; or specific historical, political, or otherwise famous people outside the novel who are not the readers.

• Unlimited: If the author uses he, she, it, or they, and tells the reader everything in every character's head and heart, then the novel is written in unlimited point of view, which has also been called third-person point of view or the omniscient point of view, since the author has been likened to an all-knowing creator God in the Judeo-Christian tradition. The author reveals every character's thoughts, feelings, motivations, and actions. This is the only point of view not limited in some fashion, hence its name.

• Outer limited: The point of view is outer limited if the author uses the grammatical third person but does not present an unlimited view of the characters, choosing instead to show only the external, observable behaviors and dialogue of all of his characters, for example, as Ernest Hemingway and Alain Robbe-Grillet do. This is also known as the fly-on-the-wall or the camera point of view since it never presents characters' interior, psychological, or emotional lives.

• Inner limited: If the author shows the thoughts and feelings of one character as if she were in that character's head, though still writing in the grammatical third person, using he, she, or it to refer to the character whose thoughts and feelings she's revealing, and presents only the external observations of the other characters, as James Joyce and Henry James often do, then the point of view is inner limited. This point of view is exactly like first person but is written in the grammatical third person.

• Combo: If the author is writing commercial fiction, especially suspense or crime mysteries, and uses unlimited point of view when focusing on the crime-fighting protagonists but uses inner limited point of view when focusing on the victims or criminals, then the author is using combo point of view, which has been recognized as its own category (sometimes called limited omniscience) by the critics.

Variations on Point of View

How many combinations of these basic points of view are there? Millions. How many subtle shadings exist within these points of view? Maybe billions. But you don't have to count them all to use them. You don't even have to be aware of all the variations and combinations to master point of view.

Why All The Confusion About Point of View?

In everyday conversation, we use the term *point of view* to refer to different sides of a situation. For example, if there's an accident and a police officer questions three people and gets three different versions of what happened, we say that he gets three different points of view. If we're having a heated discussion with someone who disagrees with us, we say, "That's your point of view." Each time we hear someone else's version of events, we say we have a different point of view.

In literature and creative writing, however, point of view is limited to how the fiction is written. So if the police officer in the previous example hears three first-person narratives about the accident, then—in literary and creative writing terms—he's heard three stories from the same point of view: first person. Each of these first-person narratives, though, is from a different perspective. So, in literary terms, the police officer has heard three perspectives from the same point of view. That distinction is critical for creative writers if they wish to master point of view.

Different Perspective, Same Point of View

An author can change perspective without changing point of view. Here are two scenes from my novel, *Only With the*

Heart, that illustrate a change in perspective while maintaining the same point of view. Each is told in first person, so there is no change in point of view from a literary standpoint. Since each narrator is giving a different version of what happened, however, there are two different perspectives. In this first scene, from the third chapter of part three, Sam, one of the novel's three narrators, is putting away a baby cradle and an unfinished rocking horse after his wife, Claudia, has had yet another miscarriage.

> Our dream of having kids was dead. After the last
> miscarriage, the doctor told Claudia to give up try-
> ing. He told her she was risking her own life with every
> pregnancy. That's why I put all the baby furniture
> up in the attic. . . . I went out to the hall with the baby
> furniture and carried it up to the attic. I set the
> cradle and rocking horse down under the eaves, next
> to the bassinet, the changing table, and the dresser.
> When I stepped back, dust swirled around in the sun-
> light and made me cough. I picked up some of the
> old blankets, shook them out, and tucked them around
> the baby's furniture. Those blankets were so big,
> and that cradle was so small. And it would never hold
> a baby. It was small and dead and empty. Like my
> life.

Sam was not aware that his mother, Eleanor, was watching him while he moved the baby furniture into the attic. In the corresponding scene in Eleanor's section of the novel (part two, chapter four), Eleanor, who is terminally ill with Alzheimer's, also describes Sam's putting the rocking horse and cradle into the attic. Since Eleanor has Alzheimer's, she doesn't remember the words for the items of furniture that her son is moving. She describes his emotional reaction to the event—something Sam neglects to do in his version of the story—and she, too, is upset, but she is unable to comfort him as he weeps over the loss of his unborn child.

> He doesn't see me. He goes past my room with it. I go after him. He goes up the stairs. To the top of the house. No one else is with him. He takes it to the corner. The sun shines on it. He makes his fingers go along the wood. When he touches it, it rocks. He wipes his face with his hand. He makes the blanket go all around it. But he doesn't get up. He stays next to it. On the floor. He puts his hands over his face. His shoulders shake. He makes a funny noise. . . . He makes that noise over and over. No one hears him. No one but me.

Since these two sections are both told from first-person point of view, there is no change in the point of view. We do, however, have a change in perspective since we have two different narrators telling the event as they remember it.

Different Focus, Same Point of View

Beginning writers also often think that describing different characters is changing point of view; so if one paragraph is about Charles, the next about Emma and the third about Rodolphe, they believe that the author has changed point of view. If the author has written about Charles, Emma, and Rodolphe in unlimited point of view, however, and not varied from that, then the author has not changed point of view. He has changed his focus from one character to another but not how he has written about them.

The following excerpt, from the first chapter of Alexandre Dumas's *The Three Musketeers*, is a description of the protagonist, D'Artagnan, written in unlimited point of view, which is always in the grammatical third person.

> A young man . . . a Don Quixote of eighteen . . . clothed
> in a woolen doublet, the blue color of which had
> faded into a nameless shade between lees of wine and
> a heavenly azure; face long and brown, high cheek-
> bones; . . . the eye open and intelligent; the nose
> hooked, but finely chiseled. Too big for a youth,
> too small for a grown man, an experienced eye might
> have taken him for a farmer's son upon a journey,
> had it not been for the long sword. . . .

Later in that chapter, when D'Artagnan meets a stranger who insults him, Dumas—still using unlimited point of view—changes focus but maintains the same point of view.

> Nevertheless, D'Artagnan was desirous of examining
> the appearance of this impertinent personage who
> was laughing at him. He fixed his haughty eye upon
> the stranger, and perceived a man of from forty to
> forty-five years of age, with black and piercing eyes, a
> pale complexion, a strongly-marked nose, and a
> black and well-shaped mustache. He was dressed in a
> doublet and hose of a violet color. . . .

Though the author has shifted his focus in order to describe different characters, he has not shifted how he has written about them, so he has not changed point of view.

Different Points of View

An author can change her focus, describing different characters, without changing her point of view. She can change perspective, giving different versions of the same story, without changing point of view. It is only when an author changes from first (I, we) to second (you), first to unlimited (he, she, it, they), etc., that she is changing point of view.

Henry Fielding does this in his masterpiece, *Tom Jones*, moving frequently from unlimited, in which the bulk of the novel is written; to first, in which he calls attention to himself as the author; to second, in which he directly addresses his audience. Here is an excerpt from the opening paragraph from book one, chapter two, written in unlimited point of view:

> In that part of the western division of this kingdom
> which is commonly called Somersetshire, there
> lately lived and perhaps lives still, a gentleman whose
> name was Allworthy. . . . From [Nature] he derived
> an agreeable person, a sound constitution, a sane un-
> derstanding, and a benevolent heart; by [Fortune],
> he was decreed to the inheritance of one of the largest
> estates in the county.

At the end of that chapter, Fielding switches from unlimited to first and second, as he will continue to do throughout the novel.

> Reader, I think proper, before we proceed any farther
> together, to acquaint thee that I intend to digress,
> through this whole history, as often as I see occasion,
> of which I am myself a better judge than any pitiful
> critic whatever; and here I must desire all those critics
> to mind their own business, and not to intermeddle
> with affairs or works which no ways concern them. . . .

William Faulkner's masterpiece of different perspectives as well as multiple points of view, *The Sound and the Fury*, is divided into four sections, the first three of which are all in first-person point of view and the last of which is in unlimited. So his novel has two different points of view: first and unlimited. The first three sections, all first-person narratives, provide three different perspectives, but the author does not change point of view.

My novel, *The Kommandant's Mistress*, is divided into three sections; but the first two, though giving different perspectives on the story, are both written in first-person point of view. Here is a scene (from part one, chapter six) in which the Kommandant is at his desk writing something late at night, from his perspective:

> When the words wouldn't come, I pulled off my ring,
> the silver band with the death's head and the *heil*
> rune, and turned it over and over in my left hand while
> I worked. . . . The words came. I slipped the ring
> back on. I saw the girl, watching me.

Since Rachel, the Jewish inmate he forces to be his mistress, is kept prisoner in his office, she is often able to tell the reader things that happen there. Here again (in part two, chapter five) is the scene with the Kommandant writing, this time from the girl's perspective. Note that since it is also in first person, there is no change in point of view.

> Often, he worked all night. The light kept me awake.
> I lay on the cot he had brought down and watched
> him. When his pen stopped, he pulled off his ring. Not
> his wedding ring. He never took that off. The silver
> band with the death's head. . . . When he saw me
> watching, he stopped writing.

The Kommandant does not tell us what he's writing, and the girl doesn't know, so she cannot tell us.

In the third section of the novel, written in a different point of view—unlimited, which is in the grammatical third person —we learn at last what the Kommandant has been writing in his office in the middle of the night.

By the time the Allies liberated the camp, [Komman-
dant] von Walther had already fled. His home and
office, however, located on the camp's grounds, were
virtually intact, and a great many incriminating
documents were recovered. Among these were two
complete manuscripts of verse, discovered under
the floorboards of his office. Though the poems in
these manuscripts are filled with intimate details of
von Walther's personal and professional life, the handwriting of these manuscripts does not exactly
match that on the other documents alleged to have
been written by von Walther, so it is highly unlikely
that the poems were written by him.

Notice that I am not analyzing the reliability of this passage
in terms of what it reveals about the Kommandant (for example, when it says "the handwriting of these manuscripts does not
exactly match that on the other documents alleged to have
been written by von Walther, so it is highly unlikely that the
poems were written by him"). It does not affect point of view
if the fictional writer of this biographical entry on the Kommandant is inaccurate in his interpretation of the facts.

What is important for our purposes here is the change in point
of view. The point of view in the first two sections of the
novel, since they are both written in first person, does not change.
Since this final section of the novel switches from first person
to unlimited, however, it *is* a change in point of view.

Point of View, Focus and Perspective

Point of view, then, is how the book is written, not who or what
it is about. When the author describes different characters or settings
but does not change how he is writing about them, then he is changing focus but maintaining the same point of view. You can

change the direction the camera is pointing—focus—or you can switch from black-and-white to color film—perspective—but to change point of view, you would have to change the camera from a video camera to an 8mm camera. Changing point of view changes the author's experience of the novel as well as the readers'.

When the author gives us different versions of the same events, perhaps all written in first-person point of view, for example, then he is giving us different perspectives, but he is not changing point of view. Only if the author writes one section of the novel in first person, with a narrator using "I" or "we" to tell the story, and another in unlimited, using "he," "she," "it," or "they" to tell the story and moving freely both inside and outside all the characters' heads (or writing any sections of the novel in any combination of multiple points of view), is the author actually changing literary point of view. Clarity about the difference between literary point of view, common usage of the term point of view, focus, and perspective will make your task easier when you write your novel.

SHERRI SZEMAN is the author of *The Kommandant's Mistress* and *Only With the Heart*. She is also the author of *Mastering Point of View* (Story Press), from which this is excerpted. She is a professor of English literature and creative writing.

Creating Four-Dimensional Characters

By Stephanie Kay Bendel

The difference between a good story and a great one is often the depth to which the author examines the characters who people the pages. Beginning writers are sometimes bewildered when they are told their characters need more development or that they haven't really allowed the reader to "know" these people. In my teaching I have discovered that a good way to make sure your characters are fully developed is to think of them as four-dimensional persons.

First Dimension—The Photograph

First-dimension characteristics are those you would observe looking at a photograph of a person. Such qualities include height; weight; age; coloring; body type; distinguishing physical traits such as scars, tattoos, or unusual proportions (for example, a man might have a large head or very long fingers); type and style of clothing—I'm sure you can think of many more. They help us form an impression of the person. More importantly, they give us concrete characteristics to visualize. All the writer can present to the reader is words on paper. The trick is to present words that will create pictures in the reader's mind. At all times you ought to be giving your reader something to look at—and not only to look at, but to remember. Accordingly, the first-dimension traits you select for your characters ought to be those things that are most memorable.

The single biggest problem in presenting the reader with first-dimension characteristics is that the traits themselves are static. It is tempting to simply stop the action of the story and tell the reader what your hero looks like:

> Roland was short and stout with a receding hairline. His eyes were blue. He wore a light gray suit that was wrinkled. He entered the newsroom and, after pausing a moment, spotted the city editor's desk.

Vague, isn't it? You can't form a clear image of Roland. It's like looking at an IdentiKit® picture the police use to obtain a sketch of someone they're looking for. The author is putting together a bunch of generic pieces and trying to give us a picture of a real live person. That may be the best the police can do, but writers can do better. Let's get rid of those inactive verbs and see whether we can describe those static traits—blue-eyed, rumpled, short, stout, and balding—in some sort of action.

> When Roland entered the room, he ran his fingers across the top of his head and arranged the few remaining strands of hair there. Then he stood on his tiptoes, his blue eyes searching for the city editor's desk. He spotted it and made a cursory effort to smooth the wrinkles where his light gray suit strained across his ample stomach.

That's a little better. We've presented a couple of first-dimensional traits without stopping the story action. The reader has the experience of seeing Roland *do* something, even if it's only to arrange his hair and smooth his clothing.

Limitations of viewpoint: The first-dimension traits you select to show the reader are limited by the point of view from which you tell the story. For example, if we were writing the above scene from Roland's point of view, we wouldn't say:

> Then I stood on my tiptoes, my blue eyes searching for the city editor's desk.

Roland would hardly be thinking about the fact that his eyes are blue, so why would he mention it here? If we want the reader to know the color of his eyes, we have to figure out a way to show that to them from Roland's point of view.

But we still have no idea what kind of person Roland is, what he's feeling, or why he's here. To answer those questions, we need to look into other dimensions of his character.

Second Dimension—The Videotape

Think of second-dimension traits as those you could observe by watching a videotape of a person. These characteristics are primarily ones of descriptive action, such as "lumbers," "ambles" or "strolls," which might show the way a person moves across a room. Now we can hear the character's voice, tone, pitch, accent, sentence structure, vocabulary, pace of speech, and so on. If she sits down, we can see whether she lowers herself gracefully onto the chair or plops onto it.

Just as we draw conclusions about a person when we look at a still photo, we draw more conclusions when we can observe that person in action.

> Julie hurried into the lab and rooted through the reports on the latest test results. She spread the sheets out on the Formica counter and studied them one by one, frowning. Occasionally she made a note to

herself on the small pad she carried in the pocket of her lab coat. When she'd finished, she went through the sheets again and double-checked her notes. Then she gathered the papers, put them in order and replaced them in the filing cabinet. She automatically straightened the row of beakers on the shelf above the counter and glanced around the lab before turning off the lights and locking the door.

In this paragraph, all we have done is watch *what* Julie is doing and *how* she does it. She isn't saying anything, and we can't read her thoughts. However, we can easily infer a lot about the kind of person Julie is simply by observing her closely. She's organized (carries a pad in her pocket and takes notes), thorough (double-checks the notes), and neat (straightens the beakers, puts things away). We have the impression that she doesn't waste time and would certainly spot something wrong.

Limitations of viewpoint: Second-dimension characteristics are not as limited by a change in viewpoint as are first-dimensional traits. If you reread the description of Julie's visit to the lab and imagine rewriting it in her viewpoint, the transition is very simple. In fact, except for deleting the word "frowning," everything else could stay as it is, simply substituting "I" for "Julie" or "she" and "me" and "my" for "her."

Second-dimension traits help the reader bridge the transition from what a person *looks* like to what a person *is* like. To discover more, we must move on to the third dimension.

Third Dimension—The Stage Play

Third-dimension traits are those revealed when you watch people interacting or reacting to circumstances, as you do in a play. Here you get some sense of a character's intelligence; sensitivity level (e.g., tactful, unaware, empathetic, uncaring); social type (e.g., extrovert, introvert, leader, follower, loner, negotiator, organizer, diplomat); the level of responsibility generally assumed; ethical, political, and religious outlook; dependency level; and educational background.

Third-dimension traits are often easily displayed in dialogue, particularly when two or more characters are in conflict. For example:

Bud slumped into the easy chair and covered his face with his hands. "I don't know how you can disappoint me like this!"

"Pop, I don't want to disappoint you. Can't you see how important this is to me? Look at me, please!"

The man put his hands in his lap and stared at them for a moment. "All these years," he said sadly, "I worked so you could have something—a future. Something I never had." He made a fist and shook it at the boy. "How can you throw it away?"

"I'm not throwing it away," Matt murmured. "It's your business, and you'll still have it. It's not like it's going anywhere."

"That's right! It's not going anywhere! How can it? I can't keep working fifteen hours a day, seven days a week, selling furniture. I'm not young anymore!"

Matt spread his hands in a gesture of helplessness. "You don't have to keep it up if you don't want to, Pop. You could sell the business. It must be worth quite a bit."

"Sell it? You cut out an old man's heart! You expect me to sell what I have spent my life building? I suppose you think then that I should give you the money so that you can do whatever nonsense it is you want."

"Write music, Pop. I want to write beautiful music.

And you don't have to give me any money. I'll work, wait tables, pump gas, sweep floors—whatever it takes so I can go to school in Milson."

"Bah! Writing pretty songs! What kind of a man does that?"

"Pop, please!" The boy's voice cracked.

Bud stood and looked his son in the eye. "Let's get this straight," he said. "Either you go to work for me this fall, or I have no son." And before Matt could reply, he turned and walked out of the room.

Notice that there is no physical description of either character in this section, and there are only a couple of gestures presented. The author is letting the content of the dialogue show what the characters—and their relationship—are like.

Bud can't see that his son is different from him. He doesn't understand why Matt doesn't want what he wants. He knows no other way to interpret the boy's behavior except as ingratitude. He's trying desperately to hold on to his control over the boy, and when all else fails, he threatens.

Matt, on the other hand, clearly wants his father's approval—or at least acceptance—of his chosen profession. Another young man might have gotten angry at his father's heavy-handed attempt to make him feel guilty. Matt, however, keeps trying to be reasonable. From his willingness to support himself in school, we see how strongly he feels about pursuing a musical career. We have a pretty good idea what his decision will be, and we know how much pain will come with it.

Habitual Behavior as a Third-Dimension Trait

Sometimes repeated behaviors, rather than the content of dialogue, can be used to show the reader third-dimension aspects of a character's personality. For example, if Alice consistently removes her husband's coffee cup from the dinner table before he's through with it, this behavior may be showing us a controlling personality, excessive preoccupation, or impatience, depending on what else is going on in the story.

Another example: If Gerald interrupts everyone, it may indicate he is an overly aggressive, controlling person, or someone who cannot tolerate disagreement, either because of a rigid personality or a fear of being proven wrong. In either case, we will chalk him up as being extremely insensitive.

Another important thing to remember is that third-dimension traits are the *public persona* of that individual. They delineate how most people perceive a character most of the time. These traits are *observable*. However, they may or may not be consistent with the inner person—that is the *private persona*, or fourth-dimension characteristics.

Fourth Dimension—Participatory Theater

Fourth-dimension traits are found in the same list as third-dimension traits, but there are two differences. The first is that fourth-dimension traits deal strictly with the *private persona*, that is, the person stripped of pretense and deception. As in participatory theater, where the audience enters into the play, the reader must enter the character's mind or discover its inner workings to explore fourth-dimension traits.

For example, Ellen is a staunch supporter of her boss's policies. She defends and praises Ms. Conklin every chance she gets. But if we were able to listen to some of Ellen's thoughts, we'd discover she can't stand Ms. Conklin. She knows that many of Conklin's decisions are bad for the business in the long run, but she can't bring herself to speak up or even confide in anyone, for fear the word will get back to her boss and she'll be fired.

Those people who work with Ellen can only observe Ellen in three dimensions and would be astounded to know what is going on in her mind. They think they know her—that she's just as arrogant and misdirected as Ms. Conklin. They don't like her.

We know quite a different person. We see that Ellen is smart enough to see the error of her boss's ways, but too much of a wimp to stand up and take a risk. We don't like her either, but for different reasons.

Answer the Question, "Why?"

There is a second important aspect to fourth-dimension traits: In order to come to the deepest understanding of the person, the author must answer the question, "Why?" Two people may behave in exactly the same way for very different reasons, and unless you understand their motives, you cannot really know them.

Let's look at two seemingly similar characters: Mabel and Agnes each live alone; they both keep all their curtains drawn, use very low-wattage bulbs in their lamps, and avoid people. Neither goes outdoors much. If that were all we knew about the two of them, we might conclude their personalities are exactly alike. But suppose we learn Mabel has a medical condition that makes her susceptible to infection and her eyes painfully sensitive to light, and Agnes has been paranoid for years and is afraid that if she opens the curtains or goes outdoors, "they" will watch her. Now we realize there is very little similarity in their personalities. In the first three dimensions, these women could be twins; it is only in the fourth dimension—when we look at the inner workings of their minds—that we understand how different they are.

Likewise, two people may find themselves in exactly the same circumstances and react completely differently because they have different personalities. Thus, it is possible to explore the fourth dimensions of their characters by contrasting their behavior in similar situations.

For example: Neil and Kevin both grew up in families who

spent every summer on Cape Cod, and both had wonderful experiences there. Now in middle age, Neil continues to return to the Cape every summer and enjoys reliving the memories of those summers. Kevin, on the other hand, spends every summer visiting a different country and hasn't been back to the Cape in years. He will tell you that the Cape is a wonderful spot, but the summers he spent there merely whetted his appetite to see the rest of the world.

Does This Person Have a Secret?

Another way to pursue fourth-dimension traits is to ask yourself, "What is there about this character that no one else knows, and how can I reveal that information to the reader?" Let's go back to our character, Ellen. We still don't know *why* she's so afraid of losing her job. Suppose we listen in on her thoughts a little longer and discover that she's a single mother who has a young daughter with an incurable medical condition that requires constant expensive treatment. If Ellen loses her job, she loses her medical coverage, and she knows that no one else will insure her little girl. Without insurance, there is no way she can get her child the treatment she needs. Now we see her toadying behavior in a different light. We realize how hard it must be to bite her tongue or even justify Ms. Conklin's actions when she disagrees with her boss, and if we write the story well, Ellen may become a quiet heroine instead of being an unlikeable woman.

How do you let your readers know why your character is behaving in a certain way? One obvious course is to get into the character's head and let the reader hear her thoughts, as we did with Ellen. But what if you need to tell the story from a point of view that does not allow you to get into the character's mind? Then you must help the reader infer from the behavior and speech of the character what is going on inside her head. Remembering that a person may speak or act deceptively, you need to present this material in circumstances where she is not likely to be doing so. For example, if in a moment of desperation, Ellen discloses her dilemma to a lifelong friend, her words will have the ring of truth, especially if they explain her previous behavior.

Examine the Character's Fantasies

Sometimes a person doesn't consciously know why he behaves the way he does. How, then, can the author show the reader what is going on without intruding on the story? A good way is to explore the character's fantasies. Remember Bud, the father who disowned his son because he wanted to study music? What could make a man behave this way? Let's see:

> Bud watched Gwenna walk away from him; her trim hips still wiggled in that fascinating way—sexy but not cheap. Definitely not cheap. If he closed his eyes just a little, she still looked like she did in high school, fresh-faced and lush. She should have been *his* girl. Would have been—if only he'd had a little more time to show her how clever he was. But Charlie Blasing had moved in too quickly.
>
> Blasing was an idiot—a goddamn idiot—and lucky as hell. Everything he touched turned into money. On top of that, Charlie had two brothers and they'd both gone into business with him and helped him become such a success.
>
> Bud clenched his fists. It was so unfair. All these years he'd had to struggle alone. And now, just when Matt was old enough to be a real help to him, the kid wanted to go away—to study *music*, for Pete's sake! How was *that* going to help him sell furniture?

Now we begin to see how Bud's mind works. He fantasizes compensating for losing Gwenna by becoming a success like Charlie, but he doesn't give Charlie any credit for business acumen. He thinks it was just luck and the help of others that got Charlie where he is. Likewise, Bud takes no personal blame for his own lack of success. If he never becomes rich, it will be because his son wouldn't help him. It is clear, too, that Matt has no chance of changing his father's mind. Our story is beginning to take on tragic overtones.

In order to continue our story, we'll need to look into Matt's deepest thoughts and discover how he'll respond to his father's ultimatum and what his reasoning is—that is, we need to examine the fourth dimension of Matt's personality.

In order to create well-rounded, living individuals in your fiction, you need to show the reader aspects of all four dimensions of their personalities. If you follow this practice, your stories will be rich and your characters memorable.

STEPHANIE KAY BENDEL is a freelance writer who lives in Boulder, Colorado. She has taught writing for eighteen years and is the author of *Making Crime Pay: A Practical Guide to Mystery Writing* and the mystery *Scream Away* (under the name Andrea Harris).

Chapter 9

Seven Tools for Talk

By James Scott Bell

My neighbor John loves to work on his hot rod. He's an automotive whiz and tells me he can hear when something is not quite right with the engine. He doesn't hesitate to pop the hood, grab his bag of tools, and start to tinker. He'll keep at it until the engine sounds just the way he wants it to.

That's not a bad way to think about dialogue. We can usually sense when it needs work. What fiction writers often lack, however, is a defined set of tools they can put to use on problem areas.

So here's a set—my seven favorite dialogue tools. Stick them in your writer's toolbox for those times you need to pop the hood and tinker with your characters' words.

1. Let It Flow

When you write the first draft of a scene, let the dialogue flow. Pour it out like cheap champagne. You'll make it sparkle later, but first you must get it down on paper. This technique will allow you to come up with lines you never would have thought of if you tried to get it right the first time.

In fact, you can often come up with a dynamic scene by writing the dialogue first. Record what your characters are arguing about, stewing over, revealing. Write it all as fast as you can. As you do, pay no attention to attributions (who said what). Just write the lines.

Once you get these on the page, you will have a good idea what the scene is all about. And it may be something different than you anticipated. Good! You are cooking. Now you can go back and write the narrative that goes with the scene, and the normal speaker attributions and tags.

I have found this technique to be a wonderful cure for writer's fatigue. I do my best writing in the morning, but if I haven't done my quota by the evening (when I'm usually tired), I'll just write some dialogue. Fast and furious. It flows and gets me into a scene.

With the juices pumping, I find I'll often write more than my quota. And even if I don't use all the dialogue I write, the better I get at it.

2. Act It Out

Before going into writing, I spent some time in New York pounding the boards as an actor. While there, I took an acting class, which included improvisation. Another member of the class was a Pulitzer Prize-winning playwright. When I asked him what he was doing there, he said improvisational work was a tremendous exercise for learning to write dialogue.

I found this to be true. But you don't have to wait to join a class. You can improvise just as easily by doing a Woody Allen.

Remember the courtroom scene in Allen's movie *Bananas*? Allen is representing himself at the trial. He takes the witness stand and begins to cross-examine, asking a question, running into the witness box for the answer, then jumping out again to ask another question.

I am suggesting you do the same thing (in the privacy of your own home, of course). Make up a scene between two characters in conflict. Then start an argument. Go back and forth, changing the actual physical location. Allow a slight pause as you switch, giving yourself time to come up with a response in each character's voice.

Another twist on this technique: Do a scene between two well-known actors. Use the entire history of movies and television. Pit Lucille Ball against Bela Lugosi, or have Oprah Winfrey argue with Bette Davis. Only you play all the parts. Let yourself go.

And if your local community college offers an improvisation course, give it a try. You might just meet a Pulitzer Prize winner.

3. Sidestep the Obvious

One of the most common mistakes new writers make with dialogue is creating a simple back and forth exchange. Each line responds directly to the previous line, often repeating a word or phrase (an "echo"). It looks something like this:

> "Hello, Mary."
> "Hi, Sylvia."
> "My, that's a wonderful outfit you're wearing."
> "Outfit? You mean this old thing?"
> "Old thing! It looks practically new."
> "It's not new, but thank you for saying so."

This sort of dialogue is "on the nose." There are no surprises, and the reader drifts along with little interest. While some direct response is fine, your dialogue will be stronger if you sidestep the obvious:

> "Hello, Mary."
> "Sylvia. I didn't see you."
> "My, that's a wonderful outfit you're wearing."
> "I need a drink."

I don't know what is going on in this scene since I've only written four lines of dialogue. But this exchange is immediately more interesting and suggestive of currents beneath the surface than the first example. I might even find the seeds of an entire story here.

You can also sidestep with a question:

> "Hello, Mary."
> "Sylvia. I didn't see you."
> "My that's a wonderful outfit you're wearing."
> "Where is he, Sylvia?"

Hmm. Who is "he"? And why should Sylvia know? (Go ahead and find out for yourself if you want to.) The point is there are innumerable directions in which the sidestep technique can go. Experiment to find a path that works best for you. Look at a section of your dialogue and change some direct responses into off-center ripostes. Like the old magic trick ads used to say, "You'll be pleased and amazed."

4. Cultivate Silence

A powerful variation on the sidestep is silence. It is often the best choice, no matter what words you might come up with. Hemingway was a master at this. Consider this excerpt from his short story, "Hills Like White Elephants." A man and a woman are having a drink at a train station in Spain. The man speaks:

> "Should we have another drink?"
> "All right."
> The warm wind blew the bead curtain against the table.
> "The beer's nice and cool," the man said.
> "It's lovely," the girl said.

"It's really an awfully simple operation, Jig," the man said. "It's not really an operation at all."

The girl looked at the ground the table legs rested on.

"I know you wouldn't mind it, Jig. It's really not anything. It's just to let the air in."

The girl did not say anything.

In this story, the man is trying to convince the girl to have an abortion (a word that does not appear anywhere in the text). Her silence is reaction enough.

By using sidestep, silence, and action, Hemingway gets the point across. He uses the same technique in the famous exchange between mother and son in the story "Soldier's Home":

"God has some work for every one to do," his mother said. "There can't be no idle hands in His Kingdom."

"I'm not in His Kingdom," Krebs said.

"We are all of us in His Kingdom."

Krebs felt embarrassed and resentful as always.

"I've worried about you so much, Harold," his mother went on. "I know the temptations you must have been exposed to. I know how weak men are. I know what your own dear grandfather, my own father, told us about the Civil War and I have prayed for you. I pray for you all day long, Harold."

Krebs looked at the bacon fat hardening on the plate.

Silence and bacon fat hardening. We don't need anything else to catch the mood of the scene. What are your characters feeling while exchanging dialogue? Try expressing it with the sound of silence.

5. Polish a Gem

We've all had those moments when we wake up and have the perfect response in a conversation that took place the night before. Wouldn't we all like to have those bon mots at a moment's notice?

Your characters can. That's part of the fun of being a fiction writer. I have a somewhat arbitrary rule—one gem per quarter. Divide your novel into fourths. When you polish your dialogue, find those opportunities in each quarter to polish a gem.

And how do you do that? Like the diamond cutter. You take what is rough and tap at it until it is perfect. In the movie *The Godfather*, Moe Greene is angry that a young Michael Corleone is telling him what to do. He might have said, "I made my bones when you were in high school!" Instead, screenwriter Mario Puzo penned, "I made my bones when you were going out with cheerleaders!" (In his novel, Puzo wrote something a little racier). The point is you can take almost any line and find a more sparkling alternative.

Just remember to use these gems sparingly. The perfect comeback grows tiresome if it happens all the time.

6. Employ Confrontation

Many writers struggle with exposition in their novels. Often they heap it on in large chunks of straight narrative. Back story—what happens before the novel opens—is especially troublesome. How can we give the essentials and avoid a mere information drop?

Use dialogue. First, create a tension-filled scene, usually between two characters. Get them arguing, confronting each other. Then you can have the information appear in the natural course of things. Here is the clunky way to do it:

John Davenport was a doctor fleeing from a terrible

Dialogue Starter

Here is a sample exchange between two characters, along with some suggested exercises:

> "Good evening."
> "Good evening."
> "I didn't know you were coming."
> "I hadn't made any plans, but I got an invitation."
> "Wonderful. Nice night, isn't it?"
> "Lovely."

1. Choose two characters who are violently opposed to one another. What sex are they? What ages? Why are they enemies? Now, set them at a dinner party where one walks in. Keep the first line, but play with the others by doing the sidestep.

2. Build on what you've done. Write more of the dialogue. Let it flow.

3. Drop some words in the exchanges. Does it sound more real?

4. Find a place for a silent reaction. Is the subtext clear? What is the character doing in the silence that is a clue to what she is thinking?

5. Finally, choose one line of dialogue for a gem. Make up several variations, then choose the best one. Does it sparkle? Sure it does. You're on your way to becoming a dialogue whiz.

past. He had been drummed out of the profession for bungling an operation while he was drunk.

Instead, place this back story in a scene where John is confronted by a patient who is aware of the doctor's past:

> "I know who you are," Charles said.
> "You know nothing," John said.
> "You're that doctor."
> "If you don't mind I—"
> "From Hopkins. You killed a woman because you were soused. Yeah, that's it."

And so forth. This is a much underused method, but it not only gives weight to your dialogue, it increases the pace of your story.

7. Drop Words

This is a favorite technique of dialogue master Elmore Leonard. By excising a single word here and there, he creates a feeling of verisimilitude in his dialogue. It sounds like real speech, though it is really nothing of the sort. All of Leonard's dialogue contributes, laserlike, to characterization and story.

Here's a standard exchange:

> "Your dog was killed?
> "Yes, run over by a car."
> "What did you call it?"
> "It was a she. I called her Tuffy."

This is the way Elmore Leonard did it in *Out of Sight*:

> "Your dog was killed?"

"Got run over by a car."
"What did you call it?"
"Was a she, name Tuffy."

It sounds so natural, yet is lean and meaningful. Notice it is all a matter of a few words dropped, leaving the feeling of real speech.

As with any technique, you can always overdo it. Pick your spots and your characters with careful precision and focus. Your dialogue will thank you for it later.

Using tools is fun when you know what to do with them, and see results. I guess that's why John, my neighbor, is always whistling when he works on his car. You'll see results in your fiction—and have fun, too—by using these tools to make your dialogue sound just right.

Start tinkering.

JAMES SCOTT BELL is the award-winning author of several thrillers, including *Blind Justice* and *The Nephilim Seed*. He also helped to develop the Writers Digest Online School's dialogue workshop.

The Art

Chapter 10

Mastering Fiction's First Rule

By Jack M. Bickham

It's one of the first things a new fiction writer hears in the way of advice: "Show, don't tell." The advice is sound. But execution is sometimes something else. There's just an awful lot of confusion about this basic tactic of effective fiction.

Let's try to clear up some of it.

The phrase "Show, don't tell" is shorthand for this advice: "Don't lecture your reader; she won't believe you. Give her the story action, character thoughts, feelings, and sense impressions as the character would experience them in real life. Let her live the story for herself as she lives real life, by experience."

That's a mouthful, and it requires some explanation.

From Facts to Feelings

First, it may help to realize that most of your formal educational training and work experience have taught you to present information in a way that's inappropriate when writing fiction.

Most of our formal schooling emphasizes *telling*. We tell the teacher the facts we learned from our textbook reading—either in class recitation or in a written test. When we're assigned to write a term paper or report, we tell the facts from a logical,

objective viewpoint—and probably try to keep our own personality entirely out of it. Later, in the business world, we are
expected to find and analyze facts, then prepare reports or mem-
oranda that are, again, designed to inform readers as factually
and briefly as possible—by telling.

That's fine, in that world. But when you start to write fiction,
you must turn the process upside down. Instead of keeping
feelings out of the process and listing objective facts, you must
be aware of feelings—your lead character's emotions and
unique viewpoint on the story action—and then you must figure
out how to make your readers experience the story world
from that viewpoint and emotional stance. Instead of presenting
facts and marshaling arguments in support of your position,
as you do in the educational or business world, you must present
the evidence and lead readers to form their own conclusions.

Thus, fiction convinces—if it does—in a way entirely different
from our usual objective writing. Fiction can only involve and
convince and excite readers if it lets them experience the story
world the way they experience real life: by taking in stimuli
and drawing their own conclusions. In real life, you don't walk
outside in the morning and experience the start of the day
with something internal like, "Cloud cover is thick. The temperature is 64 degrees, the humidity is 42 percent, traffic on the
highway is heavy, it's late September, the postman is irritable
today."

What you *do* do is walk outside and see with your eyes that
it's gray and dim; you look up and see thick gray clouds; you
feel the temperature with your skin . . . and relax, or feel warm,
or shiver. If you breathe deeply and the air feels thick to you,
you may conclude it's humid. You hear the roar of cars nearby
and conclude traffic is heavy on the highway. You see the postman
coming up your driveway. Your eyes meet and you smile at him.
His mouth turns down, his eyes squint, and he glares silently back
at you. You conclude he is feeling grumpy.

So to convince your readers, you must make the experience of the story world as much like real life as you possibly can. You present evidence. You show; you don't tell.

That's what *show* means in the broadest sense. Your readers will only believe you—be transported into your story world and be enthralled—if you convey just as much information of all kinds through this process of making it a learning experience for them.

At the risk of being repetitious, let's state again that your readers will not believe dry, objective lectures. They will only believe the conclusions they form from the evidence you carefully select and present to them.

Get Into Viewpoint—and Stay There!

This process of showing, not telling, can be broken down into four essential steps. They are:

- Selection of, and adherence to, a single character's viewpoint

- Imagining the crucial sense or thought impressions that character is experiencing at any given moment

- Presenting those impressions as vividly and briefly as possible

- Giving those impressions to readers in a logical order

Getting into the viewpoint of your central story character—and staying there—helps enormously in showing instead of telling. If you're solidly in viewpoint, you won't be tempted to lecture readers because you will be revealing that character's experiences rather than reviewing some abstract, objectively written data. If you're well inside the viewpoint, for example, you can't dump a lot of author-intrusive factual information on readers because viewpoint characters, like real people, *experience* things rather than tell about them.

Further, adherence to viewpoint largely removes the temptation to tell readers stuff that's extraneous or unknowable to the viewpoint character. This is a useful limiting device for you. You simply cannot, for example, start telling what's over the next hill, or who might be walking up behind the character, or the precise temperature, or any of a million other details that *matter* to the character.

These details will not scatter all over time and space, either. They'll be imagined at every given moment. After all, we live our lives that way—moment by moment. Your character will experience sense impressions and everything else in the same way—briefly, often in a fragmentary manner, and very vividly because it's the real world he is experiencing. So you will be less tempted to launch into long prose lectures about the exact color of the tree or panoramic descriptions covering long periods of time. We just don't live like that!

Given the fact that your showing will therefore tend to be brief, you will find yourself working hard to boil down your wordage to make it as vivid and evocative as possible. You'll be very concrete and seldom abstract. You will not, for example, write a sentence that says, "He was a very tall man." That's an objective conclusion. You will instead write something closer to, "Even though he ducked as he entered the doorway, he cracked his head on the top. As he walked into the room, suddenly the eight-foot ceiling looked like someone had lowered it a foot." (Now readers will think, "Hey, this is a tall guy" and will *believe* it.)

Finally, in showing rather than telling, you will make sure that you give this evidence in a logical order, the order that readers will need to have a lifelike experience, yet at the same time understand what's going on.

Usually this means a chronological presentation. If someone knocks on your character's front door, for example, you simply can't start the next paragraph with dialogue, and then only later mention that, oh, by the way, it was Jim at the door, and his face was twisted in anger, and our viewpoint character was concerned and invited him in, and the two of them started to talk.

Instead, you'll take it a step at a time, logically, as you (and your readers) would experience it in real life: sound of knocking at the door; viewpoint character goes to the door and opens it, sees Jim standing out there, sees his angry scowl and clenched fists, asks, "Jim, what's wrong? Please come in—." Sits him down on the couch, notices his red-rimmed, sleepless eyes, feels more worried about him, and curious, and says, "Tell me what's happened and why you're here."

The only exception to the code of logical presentation can be found in those very rare instances when you want to show readers that your character is confused—that everything seems to be happening all at once, or the character's thoughts are badly muddled. Then you may jumble logicality to baffle readers for a few moments, thus convincing them of character confusion by making the readers experience such confusion.

(In 99 percent of the cases, however, logical presentation is required. The need for logical, lifelike order is so important that I wrote an entire chapter on it when I revised my book *Writing and Selling Your Novel*.)

Divining the Dominant Impression

Of course, in all of this process you will most often be dealing with sense impressions. In working to improve your own sensitivity to vivid, suggestive sense impressions, it often helps to cultivate the habit of trying to identify, as you go through your normal everyday activities, the *dominant impression* you may be receiving at any given moment.

Consider, for example, the dominant impression you might experience turning your car around a curve in the road and suddenly having the setting sun directly on your windshield.

Or the dominant impression if you walked into an old cathedral in Europe at a quiet time, perhaps soon after a Catholic mass and benediction service.

Then imagine the dominant impression you receive when you walk into your local shopping mall.

Or the dominant impression of walking down a city street near a major repaving project.

Or the dominant impression when you walk into a bakery.

Very often, given the hierarchy of our senses, the source and quality of light is the first and dominant impression. In showing readers a room or office, for example, the brightness and source of the light often will be the first thing noticed in real life, and the first thing to be shown readers: Is it a large, dim, window-less room; a small black closet; a big office with sun-washed windows looking out onto the vast blue of the lake?

In other cases, however, the dominant impression may be dictated by the nature of the experience. Surely, in walking into an old cathedral, you would notice the vast space, perhaps dimness, perhaps vividly colored stained glass. But also high on the list to be "shown" would probably be the silence, the odor of incense, motes of dust in a stray shaft of sunlight.

Quite different from the mall. There the dominant impression might be the noise, or the crowds of people, or the ranks of glass display windows, or the garish neon, or the racket of canned music.

The major street work? Ear-shattering din of jackhammers. Roar of air compressors. Crash of debris being dumped into a truck. Smell of tar or asphalt. Of workmen's sweat or the fore-man's acrid cigar.

Or consider the bakery. Oh, my, the smell of fresh-baked bread, and rows of glistening pastries in the cabinets. You might waste a half-page trying to tell your readers about walking into a bakery when all you need to do—to thrust readers into that experience— would be to "show" the sweet aroma of fresh-baked bread . . . and maybe a touch of cinnamon in the warm air.

So every moment of showing may proceed from a different hierarchy of senses than the one that went before. Your ability to embed yourself deeply in your character's viewpoint and imagine *that moment* as vividly and truly as possible, starting with the dominant impression, will make your fiction convincing.

Revealing Characters

The same general principle applies to showing your readers your other story characters. You can lecture readers endlessly about how nervous Joe may be, and how impatient, and how driven, and blah, blah, blah. But readers don't form impressions of real people from dull, objective character profiles, so why should they believe your manuscript if you do the same thing?

Again, you have to show—present the evidence—like this:

> Joe walked jerkily into the office. The facial tic leaped under his left eye. He swooped onto the empty chair, drummed his fingers on the desktop, crossed and uncrossed his legs, and glared at Sally. "All right," he snapped. "I'm here. I don't have all day. Get to the point. I'm a busy man."

Now your readers will conclude from the evidence, "Hey, this is a nervous, impatient, driven man," and *believe* it because they were led to draw that conclusion for themselves.

Even the presentation of your viewpoint character's emotions can often be handled more convincingly through showing. It's always tempting to get inside the character and start analyzing—

"Sally was so sad and depressed," for example, or "Sally felt the anger rise up in her so sharply that it shocked her." But in such cases, it's more compelling for readers if you find a way to show, something like:

> Suddenly she realized the sound in the room was her own sobbing. She felt tears on her cheeks. She raised a hand and it trembled before her eyes. *I could end it all*, she thought without warning.

Or:

> She began to shake. The words tumbling out of her mouth sounded horrible to her own ears—language she never used, viciousness. She didn't even recognize her own voice. Her hands formed claws and she struck out at him with her nails, raking bright, bloody tracks on his face.

These quick, crude examples may overdo it slightly. But they're exaggerated to make the point: Even internal character reactions should be shown far more often than given in a dull lecture.

When to "Tell"

So, to convince, we show rather than tell.

But are there ever times when telling is all right?

Of course there are. We tell when:

• The data are objective and absolutely essential to reader understanding.

• The factual information is so fascinating that it may "sell" the story. (This is very rare.)

- The point is quite minor and we can risk "cheating."

- Economy of words is vital at the moment.

Some "objective data" may be necessary in your story. For example, it may be important for readers to know that there has been violence in the neighborhood where your character lives, and readers should worry about it. Even after presenting evidence such as extra locks on the apartment doors, a patrol car going by outside, or scared looks on neighbors' faces, you might want simply to say that there had been two murders in the past week, or that Sally was scared and wanted to move, but couldn't afford it. A little such telling takes place in most stories.

Sometimes, too, in economically characterizing someone, it may be quite okay to slip in a bit of telling, as, "Jack was late, but Sally was not surprised. Jack made it a habit to be late. It was one way he proved to the world that he didn't give a hoot about anyone but himself."

In a novel, the presentation of factual data may be appealing as interesting information in its own right, as in the books of James Michener where the historical facts form part of the fascination for readers. If your story is of this type, designed to enthrall because it contains hard-won, truly interesting information that you believe will help sell the story, then you may tell quite a lot. (My novel *Twister* was such a case. It contains more straight, factual telling than anything else I have ever written. But such a "journalistic" approach is hard to handle and risky.)

If the point is very minor, it's also fine to tell—a little—once in a while. Perhaps it's as simple a statement, as "The weather was getting colder." Or "Marie looked grumpy." Or "In a city like Zenith, with its skyrocketing population of 256,000, up 50,000 in only the past five years. . . ."

First-Person Showing

Showing strong feeling, rather than lecturing readers about it, is possibly more difficult in first-person narration than anywhere else. Because the author is deep inside the head and heart of the "I" character so much of the time, it seems natural to blurt out feelings. In fact, the stronger the emotion being portrayed, the harder it is for the author to show rather than tell.

Near the end of my novel *Breakfast at Wimbledon*, I encountered both of these problems.

A lovable old man, a British agent about to be "retired" in obscurity, gives his life to save that of our hero, Brad Smith. Brad had already loved the old man, Clarence Tune, and hated the commander who had humiliated Clarence so often in earlier scenes. Emotion was very strong. The only weapon Brad had to try to vindicate poor Clarence's reputation was information that was damaging to the insufferable commander.

It was terribly tempting to try to describe Brad's grief and anger, the sadness of Clarence's noble death, and the commander's humiliation after Brad found a way to affect Clarence's vindication. But such scenes demand restraint; a wrong word can ruin readers' own emotional imaginings.

So here is how Brad's feelings, his cold self-control, and the commander's humiliation played out, all as the dead old man was honored at last, thanks to Brad's intervention:

> On Wednesday, in a rainy little cemetery near Coventry, Clarence Tune received full military honors. A uniformed guard carried the casket to the gravesite and stood at attention. Air Force. I had never suspected Clarence might have served in the Air Force. I wondered what kind of plane he had flown.

continued

Besides Linda and myself, there were only five on-lookers: a tiny old woman who had been his landlady, Commander Fairchild and two of his dark-suited toadies, and off to one side, a sad-eyed, raincoated elderly man no one seemed to know. . . .

Afterward, Clarence's landlady came over and patted my hand. She thought I was Clarence's son. She wanted to know what to do with his cat. She said she would keep it if I liked. I said that would be grand. She said he had been a nice man and I agreed. . . .

Commander Fairchild walked over, stiffly handsome and military in his reservist uniform. He was icily under control. "I trust that was satisfactory?"

"Yes," I said. "Quite."

"Good." He started to turn away. He was very angry.

"There's the matter of the medal," I told him.

He looked back at me, red splotches appearing in his cheeks. "The medal has been authorized. Orders have been issued. The medal is to be delivered to our hall of fame, where it will be permanently displayed along with those of other men who have died in the line of duty."

I held eye contact with him. In a spiteful way I was almost enjoying this. "And the news release?"

"Damn you!" he whispered explosively.

"What?" I said.

He regained control. "The news release has been issued. It is for publication this date."

"Clarence's record is included?"

"Yes."

"His medals?"

"Yes."

continued

111

"It's made clear that he served with great honor and distinction?"

"Yes!"

"Thank you, commander." I turned the knife. "That will be all."

You could see my brusque dismissal go in like a harpoon. If he had had less control, he might have hit me. Instead, after a fraction of a second, he gave me a single killing look, wheeled and stomped back to where his aides stood waiting, unhappy and windblown in the expensively nondescript suits. . . .

There are, to be sure, a few directly emotional "clue" words hidden here: "icily," "very angry" and "almost enjoying." But the scene is much stronger for allowing the events and the cool tone of Brad's first-person narration to carry it. I could have lectured for pages about Brad's grief and anger, and about the commander's humiliation on behalf of Clarence, and not have provided the direct impact on sympathetic readers' emotions that his "showing" did. Brad's chill rudeness in questioning the commander and his final "That will be all" showed not only his rage and control, but gave readers—I hope—the deepest satisfaction in seeing the commander put down and Clarence honored at last.

These examples, in the purist's sense, constitute "cheating" a little. But they're done to get on with things. Readers will accept them if the point isn't critical to the story at the moment you slip them in.

Finally, let's admit that sometimes in a short story, you may simply be forced to tell because your total word limit doesn't allow you to present enough evidence to make the point convincingly. You may write a fine, lengthy paragraph showing David's depression, but when the story is done, you may find yourself a few hundred words too long. In such cases—if in your best judgment David's depression is not crucially important—you can get away with simply writing, "David slumped, appearing depressed, as he so often was during the long winters."

As a fiction writer, your goal is to immerse readers in your story world. That world must seem as much like the readers' real world as you can possibly make it. Readers experience your story world in a similar way: through evidence—sense impressions or whatever—that allow them to draw their own conclusions.

If you craft carefully in viewpoint and select your words well, you will show your readers not only the impressions, sights, sounds, and feelings you want them to believe, but will leave them feeling moved and satisfied.

Never lecture. Always strive to show.

JACK M. BICKHAM wrote more than eighty novels before his death in 1996. His books on writing include *Writing and Selling Your Novel* and two volumes in the Writer's Digest Books' Elements of Fiction Writing series—*Setting* and *Scene and Structure.*

Chapter 11

What Your Story *Says*

By Nancy Kress

Theme.

The most fraught word in literature. You can call it central concern or reader resonance or some such thing, but it still conjures memories of ninth-grade English: What is the book's theme? Concisely state the theme, and be sure to support your statement with specific examples in a well-written essay with topic sentence and.... No wonder so many writers go out of their way to announce their fiction has no theme. They don't want students forced to reduce their works to twenty-five words or less of platitudes.

Nonetheless, every work of fiction does have a theme. And, as a writer, it's helpful to know what yours is.

Three paragraphs into this article, and I know I'm already in trouble with hordes of would-be dissenters. Yes, writers frequently aren't particularly articulate about the larger implications of their own work. Yes, the text itself is what matters. Yes, a story can "mean" different things to different people. But I'm going to discuss theme anyway, because the lack of it is what I see crippling so many new writers' work.

But let's not call it theme, after all. Let's call it *worldview* for reasons I hope become clear as we go. And let's see why you need to think about it—if not during the first draft, then later—in order to make your work successful.

Yes, Mrs. Marblehall, There Is a Pattern

First, it's impossible to write a story, or even a few significant paragraphs, without implying a worldview. This is because the writer has always chosen to include some details and to leave out others. Furthermore, the writer has—wittingly or not—chosen a tone in which to present those details. That tone, too, implies a worldview.

Here, for example, are two descriptions of the same person. The first is from a police report. The second is from a short story, Eudora Welty's "Old Mr. Marblehall":

> Caucasian female, thirty-eight, 5'1", 175 pounds. Mole on left cheek, near eye. Described by neighbors as possessing thick shoulders, small round head. Last seen by neighbor, on own front porch, wearing sleeveless loose brown cotton dress, green bedroom slippers, size four.

> There's his other wife, standing on the night-stained porch by a potted fern, screaming things to a neighbor. This wife is really worse than the other one. She is more solid, fatter, shorter, and while not so ugly, funnier looking. She looks like funny furniture—an unornamented stair post in one of these funny houses, with her small monotonous round stupid head—or something like a woodcut of a Bavarian witch, forefinger pointing, with scratches in the air all around her. But she's so static she scarcely moves, from her thick shoulders down past her cylindered brown dress to her short, stubby house slippers. She stands still and screams to the neighbors.

The police report, through its tone and choice of details, says this about the world: Reality can be objectively observed and numerically described. The physical world is our common ground in interacting with each other. Missing persons are sometimes able to be located and therefore it is rational to devise paperwork and procedures to do so. On the other hand, the Welty description—like the story from which it's taken—implies a different view of the world: The best way to understand something is through subjective contrast and metaphor ("like funny furniture," "like a woodcut of a Bavarian witch," "so static" even though she's screaming). Ways of interacting are grounded in some unseen judgment ("This wife is really worse than the other one") that carries with it a tone of both contempt and mystery. A factual account of what the wife is shouting at the neighbors is never explained; it's the overall sub-jective impression that counts.

It's not hard to imagine a third way of describing the second Mrs. Marblehall that would be different from both these. Her view of herself as a wronged woman, perhaps. Or the view of her through the eyes of her six-year-old son as Mama, warm and loving and dependable. Each of these would imply yet another view of the world by emphasizing different as-pects of reality.

What does all this have to do with theme in your writing? Hang on. We're getting there.

It's not only description that implies a view of the world. So does the choice of story events and the way they play them-selves out in your work. Detective stories, for example, almost always end with the murderers being identified. If they did not, most readers would get quite upset. The choice of events—investigation, deduction, resolution—carries the metaview that the world is rational, and the further theme that crime doesn't pay. Romances, on the other hand, all offer the reas-suring theme that although the road to winning love may be rocky, love is possible and worth it. This is true even when the lovers end up losing each other, as in Robert James Waller's best-selling *The Bridges of Madison County.*

It's possible, however, to visualize a different choice of ending for Waller's novel. Suppose his two lovers had still ended up parting, but after Robert leaves, Francesca's husband discovers their affair. Shocked and betrayed, he divorces her. Francesca then hunts down Robert who, nomad that he is, has meanwhile taken himself to Argentina and fallen in love with a Spanish girl named Rosaria. There is a confrontation, and Rosaria shoots Francesca. In that book, the view of love—the theme—would be much different than in the one that Waller actually wrote.

So, on a macro level, the events you choose to include in your story form an overall pattern that implies a worldview. If you know what worldview you're actually creating, it can help you choose events that support it, descriptions with telling details and evocative tone, and characters who bear out your beliefs. All this gives your fiction a wholeness, a consistency born as much of patterned emotion as of rationality, which can vastly improve it.

But there's more. Pattern operates on a micro level as well as a macro level, and there, too, you have more control than you may think.

Guns and Casseroles

A famous writing maxim attributed to Anton Chekhov says that if you have a gun going off in the third act of a play, it had better sit on the mantelpiece during the first two acts. Conversely, if a gun is clearly visible on the mantelpiece for two acts, it had better go off during the third. In other words, critical plot developments and people must be clearly foreshadowed, not dragged in from left field at the end of your story. And if you spend time and verbiage on something

117

early on, we can reasonably expect that thing to figure in the climax or denouement.

Suppose, for instance, you give four early pages of a thirty-page story to Aunt Mary's shoplifting at Macy's. She stole a candy dish and a bath towel. The incident is amusing, well-written, and characterizing. Is that enough? No. You're letting us know that this incident will be part of the overall pattern of your story, and so it had better turn out to be just that. You'd better use that candy dish, that towel, or some other aspect of the escapade at Macy's as an important element of your climax. A story, like an Oriental carpet, is a pattern, and everything in it is supposed to contribute to the design.

However—and here's the critical point—not all patterns are equally tightly woven. Your theme gains or loses credibility partly on the basis of the weave you create.

Let me explain. In commercial fiction especially, *everything* in the story usually contributes directly to the plot. The shorter the story, the truer this is. Objects that receive more than one mention, secondary characters, symbols, events (even small ones), lines of dialogue, all relate directly to the main point in a tightly woven pattern that satisfies because it imposes order on life. Such fiction pleases us at least partly because it says to us that life contains patterns, order, design.

But each of us knows, in our heart of hearts, that life doesn't really add up so neatly. A real person's day (or week, or year) includes hundreds of small things unrelated in any pleasing, orderly way. Real life is messily patterned, if it's patterned at all. Aunt Mary's shoplifting occurs right in the middle of a daughter's illness, a cousin's wedding, a business triumph, a lawn-care crisis, and it's unrelated to any of them. It's not a pattern; it's a distraction. Real life is disorderly.

As a result, fiction that is too neatly patterned will not feel real. When everything in a story works out exactly, and each detail we see has a neat place in the overall scheme, we may enjoy

the story but we don't really believe it. It has a sterile, manufactured feel.

Some writers, especially literary writers, compensate for this
by including elements that are connected indirectly, often the-
matically, but not directly woven into the main plot. Anne Tyler
is especially good at this. Her novel *The Accidental Tourist*,
to take just one example, abounds with subplots and digressions
connected only loosely to the main plot of Macon's romances.
One such recurring element is Macon's sister Rose's cooking.
Rose cooks casseroles, desserts, a turkey. All of this could
have been left out, but it serves several purposes. It deepens out
understanding of Macon's background. It creates thematic
design; much of the book concerns how people nurture each
other (or don't). And, more relevant to my point, it gives the
book the feel of the multidistraction that is real life.

However, fiction in which there is no order whatsoever—in
which things just seem to happen without connection or thematic implication—isn't satisfying either. Why should it be? It
may look like life, but we want something more from fiction.
We already have life.

The result is that every writer walks a tightrope between arran-
ging the elements of his story in too tight a pattern or too
loose a pattern. Too tight, and the story feels contrived. Too
loose, and it feels pointless. And, to complicate matters more,
different kinds of fiction define "too tight" and "too loose" in
different ways. Romance novels usually require tight pattern-
ing; literary short stories allow very loose design.

Theme is how much order, how stringently you've imposed
on your fictional universe. It's also what kind of order: happy,
malevolent, despairing, random, hidden-but-there, and so on.

Some writers find that they don't know their themes until they've
finished the first draft (I am one). They then rewrite with an eye toward
balancing on that tightrope: not too contrived, not too rambling;
does what I'm saying about the world below me actually add

up to anything? Other writers pay attention to these things as they write the first draft. Either way, an awareness of the macro and micro levels of theme can provide one more tool for thinking about what you should write, and how.

NANCY KRESS is the author of many short stories and books, including *Dynamic Characters* and *Beginnings, Middles & Ends* (both Writer's Digest Books).

Chapter 12

Killer-Diller Details Bring Fiction to Life

By Donna Levin

There's an expression, "God is in the details," and it applies to nothing more than it does to the writing of fiction. To that and to the art of telling good lies. And what is fiction but the telling of lies?

Well, not exactly, but fiction writing and lying do have something in common. (Picasso said, "Art is a lie that lets us see the truth.") In both cases you are making something up and trying to make someone believe it. Even when you write about something that "really happened" in your personal life, in fiction you will find that making the reader believe it is one of your chief tasks.

Now, I mean "believe" in a specialized sense. A reader picks up a book in a store knowing it's fiction, or fictionalized. But when the reader actually buys the book, he's in effect saying to the author, "I'm going to give you a chance to tell me a story that I can at least pretend is real for the duration of the book."

Providing the details is how you make your reader into a believer. Why? Because it's how you put your reader into the action.

As a writer, you should know that if you really want the reader to believe he's reading about an African safari, you'd better describe the long purple tongues of the giraffes. You must learn that giraffes have purple tongues, or imagine they do, or remember that detail from your real-life safari or trip to the zoo. The purple tongue of the giraffe lets us see the giraffe. The wind in the face of our heroine lets us stand out on the savannah with her.

A detail doesn't need to be real in the conventional sense in order to have power. Science fiction and horror writers know very well the power of invented, but authentic, details.

One of the most compelling aspects of Anne Rice's *Interview With the Vampire* is that Rice really makes you believe that vampires exist, and she does so by the exquisite detailing of the way they live (or, we might say, *un*live) and function. She casually dismisses any familiar Hollywood notions or even any traditional ones that don't suit her. "Forget that," she says, "this is the way it is." And then she follows her own rules with a steely consistency.

In the same way, the science fiction writer has to let us know that the South Forkorian qebor eats yodels and that yodels eat mordons in order to establish the food chain on the planet Zen.

When writing historical fiction, you must weave in as many of the factual details as you can. But sometimes you will be called upon to fill gaps that history has left. Your inventions—whether they are to surmise the way that the Huns celebrated wedding ceremonies or to recreate dialogue spoken by Charlemagne—will also make history seem real.

Quality, Not Quantity

When it comes to details, more is not necessarily better. The number of details you need to describe a person or to dramatize an event is a result of several factors. The first is your writing style. Some writers like to give the reader just enough of the bare facts to keep from getting lost. Others like to write lavish descriptions of every crinoline.

Both the amount and type of details you include will also be a function of the genre you're writing in. The readers of a Judith Krantz-style "sex and shopping" novel will be looking for lots of brand names, especially of designer clothes. A sword-and-sorcery novel will require you to authenticate the magic by inventing the details of how it works. A police procedural requires the details of how evidence is collected, suspects interviewed, and bodies autopsied.

Another factor in gauging the amount of details you need is to ask how familiar or unfamiliar the situation you're writing about is. The more unfamiliar, the more details you'll need to give. For example, I had a student who was writing about a mythical colony of semihumans who lived underground. She needed to describe their underground life in fairly thorough detail. By contrast, a book about modern life may require fewer details because we already know what a McDonald's looks like and how fast the average car can drive.

That doesn't mean you should eliminate all the details about contemporary life. It's the job of literary writers in particular to let us see commonplace occurrences as if for the first time—and they can often do that by their careful choice of details. The novelist Sue Miller has a gift for it. In *The Good Mother*, she describes a laundromat: "The long row of gleaming yellow washers sat silent, lids up, open-mouthed." Elsewhere: "I liked the laundromat—the way it smelled, the rhythmic slosh of the machines, the ticking of buttons, zippers, in the dryers. . . ." There's more, but not much, because we've all seen laundromats. But by honing in on a few details, Miller brings this ordinary setting to life.

Whether your style and genre dictate that you shovel or sprinkle on the details, it's still important to choose well, to make your details earn their living by revealing much in a few words. One well-chosen detail can do the work of twenty banal ones. And when they do, I call them "killer-diller details."

Specific Details

Sometimes you can turn a banal detail into a killer-diller one by being specific. Don't tell us there were flowers in the yard—

name them. Don't say the man was wearing a suit—tell us it was double-breasted chalkstripe.

Challenge yourself to see just how specific you can get. "A red scarf" might be adequate, but how about a vermilion, crimson, or raspberry one? You might get away with "a stylish car," but a 1996 Mercedes 450SL in aubergine is bound to tell us more about the person behind the wheel.

Metaphors and similes can help make your details more specific, too. To be precise, "He ate like a pig" is a simile, and "He was a pig" is a metaphor. In both cases, the writer is taking a person and comparing him to something else that isn't there (presumably there's no pig in the restaurant).

If you write, "her face was as expressionless as a hard-boiled egg," the image of the woman's face lodges much more solidly in our minds than if you write, "Her face was blank." The latter, being a familiar idiom, passes through the reader's consciousness without even leaving a footprint.

Anne Tyler, in *Dinner at the Homesick Restaurant*, writes of "a spindly, starved cat with a tail as matted as a worn-out bottle-brush." Forever and ever I can perfectly see that cat's tail.

Beyond Blue-Eyed Blondes

Killer-diller details are not the obvious ones. Say your character is walking into a kitchen. Most kitchens have stoves and refrigerators and to tell us that this kitchen does, too, isn't telling us much. In the name of being specific, you might tell us that the kitchen has a restaurant-style oven with a six-burner range top, or an avocado side-opening General Electric refrigerator, and you'd be telling us more. But you might also try to zero in on what's in this kitchen that is not in the usual kitchen. A bowl of strawberries from the owner's own garden. A child's artwork on the refrigerator (and what does the artwork depict?). A manual Smith-Corona typewriter on the Formica table.

When describing people, beginning writers usually check off hair and eye color. "She was a redhead with green eyes." Then, if they have any energy left, they may get into general physique and cite the character's age.

I had a student once whose character descriptions were so formulaic that I suspected her of having created a format in her computer for them. "The thirty-six-year-old brunette mother of two was five-five." "The twenty-five-year-old blonde beauty was five-foot-eight."

I had a devil of a time breaking her of this habit, which to her seemed efficient, since it covered a character's vital statistics in a few words. When I first encouraged her to vary the description, she came up with, "At six-four, the hulky forty-year-old had gray hair and blue eyes."

It's true that in real life we often appraise the people we meet casually. If you tried to remember what the waitress at the coffee shop this morning looked like, you might come up with hair color and approximate height, if that. If you're not "into" houses, you might not remember much about your neighbor's living room beyond the color of the couch and wing chair.

But paradoxically, in order to make your reader believe in your fiction, it has to be more intense than real life. Documenting only the obvious facts about a character or an environment isn't enough. Sure, we often want to know what a character's hair and eye color are, her age and height. But we also need to know what it is about this character, or this couch, or this bowling ball, that is unlike any other person, couch, or bowling ball in the universe. We want to see the one loose button on a man's shirt. The graffiti scratched in the wood (and perhaps what it says). The Band-Aids on the fingertips of a nail-biter.

Details as Information

The facts of how things work are important details, and sometimes they can be killer-diller ones. When Tom Wolfe wrote

The Bonfire of the Vanities, he made us believe that Sherman McCoy was a bond trader by carefully detailing just how bonds are traded, giving us information that only a bond trader (or someone who had done thorough research) would know.

If you ever saw Billy Crystal and Danny DeVito in the movie *Throw Mama From the Train,* you know what I'm talking about from its opposite. Billy Crystal is a teacher of fiction writing (there should be more movies about teachers of fiction), and in an early scene in the film, one of his students has written a story about men on a submarine. She reads with great energy. " 'Dive! Dive!' yelled the captain through the thing. So the man who makes it dive pressed a button or something and it dove. And the enemy was foiled again."

Billy Crystal tactfully points out, "When you write a novel that takes place on a submarine, it's a good idea to know the name of the instrument that the captain speaks through."

In this case, knowing the names of the various equipment on a submarine is a necessary starting point. If the writer here can also provide the slang expression that Navy personnel use under stress, that would be a killer-diller detail.

How the Part Becomes the Whole

In a novel by Ken Kulhken, *The Angel Gang,* an old man, Leo, receives a beating at the hands of some thugs. At one point, the author describes how the thugs cut a slit in Leo's eyelid. When Leo closes his eyes, he can see through his eyelid. The image is horrific, but also very specific and concise. The one detail stands in for the whole beating.

That doesn't necessarily mean that you then eliminate all the rest of the description of that beating. As we've discussed, the exact number of details and the amount of description you include is a function of your style, the genre, and the content. But always be on the lookout for the killer-diller details that can encapsulate a person, environment, or incident.

In Barbara Kingsolver's novel, *Animal Dreams*, the narrator describes how her sister Hallie was so honest that, "I'd seen her tape dimes to broken parking meters." This killer-diller detail becomes the whole person for a moment, allowing us to imagine how she'd act in a hundred different situations. That doesn't mean that we don't want or need to know more about Hallie —of course we do, and the more important she is to the book as a whole, the more we'll want to know. Kingsolver in fact gives us many more killer-diller details to describe her.

An Exercise for Detail-Spotting

There's a technique for training yourself to produce these killer-diller details. Around dinnertime or later (if you're a night person), take ten minutes to note the five most interesting things you observed that day. Make this a rigid habit for at least a month.

Now, when I say write down what you observed, I don't mean the weighty insights you had while watching the clerk bag your groceries. I mean the most specific, and sometimes off-beat, details that you see (or hear, or taste, or smell, or touch). It doesn't have to be the color of the hold of an alien ship. I'm talking about details you might miss if you weren't paying attention. How *does* the clerk bag the groceries? Did he put the bread on the bottom? Did he have any unusual physical features? Did he ask you a too-personal question that made you uncomfortable?

Maybe while walking up and down the aisles at the store, you noticed that someone had stuck a package of linguine on top of the canned pineapple. Maybe you overheard a pair of twins fighting over who would get to ride in the cart. Those kind of details are hardly earth-shattering. But they're real and not immediately obvious, the way that writing, "It was a big, crowded grocery store with Muzak playing," *would* be obvious

—and banal. As you learn to add these types of details judiciously to your scenes, they, too, will become more real.

Here are some things I observed in the past couple of days:

• Two women were talking in Vietnamese, peppering their speech with "Wow!" and "Okay."

• The bus driver wore a royal blue-purple cable knit sweater that washed out her pale skin and white-blond eyebrows.

• My wedding ring tapping on the banister as I went down the stairs.

• An old man wearing a cardigan that used to be a woman's; the giveaway was that the buttons were backward.

• A red Ford pickup covered with bumper stickers: FARMS NOT ARMS, ABOLISH APARTHEID, ARMS ARE FOR HUGGING, ONE NUCLEAR BLAST CAN RUIN YOUR WHOLE DAY, I ♥ MY PSYCHOANALYST.

• A man with a belt-length black beard and a parrot on a leash.

• Walking down the street, I heard someone shuffling behind me. The whispery sound made me realize that the person was wearing bedroom slippers.

• At the deli, there was a woman wearing the jumpsuit of an American Airlines mechanic. Her name patch said, "Cupcake."

Remember as you practice observing that it's not a contest to see what offbeat or dramatic occurrences you can witness.

(No extra points for going to a hospital emergency room.) Nor is the goal to come up with details that you can actually use in your novel or story, although you may do that in the process. Rather, the point is to become more aware of what's going on around you. The point is to learn to mine even familiar surroundings for what's specific and unique about them. Then use those details in your writing to go beyond blue-eyed blondes, a description that probably fits 15 percent of the population.

Observing and recording your observations are also helpful exercises to get you back into a writing routine when you've been away for awhile, or when you're feeling stuck. But the greatest value lies in how your observations will translate, over time, to an improved ability to invent precise, informative, unpredictable details—in other words, killer-diller details that make the reader take notice.

And that's no lie.

DONNA LEVIN is the author of *Get That Novel Started!* and the *Get That Novel Written!* from which this article was adapted. She has also written two novels: *California Street* and *Extraordinary Means*.

Chapter 13

Sense and Sensuality

By Janet Fitch

Our lives at the millennium in advanced Western culture are the most senses-deprived of any on earth. Biologically and psychologically, the human organism was designed for intense experience in a richly sensual world. But we find ourselves in a senses-depleted world, a world limited largely to visuals, and ersatz ones at that.

Our senses aren't mere perceptions. We're not robots. The senses act upon us; they stimulate us in countless ways. We are the instrument the music is played on, not merely the listener to what's being played.

Think how sensually paltry our lives have become at the end of the twentieth century, compared with the world inhabited by our ancestors, or even of our "less privileged" brothers and sisters in other regions of the world still rich in uncensored sights, sounds, smells, textures, tastes.

As creatures of our time and place in Western civilization, we're cut off from the full spectrum of life by our very affluence, by our control of our physical environment. The most primitive senses especially—touch and smell—have been relegated to tiny islands of experience, as opposed to the range of these stimuli when we were open to the vagaries of physical reality.

Take touch. We wear shoes, clothes; our homes are weather-proofed. Our environments are "smoothed" for us. We don't work manually, we don't live among livestock and seasons. As small children, we're told to "look but don't touch." In our culture, sight is "good" but touch is "bad." Stop touching yourself. Don't handle your food. Keep your hands to yourself.

Smell is also "bad." Our culture deodorizes life. We don't cook things for hours so the smoke and the scent won't clog the interior. Our wools don't smell of lanolin. We live in cities, we don't smell the earth warming in spring, we don't appreciate the variations of body odor, even traditional strong-smelling foods. We avoid the least "stink."

The millennial reader is starving for sensual information. He wants the world back. And this is what good writing gives us—a rich, "full spectrum" sensual experience. Appealing to the five senses is the feature that will always set writing apart from the visual media. A good writer will tell us what the world smells like, what the textures are, what the sounds are, what the light looks like, what the weather is.

In sensual writing, the reader doesn't simply watch a character; he enter the character's body. If the character is cold, the reader is cold. If she's hungry, the readers experience her hunger. Sensual writing satisfies the reader's need to be in the flesh of a story, experiencing a richness of life that has often been robbed from his daily environment.

How do you describe a sense impression? How hot is hot? How sharp is sharp? How blue is the sky? What is the taste of a peach in summer? How would you describe a sunset to a blind man, the mockingbird's song to the deaf?

Angling for Description

You can get a certain distance with literal descriptions, but the truth is, most sense impressions cannot be directly described. So how do you achieve this necessary sensual writing? The first clue is to come in at an angle, obliquely, the way you approach all things evanescent. The quality of *synesthesia*—using one sense to describe another—comes to our aid in a big way.

Wine reviews provide excellent examples. Ever notice the things that critics taste in a glass of wine? Baritone notes, grass, daisies, butterscotch. A blonde wine. Sunshine. They find a wine crisp, or strawlike, or oaken or flaxen or young. Sprightly (Does that mean that it's going to bound off into the distance?) or sharp (Does this mean that they're going to stick themselves on the Chardonnay? That they're going to need a tetanus shot?).

What these critics are doing is using the other senses—textures, smells, sounds, and visuals—to describe a taste, something very difficult to describe. A review might start with the literal—"tastes like apples" or "tastes tart"—but this is an area quickly exhausted. So synesthesia is brought into play. From there it's a short leap to the fiction writer's best tool—fantasy.

Back to the wine review example. After pursuing the literal, move into synesthesia—the chocolatey, oaken, baritone notes of the cabernet, the rich brocade of its velvets. But that's not the end. As a fiction writer, go one step further. Think through the thing itself and travel to its point of origin, the soil where it grew, the small village, the hands that picked the grapes, the time of year, the time of day, and emerge with a whole secondary series of sensual information. You drink the wine and go through it to Burgundy, where you stick your hands in the soil and raise them to your nose, you talk to your French grandfather Jean Luc as you have lunch on the red-and-white checked tablecloth during the harvest season.

For fiction writers, the senses are not only a window onto external reality, but also the gateway into the inner realms.

Exercise 1

Try this exercise to reach through a sense into fantasy. Take a food, preferably something strong enough to "reach through" into the imagination. (I've found the more processed

and denatured, or desensualized, the item, the more difficult
it is to "reach through.") Describe the taste first in literal terms.
Then describe it synesthesially. Finally, move into the imagination.
Take your time. See if you can reach through the taste into a
complete scene, a time of year, a time of day, a place and
people as you stretch out from your sense data.

I recommend you keep all these sense exercises in a three-ring
binder, organized by category ("touch," "smell") for reference. You'll be surprised how useable this information will prove
to be in your fiction writing.

Exercise 2

Practice this exercise using various fragrances. Try writing about
simple scents, rather than perfumes, which already have implied moods and narratives. Sample essential oils, spices, herbs,
even common household substances such as bleach, vinegar,
or ammonia. (Don't sniff straight from the bottle, whether it's
cologne or something toxic like bleach or ammonia! Do as chemists
do: Hold the open bottle away from your face and then waft the
scent toward you with your hand.) Use your impressions to
give your characters distinct scents, bringing another dimension
of the sensual world into play.

A tool I regularly use is a "scent organ." At a garage sale, I
found a box with ten small bottles that had once been used
for ginseng. I put a wad of cotton in each one, and went to a
local purveyor of body products and essential oils and paid
them five bucks to give me a few drops of ten different fragrances
in those vials. I took great care to select scents that were most
evocative for me. Hawaiian pikake (my mother's perfume was
pikake when I was a child), almond, rose, eucalyptus. Bitter
California orange that smells like my old neighborhood here in
L.A. where people didn't pick the fruit, just left it to rot on
the trees. Whenever I open that vial, I am fifteen.

Making Sense of Memory

Nothing stimulates memory like sense data. Memory lies coiled within us like a magician's trick handkerchief, and a simple smell or taste can pluck the tiniest corner and pull out the world. When playing with sense exercises, watch for memories as they begin to emerge. Remember, Proust started with that little madeleine dipped in tea.

As you read over your sense exercises, you'll notice something readers have always instinctively known. The most interesting smells/colors/sounds are those that are not strictly speaking sense impressions at all, but instead, memories and fantasies, purely psychological matters.

Think of baby powder. You can describe it literally: sweet, chalky, talcy, dusty, sneezy. You can do synesthesias: smells pastel, smells tender. Then move to the psychological element. Take an attitude on that smell: insipid, cloying, stultifying, like diaper rash, airless. Try a different attitude: sad, lost, vulnerable, hopeless, eradicable. This is the Heisenberg aspect of description—a sense impression can be colored by the observer's take on that information, so that the description can reveal character as well as define the exterior experience.

Finally, move utterly into the realm of memory and fantasy, working to the associations of that smell: It smells like children, like bath time, like rabbits, bubble bath, lullabies, soft towels, the bluebirds over the dressing table, my mother's face, powder on my father's suit, bare bottoms of grandchildren, my own early motherhood, how tired I was, the fourteen diaper changes a day, my insecurity and fears, marital problems with the new father who wasn't used to being second banana. I imagine throwing the powder at him and how it fountains through the air.

The smell is merely the stimulus. Describe the stimulus, and then move to the psychological component.

The Intensity of Touch

The sense of touch is the most vivid and direct source of information about the world. It is also the most neglected, the most taboo. Touch is pain and pleasure, the most intense source of direct stimuli.

Keep a running list of vocabulary to describe aspects of touch, texture, and shape. You'll use it over and over again. Start by listing dichotomies: Hard/soft, smooth/rough, straight/curved, hot/cold, wet/dry, heavy/light, give or no give.

Exercise 3

Amass items that are texturally interesting: sand, a rock, a hammer, a feather duster, a piece of lace, a baseball, a sponge, a wooden spoon, a rubber duck, a nylon stocking, a stuffed animal, gravel, marbles. With your eyes closed, pick up one and really feel it. Experience it, finding the words to describe the sensations, both literally and synesthesially. Notice details, referring and adding to the list of texture words above. Exhaust the physical. The purpose of this exercise is to train your ability to write literal description.

Touch is an activity as well as a sensation. We can enjoy the fine sponginess of a piece of steel wool with our fingertips, or we can scrub it up and down the insides of our arms for a very different sensation. A strip of leather can be soft and pliable to the fingers, but if someone whips us with it. . . . So touch is a gesture as well as the thing touched. It is also the impact of an object on the skin, the largest organ of the body.

Exercise 4

This exercise illustrates touch as a springboard to fantasy/memory. Take a piece of fabric. Close your eyes and feel it. Feel it with your hands, with your arms, across the back of your neck, under your feet, behind your knees, across your chest. Press it to your cheek, your lips. Ask yourself, what is this cloth? A piece of scratchy wool might end up being a school uniform; a piece of velvet might be a theater chair or your grandmother's couch. Take an attitude. What's happening here? Be a character who is touching this cloth. Who are you? Where are you?

As you develop your awareness of the senses, you will find yourself collecting a vivid sensual vocabulary. As you read and write, you may note that the richest, most vivid words are those that use more than one of the senses at a time. For example, a yellow sky—how many senses does that appeal to? One—the visual. However, a lemon sky refers to color, taste, smell, and even texture. Four senses implied in a single word. Or take a brassy blonde—brass implies a sound, a color, and a texture, even a taste (if you've ever licked brass, you know what I mean). That's four senses. In this way, the synesthetic layering effect adds depth and dimensionality to your sensual world on the page.

What Aren't You Hearing?

Our world is a chaos of noise. In fact, we even use sound—music—to drown out the ambient sound as a way to control our environment, just as we use deodorant to cut us off from smell, and air conditioning and heating to alter our tactile environment.

But as writers, we want to pay attention to this neglected sound so when characters pause in dialogue, or when they are alone, they hear something in the silences.

Exercise 5

Take ten minutes and just listen. List what you hear. Record this ambient sound at various times of day, in various places, keeping this data for your sense notebook. Note over time the audible difference between summer and winter (summer is louder because the windows are usually open). Note the difference between morning ambient sound and that at 3 A.M.

Many writers are fond of playing music and writing to it, using it to control mood. As an exercise, I find I get more out of unfamiliar music, or music I don't like, more than old favorites. If you hate polka, try playing polka and see what kind of a reaction you can get out of it!

Look to the Light

What can I teach you about seeing? As writers, we need to begin to see richly, the way a painter or photographer sees. We need to analyze what we see.

The first lesson of the visual is that all seeing is seeing light. We need to be continually conscious that what we see is the effect of how light strikes objects within our visual range. Think of how Rembrandt sculpted his light. Instead of writing about what things look like, try writing about the light and how the light strikes the objects.

A good way to expose yourself to the vocabulary of light is to read books on art. For example, water words describe light: it pours, it washes, it splashes, it soaks, it plays. Light is a painter, a sculptor: it strokes, it daubs, it rubs, it burnishes. Light does things to objects, so its verbs are quite active. Examination of light in describing a scene will eliminate once and for all the static descriptions because there can always be something active in a scene, if only the light itself.

Exercise 6

To write effectively about light, you must develop vocabulary to describe how light affects what you see. Light a candle in a room and "paint" what you see. Describe the angle at which the light falls. Note precisely what is illuminated and what is left in shadow. What is the quality of the light? What direction is the light coming from? What is the color of the light?

I've only touched on the coastline of the vast continent of sense exploration. I urge you to don your pith helmet and explore the interior, and use what you bring back in everything you write. If you learn to properly play your own instrument, your own five senses, you will be able to move another finely tuned instrument—your reader.

JANET FITCH is the author of *White Oleander*. Her short fiction has appeared in *Black Warrior Review, Rain City Review,* and other journals.

Chapter 14

Why True-Life Stories Often Don't Make Good Fiction

By Alyce Miller

How many times have you been inspired to turn a true story (amusing anecdote, tragic episode, personal experience) into fiction? Or after hearing a particularly good story, one that moved you to laughter or close to tears, you've thought, "Wow! Now that would make a good piece of fiction"?

Why is it that after transcribing the story to paper, you discover it has failed miserably on the page? Worse, readers and editors conspire to tell you the story is boring (nothing happens), improbable, predictable, or even *unrealistic*. How can real stories seem unrealistic? Don't most fiction writers borrow material from real life for their stories?

The answer is yes, but fiction writers draw on many other sources as well. Often what appears in works of fiction is a combination of "true stories," imagination, and invention. This is what distinguishes fiction from much nonfiction.

Probably six of the biggest pitfalls in writing directly from true life are as follows:

1. Writing stories from which you have either too much or too little distance. With too much distance, you may not know enough to flesh out the story beyond anecdote; with too little distance, your familiarity may get in your way as you assume your reader will automatically feel the same way you do about the material.

2. Relying on and allowing the "real life" plot to drive the story toward "the way it really happened," rather than exploring alternate routes.

3. Neglecting character development; assuming that because you think a real life person is funny or tragic, your reader will too.

4. Wanting to stay in control and explain why everything happened the way it did; overlooking the wonderful possibilities of ambiguity, irony, and understatement.

5. Straitjacketing the writing itself because you know exactly where the story is going.

6. Failing to include essential details that convince and give texture. Again, relying on your own emotional response to a real-life situation, rather than to the careful detail and development that move the story machinery.

Inventing Another Kind of Truth

It's helpful to remember that one of the shifts that marks so much contemporary fiction is from "what the writer already knows and wants to impart" to "what the writer discovers." Contemporary fiction typically resists demonstration and instruction, and leans more toward exploration and open-endedness. Readers of contemporary fiction expect to play a very different role from their nineteenth-century counterparts.

Writers who get stuck in transcribing real-life stories cheat themselves and their readers of the potential for mutual discovery.

My creative writing students frequently express frustration with their flawed attempts to transform real life to fiction. A student in an adult fiction class I recently taught dismissed all critiques of weak moments in her stories with this rationalization: "But that's the way it really happened. It's the truth." Her readers' responses were, "But you haven't convinced us."

What my student forgot is that fiction is, as the adage tells us, a means of transforming, not simply transcribing, life. "Truth" is always prismatic. Fiction, by its very nature, alters and falsifies. The fictive dream offers the illusion of truth. It is very different from factual reportage.

Certainly, fiction writers often borrow ideas from real life, but they also mix and blend real-life events, characters, and images with what they invent and imagine. Often, writers may start with a snippet of conversation or an interesting image from real life and work from there, allowing each idea to choose the next. Fiction writers must always be open to possibility. Perhaps in real life the main characters of your story live in southern California, but if you know little or nothing about southern California and the landscape and culture of southern California are not essential to the story, you might consider choosing a setting you are more familiar with. Readers can tell when you're stretching thin what little you do know.

Sculpting real-life events and characters is a given in fiction. Remember, you're not a journalist concerned with the exact recording of "facts." Fiction writers are inventors of another kind of truth.

Examining the Truth

Another student of mine recently wrote a long, involved love story based on an emotional experience that really happened to him. The story failed on many levels.

It opened with the accidental reunion of two high school sweethearts in a small western town that they just happened to find themselves in. The woman now worked as a waitress in a bar where the man had coincidentally stopped to gamble. We are told in the second paragraph that the woman had jilted the man eighteen years before, and the man was still nursing a broken heart. By page three, the couple had slipped off to a motel and fallen into bed together. In the afterglow of sexual ecstasy, they realized they had never stopped being in love. By page five, they were living together. The woman had a young daughter, by another lover, named Valentine. The little girl immediately became attached to the male protagonist, no questions asked. The three lived in perfect familial harmony for a year until the final pages when the man realized he simply could not make a commitment. We never knew why, since up until that point everything seemed to be going along swimmingly. The story ended with the departing man promising the little girl he would send her a card every year on her birthday, which fell on Valentine's Day.

So how did the story fail?

First, coincidence (in this case, the accidental meeting) is always difficult to pull off in fiction. Handled carelessly, it comes across as a trick, or even laziness on the part of the author (the way the line, "And then I woke up," does). The coincidence in the student's story, even though true, rightly struck the readers as "hokey." But because it "really happened," the student was reluctant to part with that detail.

Since the coincidence was not essential to the story, the student might have considered other possibilities that would have helped the character development. Example: What might happen if the man deliberately came looking for the woman? What if he had been seeking revenge? What if he was happily married to someone else? What factors in her present life might have prompted him to seek out the old girlfriend? What if the reunion took place in their old home town, which the woman had never left, making it logical for the two to be in the same place simultaneously? What if the man didn't recognize the woman right away, or vice versa? What if she had come looking for him?

A second problem: The student relied on the weight of his

own emotional attachment to the situation, rather than character development, to convince the reader to care about the two characters. He assumed the readers would automatically accept the man's passion for the woman. What he forgot is that the real-life subject matter was not loaded for his readers in the same way it was for him.

Third, his choice of perspective through a thinly disguised version of himself as the male protagonist allowed him no opportunity to play with point-of-view possibilities. Writing "himself" restricted him. The issue of distance arises here. Perhaps because he felt so emotionally linked to the situation, he found it impossible to write with a certain necessary detachment that might have led him to a more fully realized character. As a result, he ended up with a shamelessly bland protagonist whose motives were vague and whose actions seemed unfathomable. Hard to feel sympathy for such a character!

Fourth, the dialogue between the two lovers showed none of the tension or irony that this strained situation would ostensibly produce. The student stuck pretty much to "real-life small talk," which may have been true to life but is rarely of interest. Fictionalized dialogue *simulates* real-life dialogue, but must be carefully selected for the way in which it serves the story. A line like, "What a nice house you have" could work if it was, say, ironic, for example, if we knew the woman lived in a rundown trailer. But the student's dialogue consistently mirrored the action ("Would you like some lemonade?" she asked, handing him a pitcher) and revealed nothing about the characters' feelings or true motives. When in conflict or crisis, people often don't say what they really mean and this can be used to great advantage by writers in developing tension. Many times actions speak louder than any words. For example, how would the reader have read the same scene if the woman offered the man lemonade and her hands were trembling? Or she poured him a glass of lemonade without asking him if he wanted any? Or she gave him a glass of lemonade while she drank beer? Or she gave him lemonade that was too sour?

Fifth, the student failed to develop the dynamics inherent in the main conflict between the two characters. After all, the man had been jilted by the woman. What must he be feeling? How would he behave? When he jumped in bed with her, were his motives mixed? The setup offered tremendous potential for the subtle expression of complex dynamics, but the story as the student wrote it lacked any of the tension suggested organically by the circumstances.

Finally, the student relied on a cliché at the end as a stand-in for the complexity of the man's sadness at leaving the little girl named Valentine. Even though in real life the child's birthday fell on Valentine's Day and her name was Valentine, the device felt corny. Readers objected that the story had descended unforgivably into bathos. How to get away from that? The student might have reconsidered whether the Valentine's Day detail was crucial to the story and discovered he was using it as an easy stand-in for more complex dynamics yet to be explored. Or he might have set out to discover what would happen if the little girl were not so likable. Or what if she weren't six (as she was in "real life"), but ten or fourteen? What if she had been omitted entirely from the story?

Avoiding the Clichés of Life

Writers must be attentive to the clichés that real life serves up and either make something of them (freshen them, challenge them, work against them) or abandon them altogether.

Speaking of clichés, the love story is by its very nature already a cliché. How to work against that? Consider a piece as poignant and disturbing as Chekov's "The Lady With the Dog" or Lawrence's "Horse Dealer's Daughter." Both are love stories. But both leave the reader uneasy by resisting what is expected and

challenging the reader to think beyond the narrative lines of
"boy meets and gets girl."

Another problem with translating directly from real life is that
it is only infrequently punctuated by trouble that is interesting. A happy family reunion in which all the relatives are thrilled
to see one another, true as it may be, is boring to read about
because nothing happens. It lacks the critical elements essential
to fiction: conflict or crisis. A conflict or crisis can be as subtle
as the boy narrator's thwarted romantic quest in Joyce's short
story "Araby," or as shocking as the murderous jealous rage
of Tolstoy's protagonist in "The Kreutzer Sonata."

At the other end of the spectrum, remember that real life can
be stranger than fiction. "Trouble" in real life may be far too
complicated or unbelievable to translate directly into fiction. It
may need condensing and distilling in order to make it work.
Again, the very strangeness of real life may be a stumbling block
unless the writer can work in the details that convince, or
push the strangeness to new levels.

I have often wrestled with the challenges of fictionalizing the
complexities of real people and events. For example, I tried to write
about a woman I know who has been kidnapped, raped, and
beaten; who has had seven abortions and three children, all by
different men; who has struggled with alcohol and drug abuse;
who finally shot to death her abusive common-law husband
and spent four years in prison, where she was impregnated by a
guard. When she gave birth in the prison hospital, her family
had only a couple of days to make arrangements to get the baby
out. After the woman's release from prison, she dated an ex-
prisoner who, at age fourteen, had bludgeoned his grandparents
to death. Shortly thereafter, she slept repeatedly with her one
sister's husband, also an ex-convict. She had a second sister who
was an alcoholic and lived with a string of abusive men.

All of the these facts are drawn from real life, yet their very
volume proved distracting. I discovered that the undiluted,

untransformed truth was far too complicated and implausible to work as fiction. I realized I would have to stretch my readers' credibility too far and run the risk of disrupting the fictive illusion. I might easily be accused of contrivance or soap-opera camp.

When working from complicated real-life stories, you might consider simplifying and concentrating on one event, allowing the story to blossom from that point. Discover what it is that interests you most. For example, I might have chosen to focus on the moment when the woman's baby was born in the prison hospital. Or the moment when she had to hand the child over to her alcoholic sister. Or I might have focused on the hours leading up to her sister's discovery of the adultery.

Some of the other real-life events might work as texture, woven into the background fabric. By narrowing the overwhelming number of explosive facts about this woman's life, I would be more likely to develop the story with depth and not rely on a barrage of sensational events to pump up emotion. And I could have made use of some of the other details through implication and understatement.

Remember that writing fiction is a selection process. Writers sift through a vast array of experiences (real, imagined, and borrowed) and choose the details that serve the story. Real life has no such filters. It comes in gusts and storms.

Fiction, like life, is not static or fixed. Writing is an act of discovery in an infinite field of possibility. Telling a story exactly as it happened may put a stranglehold on the sheer delight and pace of invention. Don't suffocate the life out of interesting stories. Allow them to breathe and grow.

Some Things to Remember
• Real life is only one source for your story ideas. Combine what you observe in real life with what you invent and imagine. Keep a writer's notebook. Collect ideas.

• Truth is often stranger than fiction. Create composites of people and events by finding their "essence." Simplify without flattening. Say more through less. Allow implication and nuance, not volume, to create texture and depth.

• Real life happens a day at a time. A hundred years can pass in a fictional sentence. An hour can be elongated to last an entire novel. Time in fiction is often collapsed or prolonged. It does not adhere to the neat little increments of real life. Condense or skip over periods of time that have little bearing on your story.

• Complexities and contradictions of human beings must usually be refined in fiction without reducing characters to attributes. Consider what is most interesting about the characters you're working with. Resist the urge to overexplain, a habit with tellers of real-life stories. Allow your curiosity to roam freely. Allow real-life characters to be transformed. Don't hold any real-life detail too precious. Be ruthless. If it's not working, abandon it.

• Try starting with the kernel of a real-life story. The best way to enter a story is through your own curiosity. In real life, you know Aunt Carol wept at Grandma's funeral because she was sad. But your curiosity might suggest that maybe Aunt Carol's tears signified something other than sadness. What if she was actually elated Grandma died and her tears are tears of joy? Or she's crying out of guilt because her last words to Grandma were cruel? Or perhaps her tears have nothing to do with Grandma at all, but with the unexpected presence of her ex-lover at the funeral.

• If you've conveniently entered the story from your real-life point of view, try telling the story through another character's eyes. Explore different "I" narrators. Explore the use of third person (both limited and omniscient). Notice how a change in point of view allows the thinly disguised version of yourself to become someone else.

Finally, don't get stuck in real life. Keep your fictive possibilities open! Real life is only part of the story

ALYCE MILLER's fiction and poetry have won numerous awards and have appeared in such journals as *Story*, *The Southern Review*, and the *Kenyon Review*. She is the author of *The Nature of Longing*, winner of the Flannery O'Connor Award, and *Stopping for Green Lights*.

Chapter 15

Fiction's Connecting Link: Emotion

By Kathy Jacobson

Without emotion, fiction becomes flat and boring. With it, you hook your readers, pull them in, hold them to the end, *and* make them eager for your next story or novel. So let's look at how you can enrich your writing by increasing the emotional level.

First of all, consider emotion as a triangle. One side represents the emotion of the author (your enthusiasm for the story), the second represents the emotions of the characters (how they interpret and respond to the events of the story), and the third represents the emotion of the readers (how closely they will identify with the characters). Your challenge is to make each side of the triangle strong enough to ensure the book doesn't collapse on itself (fail to interest an editor).

Your Enthusiasm

Do you love the genre you've picked? Are you an avid fan? You must have passion for the *type* of novel or story you plan to write or your work will lack excitement. The subject matter must fill you with enthusiasm, or the task of putting words on paper will soon become drudgery.

Love your work, love your story, love your characters, love the challenge of creating a book. Even when things don't go well, or you get a rejection, or your critique group discovers holes in your plot, remember that you write for the joy of it.

Also, don't be afraid of your own emotions. In the course of living, you've experienced hate, love, joy, anger, success, disappointment, fulfillment, and heartache. Strip away any inhibitors and screens you've developed to protect yourself from those who don't understand you, and let your feelings pour out on the page.

The Character's Emotions

Stories are about people. They tell the stories of the characters that fill them. They describe who the characters are, where they go, what they do, who they encounter. But most important, stories portray *why* characters behave in certain ways, and the *why* always arises from emotion.

Suppose your character gets shoved while walking down the sidewalk. Will he beg pardon, swear but hurry on, shove back, or pull a knife? His reaction will come from his unique emotional state, whether he's frightened, harassed, or angry, or whether he views himself as a victim or a fighter. Obviously, the better you know your characters, the more surely you'll give them the right emotional reaction.

Unlike real life, where human beings often act irrationally, story people must behave with a certain consistency. You can't have your young heroine be naive one moment and seductive the next. If she's shy and innocent, she'll be horrified by violence and profanity. On the other hand, if she's streetwise and cynical, she won't be looking at the world through rose-colored glasses. Her behavior will be believable because it will match her emotional reactions.

Reader Identification

Readers like books to carry them into the unknown. They like characters who are unusual, who open new arenas for them, who introduce them to situations they might never personally experience. This means that as writers, we have unlimited opportunities to explore new worlds. But we must also give readers something they can relate to, something that will form a bridge between the familiar and the unknown. Emotion will *always* create such a bridge.

When the Triangle Doesn't Work

Okay, so you're passionate about your story, your character's emotions are well motivated, and you believe any reader who picks up your book will be entranced by it. Then you give your manuscript to a friend (or your spouse or your mother) who returns it with an enthusiastic, "What a nice little story." Or worse, "Well, you know I don't really like romances, but this one seemed okay." Or more obtuse, "You really made me see the setting." Or you might be lucky enough to have a reader with guts enough to say, "You've got some good stuff here, but something's missing. I just don't know what it is."

When this happens, it is most often the second part of the triangle—the character's emotional response—that you'll need to shore up. So let's see how you can build your character's emotions into a strong connecting link between you, the writer, and your reader.

Conveying the Character's Emotions

Your first challenge is deciding what the character feels. If you were to identify the character's primary driving emotion, what word would you use? Is he angry, eager, curious, hurt, happy, depressed? Try to find *one* adjective that best fits his emotional state, then identify how that one emotion defines his character.

If he's angry, how does he express that anger? Does he wear

it like armor to deflect all attackers (real or imaginary)? Does he keep it locked tightly inside, like a bomb ready to explode? Or does he use it as a weapon, coldly and with firm purpose to get what he wants?

If he's eager, does this make him confident, aggressive, responsive to others, indifferent to roadblocks?

If he's hurt, does he keep a running total of insults and slights, letting them become the entire focus of his life? Or is he hunting for a cure, moving from psychiatrists to self-help books to love relationships to drugs, always looking for something outside of himself to solve his problem?

As you can see, the primary driving emotion gives you a cornerstone, and developing an emotional profile becomes your foundation. Once you have this foundation firmly in your mind, build the emotional framework by considering the following:

1. Identify Your Character's Worst Fault

To help you pinpoint the characteristic that will serve you best in looking for such a weakness, look to the end of your story. What insecurity, blind spot, failing, or fear will propel your character into the final crisis or black moment? He'll need to be working from some expectation or agenda that keeps him from resolving his problem until circumstances force him into it. What inner failing drives that expectation or agenda? What keeps him from making the choices that would have prevented the crisis?

Depending on the type of story you're writing, you may have to present the worst fault in a way that keeps the character likeable. For instance, in a romance, you can't allow your heroine to come across as a whiner or have your hero still needing to prove himself to his father. But don't short-change your characters by choosing tepid weaknesses. Remember, the harder the struggle, the more emotion you can build.

2. Recognize Your Character's Greatest Strength

What sets your character apart from the crowd? What inner emotional resource does your hero have that he can call on or discover to help him conquer in the end? Again, look to the final crisis of the story and consider what it will take for him to win. Just as you've given your character a fault to propel him into the black moment, give him a positive trait that will provide him with the power to overcome both his opponent and his own weaknesses.

3. Give Your Characters Specific, Urgent Goals

What the characters want must be strong enough to drive them to get it against all complications, all adversity, any danger, and often in spite of their better judgment. Does your character want anything that intensely?

Don't skimp. Make the goals important. Make them believeable, and make sure they'll have emotional impact for the reader. If the character's long-range goal is to find happiness or inner peace, you'll have to give him a dramatic, difficult history that will infuse the goal with power through contrast.

No matter how important the goal is, it has to be urgent in order to have emotional force. Put pressure on the character's ability to achieve the goal. Make it a race—against time, an enemy, his own mental stability, financial security, danger, another's choices—to keep the tension high.

4. Consider How Your Character Will React in Various Situations

Is he likely to become insecure or belligerent when threatened? How does he react to generosity? When he's angry, does he erupt or hold it in? How can you tell if he's bored? Excited? Frustrated? Annoyed? What mannerisms does he adopt? What physical manifestations will his body exhibit?

Make sure his reactions are consistent. The reader will believe a character who trembles with anger, fidgets when bored, and cries for victims *if* you've shown that he wears his emotions on his sleeve. If he's built an emotional shell around himself so his eyes never fill with tears and he never raises his voice, we can believe he'd kill the man who raped his daughter *if* you show that by holding his emotions in, they've reached fever pitch.

5. Give the Character an Inner Conflict

Why is the character insecure, unhappy, angry, afraid, or frustrated? What motivates him to act? Will he fight or flee? Why? Can you force him into a situation (the conflict of your story) in which he must act against his true nature? If he's a fighter, what would it take to make him run? If he'd normally take flight, what circumstances would make him stand his ground?

6. Integrate Your Character Well

Since good fiction depends on good conflict, you want to build conflict wherever possible. But even when your fighter must flee, you have to make him self-consistent. You have to motivate the conflicts within your character as well as without, so make sure his goals reflect his personality and his strengths don't preclude his weaknesses. Make him as complex as you want, but be sure his personality reflects his background and motivations.

Connecting With the Reader

Once you know how the character will react, you have to present the emotions behind the reactions in a way that makes the reader *feel* what the character feels. You can do this in a number of ways, and showing is better than telling.

Some verbs always tell and never show, especially any form of *to be* or *to feel*. For example, if you write, *Mark was bitter*, or *Mark felt bitter*, you're telling. If you write, *Mark crumpled the letter from his father, vowing never to return home again*, you've given him two specific actions that *show* his emotion and help the reader *feel* Mark's bitterness.

Use verbs that connote emotion rather than merely describe action. For instance, strode, paced, ambled, marched, strolled, and tromped are all better than walked. In order, they convey purpose, anxiety, contentment, anger, leisure, and duty, while walked only shows movement.

Use adjectives that indicate the character's emotional interpretation. A room can be dingy, sterile, homey, oppressive, crowded, busy, inviting, silent, tacky, impressive, or intimidating, depending on who's looking at it. Be sure to choose adjectives that reflect the character's view and not your own, since the emotional bridge you want to build is between the *character* and the reader.

Watch Your Point of View

Recognize that the character is a stronger narrator than the author. Any time you start describing the action rather than letting the character experience it, you're distancing the character from the reader. This will cost you both immediacy and emotion. Look at this example in which an omniscient narrator describes Mark's situation:

> Mark's father had always ordered him around, and this letter was just another good example. Mark read it again and again, and bitterness grew acrid inside him. The daughter of one of his dad's old cronies would be visiting next week, and Mark was instructed to come home and meet her. Crumpling the letter, he decided the time had come to make a break.

Now look at it from Mark's point of view:

Mark crumpled his father's letter and lobbed it into the garbage can. After two years, the old man still didn't get it. Mark made his own decisions now. He chose his own girlfriends. He sure as hell didn't rush home to meet the daughter of one of his dad's old cronies.

Can you see the difference in these two exmples? Although both are well written, one pulls the reader tighter into the character's point of view and, therefore, his emotional state. Where the first describes the emotion, the second lets the character experience it.

Apply the Emotional Filter

Everything in your story will have greater impact if you have your character interpret it emotionally. Involve the five senses to give your writing strong sensory texture, then make sure you convey your character's emotional assessment of what she experiences. For example, on assignment for the Star System Regulatory Agency, Lily lands on a planet she's never visited before. She's going to notice the color of the sky, the bleakness of the landscape, the odor of the air, and the flavor of the water, but her impressions are going to be more important than the details in drawing your reader into the scene. Let's see a simple description first:

Lily stepped through the Theta Gate and took in the scene before her. Humanoids from a dozen planets mingled with multi-pods, avians, and the local Zerips. Pink clouds floated across the red sky. The air had a distinctly chlorine odor, and a few leafless trees lined the main route into the city.

Now let's run the scene through Lily's emotional filter and see how much richer it becomes:

> Lily stepped through the Theta Gate and wrinkled her nose in distaste. Humanoids from a dozen planets mingled with multi-pods, avians, and the local Zerips, but only the Zerips looked at home under the hideous red sky. She tried to filter enough oxygen out of the chlorine-heavy air to satisfy her lungs, but gave up after a few breaths. The air mix wouldn't kill her, although it didn't seem to do much for the few leafless trees that lined the main route into the city.

As a rule of thumb, if your character doesn't care enough about what she sees, hears, tastes, touches, and smells to give some emotional assessment to it, the reader won't care either. And this applies to everything—action, dialogue, description, and other characters. Here's an example of an exchange between two characters:

> Angie watched Hugh stride between the rows of computer terminals. He didn't glance at any of the data operators, but kept his eyes fixed on her. When he reached her desk, he smiled.
>
> "We brought Williams in last night," he said.
>
> She pressed her palms flat against her thighs. "Did he confess?"
>
> "Not in so many words." Hugh lifted his hand and examined his nails. When he spoke again, his eyes were serious. "He said Charlotte Mason was having an affair with Johnny Keno."
>
> Angie let the information sink in.

We have dialogue and action, but no emotion. We don't know

Angie's opinion of Hugh, or his of her. We have no hint of whether she's glad or sorry to hear the news about Williams, or what effect the information about Charlotte has on her. To give your work more potency, run it through your focal character's emotional filter. Keep the reader constantly connected to the character by giving the character opinions and judgments. Let's look at the previous exchange again, this time with Angie's emotional filter in place:

> With her heart beating double time, Angie watched Hugh stride between the rows of computer terminals. Until yesterday, just being in his presence had sent her heart racing. Today, she feared what he would tell her.
>
> He didn't glance at any of the data operators, but kept his eyes fixed on her. When he reached her desk, he smiled. "We brought Williams in last night."
>
> Max Williams knew everything, but how much would he tell? Angie cleared her throat, hoping no trace of her fear would show in her voice. "Did he confess?"
>
> "Not in so many words." Hugh lifted his hand to examine his nails and let the suspense build.
>
> Suddenly she saw his hand in the whole sordid affair. He'd seduced her for what he could get from her, and now he toyed with her like a cat who'd cornered a mouse. She pressed her palms flat on her thighs to keep from wringing her hands together.
>
> When Hugh spoke again, his eyes were hard. "He said Charlotte Mason was having an affair with Johnny Keno."
>
> The words flowed through Angie's mind and pooled near her heart like congealing tar. So Charlotte had been in on it all along.

Notice in the second version that Angie interprets her own reactions for the reader *and* conveys hints on Hugh's agenda. Since you don't want to go into Hugh's mind while in Angie's point of view, she has to transmit his behavior. Since she can't know what's going on in his head, she has to interpret it based on her on assumptions, which means we see him through her emotional filter.

Opinions and Judgments

The emotional filter is always subjective. It presents your focal character's view of your story world, the situation, the other characters, and the conflicts. By attaching his opinions to his observations and having him make judgments on everyone else's behavior, he not only becomes a stronger character, but your reader will form a stronger emotional bond with him.

Every once in a while, you may find yourself writing a scene through the eyes of your villain or some other unsympathetic character. Be sure to make his filter true to him. Present his warped view in the living color of his hang-ups and destructive agenda. If you do this well, the reader will love reading about him because he will be so compellingly *un*likeable.

If you find it difficult to include the subtleties of an emotional filter while writing your first draft, don't self-edit during the creative process. Write your dialogue or your action and add opinions and judgments on the second or third time through. Invest heavily where you have the most control (your own effort and emotion), and reap the benefits when the reader connects emotionally to your characters and loves your story.

KATHY JACOBSON is the author of *A Novel Approach: Blending Emotion and Structure to Create a Salable Novel.* She has also written novels for Harlequin, including *The Sheriff With the Wyoming Size Heart* and has taught novel writing since 1991.

Chapter 16

Location, Location, Location: Depicting Character Through Place

By Richard Russo

My first novel, *Mohawk*, as it was eventually published, was a kind of ensemble novel that had a dozen or so important characters and employed numerous points of view. Put all the stories together and you had at their center a portrait of a place, a small fictional town in upstate New York, and in the center of that town a dive called the Mohawk Grill.

The town and the grill proved so compelling, at least to me, that I set another novel there. But you may be surprised to learn that the first completed draft of the novel that was published as *Mohawk* was set in Tucson, Arizona, where I happened to be living when I wrote it. The book was about an elderly woman named Anne Grouse, who began the book bitter and ended up more bitter still—not an emotional trajectory I particularly recommend, though it describes a fair number of contemporary novels.

Beyond these few facts, I don't really remember much about this early draft. I gave it to a friend and mentor, who read it and told me what I suspected and maybe even knew but certainly didn't want to hear. He explained that the book wasn't very good, that being in the company of a bitter person in a long work of fiction isn't much more fun than being in the company of a bitter person in real life. Also, my writing betrayed a tourist's knowledge of the Southwest, where I had spent the last six years in a study carrel at the University of Arizona library. On the slender plus side, my friend noted that Anne was a much more interesting person when she was younger, when she still had hopes and dreams and hadn't managed to mess up her life. About the only scenes that really lived were set in the upstate New York town where Anne was raised—one in a glove shop where Anne's father worked and the other at a down-at-the-heels amusement park on the lake.

Also, he told me, the minor characters were far more interesting than the major ones.

Well, this brutal honesty pretty much squared with my own sense of the book. The minor characters—mere functionaries, I'd thought—were people who grew out of the place and the necessity of the place. The glove shop where Anne's father worked was the one my grandfather had spent his entire adult life toiling in, and the dying amusement park, along its shabby midway, was where both my mother in the 'thirties and I in the 'fifties had learned to dream among the fluttering lights and the rigged games of chance. I was no tourist on that midway, but there was a problem: I *wanted* to be a tourist there. I'd left my hometown of Gloversville, New York, when I was eighteen, enrolled in a university twice the size of that town, and by the end of my first week there, learned my first lesson: that I'd do well to hide where I was from. For the next ten years, first as an undergraduate, then as a graduate student, I walked backward, erasing my tracks with that wonderful switch we call education. I learned how to read carefully and talk to smart people and work from the outside in when confronted at a table with more than one fork. In becoming a writer, I had intended to make use of these lessons I'd learned and for this reason, I was not pleased to learn that the only things I'd managed to bring to life in my first novel were the things I'd hoped—Judas that I was—to deny.

Discovering Your *Place*

Intellectually, of course, I already knew that place *was* character. That's Intro Fiction 101. I could illustrate the point with numerous examples from my reading. I knew that London was a character in Dickens, and that it spawned Mr. Micawber, and Crook, and Scrooge. And I could tell what happened to Dickens when he ventured too far from the place that gave him the majority of his people. There's only one reason people read and teach *Hard Times* (the only Dickens novel not set, at least partly, in London) when the rest of the Dickens canon is available: It's short.

And there were plenty of contemporary examples. I could see Larry McMurtry's characters growing directly out of the west Texas soil, and its windswept small towns, and then saw what happened when he tried to set a novel in Las Vegas. I'm sure McMurtry spent serious time in Vegas, and not in a study carrel either, but still.

Yes, I knew that place was character, but I knew it without, somehow, believing it. Otherwise, how to explain the sense of wonder I felt in the rewriting, the reimagining, of the book I eventually published as *Mohawk*? How else to explain the surprise I felt when, having created the Mohawk Grill from the memory of the half-dozen greasy spoons I frequented with my father, I discovered enough vivid characters to occupy every stool at the Formica counter?

Interior Place

There's a distinction that's often made in discussions of place—that is, the difference between *interior* and *exterior* setting. Interior setting has come to mean, basically, an indoor place. The setting of *The Glass Menagerie* is primarily an interior one—Amanda Wingfield's apartment. We never leave it, never venture out of doors. We're told the action takes place in St. Louis, but it could be any city. Usually the play is staged in such a way that we glimpse an urban view from the windows of the Wingfield apartment—close brick walls and dark fire escapes

and neighboring windows with tattered shades. The Wingfield apartment also has a fire escape, where Tom retreats to
smoke, but the play makes clear that the fire escape is an illusion.
There's no real escape for the characters, and none for viewers
while we watch.

Most beginning writers do a pretty good job of interior setting
because they understand that the objects people own comment on them—at times, even define them. Anyone who needs
convincing might take a look at Mary Gordon's "The Important Houses," included in *The Best American Short Stories 1993*.
In the back matter of the book, Gordon admits that the story
isn't really a story at all, but rather an excerpt from a long memoir that happens to read like fiction, despite its lack of anything like plot or chronology or scene. What's amazing is that
we get a marvelous sense of character despite the fact that
we never meet any of the people, either directly or dramatically,
who live in the houses she describes. The very contents of the
grandmother's house offers us a portrait of the woman who owns
it—honorable, harsh, judgmental, daunting, repressed, dark.
The narrator describes the house:

> . . . every object in her house belonged to the Old
> World. Nothing was easy; everything required
> maintenance of a complicated and specialized sort. . . .
> Each object's rightness of placement made me feel
> honored to be among them.

The other important house is the residence of the narrator's
aunt, whose husband owns a liquor store:

> The house was full of new or newish objects: the plastic
> holders for playing cards, like shells or fans, the
> nut dishes in the shape of peanuts, the corn dishes in
> the shape of ears of corn, the hair dryer like a

rocket, the make-up mirror framed by light bulbs, the bottles of nail polish, the ice bucket, the cocktail shaker, the deep freeze.

Though an apprentice writer's descriptions may not be as lush as Gordon's, even beginners understand and accept the basic principles of interior setting—that a person who owns an ice bucket and cocktail shaker is different from someone who owns a claw-footed tub for bathing.

Exterior Place

The relationship between character and exterior setting is more mysterious. We don't own a landscape, a street, a neighborhood, or a river in the same sense that we own a cocktail shaker or a claw-footed tub. Nor can they be said to own us, in the way Thoreau meant when he observed in *Walden* that the things we own can own us in return. True, exterior landscapes can "run through us," in the sense that the river runs through the two brothers in Norman Maclean's memoir. But because the relationship is more tenuous, less sharply defined, it is more likely to be ignored, either in whole or in part, by apprentice writers. I'm forever asking my undergraduates very literal-minded questions about their stories, and the thinly veiled irritation with which these questions are often answered is suggestive.

Where does this story take place? I'll ask innocently, especially when it doesn't seem to have taken place anywhere. Well, I'll be told, it's really more about the people. In a story with a vague urban setting, I'll ask, Which city are we in here? It doesn't really matter, I'll be informed. Well, okay, but I need to know.

In fact, the need to know is not universally conceded. There are examples of great works of literature where the external setting is not specified, the city is not named, the landscape more symbolic or moral than real. My more sophisticated students will dredge up the ghost of Kafka. Where is the penal colony? We don't know. We don't need to know. Okay, I concede the point, but only after sharing an anecdote and some speculative theorizing.

Some years ago, I was making small talk with an influential New York editor, and I asked him what books he was excited to be bringing out on his spring list. He named and described half a dozen. I don't remember any of the books he wanted to recommend, but I do remember the way he talked about them. The first thing he'd say about each one was where it took place, a fact I remarked upon because it's often the way I begin talking about books I like and the way people often begin talking about my own books. I hadn't really given the matter much thought beyond the fairly obvious fact that the "where" of a book is an easy starting place, certainly easier to describe than the "who." But for this editor, it went much deeper, and it turned out my small talk had opened, or reopened, a vein. All the books he published and wanted to publish, he informed me, were ones with a strong sense of place. He said he had little faith in the vision of writers who didn't see clearly and vividly the world their characters inhabited. His most powerful need as a reader, he claimed, was to feel oriented. We agreed that we could do that anywhere—on a street in Calcutta, in the middle of an Iowa cornfield, on a boat in the ocean (that is to say, one place was probably as good as another)—but we couldn't feel oriented if we were nowhere or anywhere.

We discovered, too, that we had similar habits. We often didn't read very far into books that were set in places we'd never been before putting the book down long enough to consult an atlas. And we also agreed that we didn't care whether the place in question was fictional or real; we still wanted to know where it was located geographically. We'd both consulted maps of Minnesota to locate Jon Hassler's Staggerford, and I explained that my Mohawk was located north of the New York State Thruway in the foothills of the Adirondacks.

Universality in a Small Town

With some graduate student writers I've taught, the prejudice against rich, detailed, vivid exterior settings was also rooted in the fear that the more specific the setting, the more regional and less "universal" the story's appeal. Nobody wants to be labeled a regional writer. At one point in his career, McMurtry announced his intention to leave Texas and never return in his fiction. He had his reasons, among them, I suspect, a desire to be more a citizen of the world than of Texas. If so, who can blame him?

But a moment's reflection will suggest the truth of the matter, and that is that there's no reason to fear the regional label. The American writer of the twentieth century who is the most universal in his concerns is probably William Faulkner, who is also the most regional, having seldom strayed imaginatively outside a single county. The real fear of being labeled regional—in the sense of, say, Hamlin Garland or Sarah Orne Jewett—is its unstated implication. These writers weren't more regional than Mark Twain and Faulkner; they, I believe, were less talented, less visionary, less true. It's *this* kinship with them that we fear, and it's not a fear that's rooted in geography. Writers have to recognize and accept an essential artistic paradox— that the more specific and individual things become, the more universal they feel.

The clearest expression of this that I can share with you is in the form of the two most consistent compliments from people who have read my work. "Boy, you really know those small upstate New York towns," they tell me. Often they explain how they know I know. "Hell, I've lived up there all my life," they say. Or, "I've got relatives in Utica and we visit them every year. It's like visiting a Richard Russo novel up there." The second group of people pay me what appears to be on the surface a contradictory compliment. "I thought that was my hometown you were writing about," they'll say about my Mohawk or North Bath, then they'll tell me about their hometown in Georgia or Oregon. Even in England I get this. My advice? Don't try to resolve the paradox of things that are vividly differentiated seeming more universal and familiar as a result. There's neither mathematical nor scientific logic to this. Just take advantage of it.

Destiny in a Place

In the end, the only compelling reason to pay more attention to place, to exterior setting, is the belief, the faith, that place and its people are intertwined, that place is character, and that to know the rhythms, the textures, the feel of a place is to know more deeply and truly its people. Such faith is not easy to come by or to sustain in this historical period.

Most people, in any historical period, seem able to focus on only one or two ideas at a time. In the matter of human destiny, an issue of some concern to fiction writers, the question of how people become what they become, why they do what they do, has been settled. In our time, the two great determiners of destiny are race and gender. It was not always this way, of course. There was a time in the not-too-distant past when social class was thought to have been a determining factor in human destiny. Remember the great proletarian novels of the thirties and forties? They seem dated now, in part because the idea of seeing human destiny as determined by class seems not to have survived the second World War and the GI Bill— this despite the fact that in the last two decades, the gap between the haves and have-nots has widened.

For my mother and many others of her generation, the issue

is time. Since his death, my mother and I have spent many hours talking about my grandfather, a man who played a central role in our lives. Her devotion to his memory requires fierce loyalty, which in turn makes it difficult for her to admit her father's frailties. When she's able to do so, it's always with the same proviso. "Well," she says, "I guess he was a product of his time." She never lets it go at that either. She fixes me with a motherly gaze. We're *all* products of our time, she reminds me.

The truth, of course, is that we're products of a lot of things—race, gender, sexual orientation, time, genetics, and chance among them—and we're under no obligation to rank these larger forces. What's interesting to me is that just about the only people I know who seem to believe that place is crucial to human destiny and the formation of human personality are fiction writers. Admittedly, I intuit this from their work, but I think it's true.

Take Annie Proulx. *The Shipping News* is, at one level, the story of a man who manages to conquer a gesture. Her protagonist, Quoyle, has a huge jutting chin, courtesy of his Newfoundland genes, and we find him at the beginning of the book self-consciously covering his chin with his hand. Returning to Newfoundland, he finds a place where his movements, clumsy and awkward in New York, feel natural and graceful, a place where he can live without apology, without undue self-consciousness.

Ivan Doig seems to believe in place as a determiner of behavior. Like many western novelists, he suggests that the physical landscape of the West is responsible, at least in part, for philosophical, emotional, political, and spiritual differences between East Coast and West Coast mentalities. Danish author Peter Hoeg is also a believer. No work of fiction I've read in recent years is so dominated by a sense of place, where landscapes, interior and exterior, loom so powerfully over character, as in *Smilla's Sense of Snow*. Race, gender, and social class are also powerful

forces in the novel, but in the end, it is literally Smilla's sense
of snow—of the properties of snow, as well as her ability to
navigate in a blizzard that is both physical and moral—that
saves her, that provides her with the answers she's been looking
for from the beginning.

Where Have All the Places Gone?

Running contrary to such wisdom is our entire cultural climate,
which minimizes the importance of place. Witness all those
IBM commercials advertising "Solutions for a small planet." In
these ads, we listen to people in other cultures speaking in
foreign languages. Only the clever running subtitles reveal that
the people are talking about their computers, their computer
needs, which, it turns out, are the same as ours. We all yearn for
more megabytes; it doesn't matter where we live. This message
—it is a small world, it doesn't matter much where you are—is
being reinforced by both perception and reality. As James
Howard Kunstler points out in *The Geography of Nowhere*, the
interstate system of highways that allows us to travel five
hundred miles a day in about half the time it would have taken
thirty years ago has also had the unintended effect of making
it seem, when we get to our final destination, that we haven't
really gone anywhere. The exit where we get off the interstate
is a dead ringer for the one where we got on, their being fifteen
hundred miles apart notwithstanding. Interstate travel (even
more than air travel, I suspect) also suggests that the places we
bypass aren't worth pausing at, a conclusion difficult to reconcile with the growing sameness of our major destinations.

A few years ago, I was invited to attend the Nashville Book
Fair. I'd driven through, or rather around, Nashville many
times, but I'd never stopped, never visited. I was put up in the
Hilton, which was a lot like other Hiltons I'd stayed at, except
you could get grits. The cable TV offerings were identical to

those offered by our local cable company in Maine, including the Nashville Network. The first of the conference sessions I attended was one on contemporary Southern writing. Several writers I'd long admired tried to identify what made Southern writing southern and to offer suggestions for how to preserve it. I have to say it was one of the stranger discussions I've ever listened to, and not just because I was a Yankee. There was little talk of landscape, or the rhythms of daily life, or architecture, or occupations. Members of the audience wanted to discuss the scent of magnolias and the redness of the earth, and a couple of members of the panel nervously admitted to having relocated to places like Massachusetts.

I came away with the distinct impression that even to articulate people who cared about it, our sense of place and what place means is rapidly eroding and that even our vocabulary for discussing place may be gone with the wind. One of the ideas I kept hoping would crop up was the question of how writers should handle the Wal-Mart sameness that is creeping into our cultural life, regardless of where we happen to be located. If what made Southern fiction distinctly Southern was being subtly eroded, couldn't the same be said for the notion of place in general? There may be a Burger King in every small town in America, but does that mean they should be similarly ubiquitous in our fiction?

I am of two minds on this subject. Personally, I avoid Burger Kings in fiction as I do in life, and for the same reasons. To me, they are neither nourishing nor enjoyable. I am suspicious of the fact that all you have to do is name such places and the reader is located, a kind of cultural shorthand. I prefer places that require and reward lots of description, and my own novels are strewn with the kinds of establishments that are poised on the brink of extinction. This may explain why I'm occasionally accused of harboring a nostalgic view of America. It's true that I become more curmudgeonly every year, and what's needed may be younger eyes. I still remember chortling with glee while reading the Sam Hodges novel of the new South, *B-Four*. Several of the scenes are set in a local IHOP, where the pancake syrup containers are so stuck to the Lazy Susans that grown men have all they can do to liberate them.

The simple truth may be that there's no place in the world, and no object either, that can't be brought dancing to life when seen by the right eyes. Whether or not Burger Kings deserve a prominent place in our literature is less the issue than whether place itself, which is under siege both in reality and in metaphor, can be rescued from the endangered species list of important concepts.

Advice

If I have convinced you that place is an important resource for fiction writers, consider the following practical tips on how to handle place in your fiction.

1. Describe Selectively

The relative importance of place to any given story is independent of the amount of description given it. The best examples I can think of are John Cheever's Shady Hill stories. They are, in my opinion, the best stories in the Cheever canon. I've read and reread them and taught many of them. When one of my students wanted to write a critical essay on the importance of setting in fiction, I suggested the Shady Hill stories, picturing the vivid sense of life's rhythms that Cheever had created through what I remembered as lush descriptions.

The problem was that when my student read those stories herself, she found very little description. She couldn't, she told me, find a single sustained passage of description in any of them. Preposterous. "You've read 'O Youth and Beauty!'?" I asked her. " 'The Housebreaker of Shady Hill?' " She had.

Closely. Which forced me to go back to the stories myself and, of course, she was right. There were very few descriptive details, and those were woven so skillfully into the stories' drama, in such seemingly subordinate ways, that they were difficult to extract, like molars in the back of the mouth, unseen but with the deepest roots imaginable. What kind of furniture does Cash Bentley hurtle in his friends' living rooms before his wife shoots him in midair? What's the architecture of the houses that Johnny Hake burgles? I'd had the impression that such information was offered in these stories. The deep sense of place that emerges from the Shady Hill stories has more to do with life's rhythms, where things are in relation to other things, whether the characters can walk there and how long that will take, whether they'll drive or take the train. We won't be told that the cocktail shaker is pure silver; we'll be told that it's sweating in the lazy Sunday midmorning sun. Rendering such passive details active makes us insiders, not tourists. We become giddy, well-heeled drinkers trying to banish hangovers, not sober, anthropological observers of curious behavior.

2. See Clearly From the Start

Something to guard against: My own experience of writing, which may be different from yours, is that even when I acknowledge the importance of the physical world, even when I make mental notes and scribble reminders, I still have to guard against the temptation to believe that I'll be able to add onto a scene later, and flesh it out after I've attended to other matters. If the scene is talky (too reliant on dialogue) or if it's too interior (too reliant on a character's thoughts at the expense of the physical world), I'm often tempted to let it go, move on to the next scene, promising to return later with a bucketful of descriptive details.

I know I'm not alone in this. When I complain to my students that their scenes are vague, that the dialogue seems to be coming out of thin air, as if the scene were wired in such a way that we had to choose between the audio and the video, they frequently tell me not to worry, that they'll go back and add the details of the physical world later. What they want to know is whether the characters are doing and saying the right things. Such an attitude not only ranks the various tasks of the fiction writer, subordinating the objective world, but it suggests something about the process that I've never found to be true. When I'm writing badly, I'm almost always in a kind of fast-forward, taking shorthand notes on what the characters are doing and saying. The edges of the picture are fuzzy and blurred by speed. Later, when I realize the scene isn't working, when I go back and try to "fill in the details," I find that the details I fill in often invalidate what the characters have said and done. Better and more efficient to slow down and see clearly to begin with. If character can grow out of place, as I've suggested, it follows that place cannot be the thing that's "grafted on" late in the process.

3. Create Distance

My own experience has been that the place I'm living is probably not the place I'm writing about. Now that I've lived in Maine for several years, I'm often asked by people who consider me a Maine writer by virtue of my address when I'll be writing a novel set in Maine. They don't realize what they're probably asking is when I plan to leave the state. The simple truth of the matter is, I've never written effectively about any place I was currently residing in. I not only need to leave but actually need to have been gone for some time for my imagination to kick in, to begin the process of necessary tempering knowledge.

It may be different for you, but the ability to look out my window and see what I'm describing in a story is not an advantage. If what I'm describing is really there, I'm too respectful of and dependent upon the senses, and the thing described, as a result, will often not have the inner life I want it to have. I'd rather make a mistake, get something physically wrong, put the button on the wrong side of the sleeve, than be dictated to by literal reality, than place intuition and imagination in a straitjacket. Maybe this is just a feeble justification for the many things I get wrong as a result, but I don't think so.

4. Use Research Selectively

Just as the importance and vividness of place is independent of the amount of description given it, there is also no direct correlation between the vividness of your setting and comprehensive, factual knowledge. Granted, throughout this essay, I've been insisting on the essential relationship between place and character, but I'm not particularly advocating Micheneresque research. An intimate understanding of place can lead to character breakthroughs, but that's not the same as to say that encyclopedic knowledge of the facts of place will yield interesting characters.

Often, the exact opposite will happen. Too much knowledge of the literal can stifle the metaphorical. Many best-sellers give the impression of having been written by tourists for tourists, and such books, for all their insistence upon location, somehow locate me in a world that's halfway between a library and a good travel agency. The difference between the places in these novels and the places in reality is the difference between the place itself and the picture of it on a color brochure.

A Product of Place

Finally, even those among you who are convinced by the argument I've been articulating about the importance of place and the link between place and character, may not end up as place-oriented in your fiction as I am in mine. The writers I've discussed above are, as I'm sure you've noticed, like-minded. If

I'd chosen different writers to draw examples from, my conclusions might have been different.

I can only give you my sense of how profoundly important
place has been to my own life and my life as an artist. If I
were black or gay or a woman, chances are my life as a person
and as an artist would have been shaped more dramatically
by race or gender or sexual orientation. But insofar as I'm a
"product" of anything, to borrow my mother's term, I feel
I'm a product of place, of places. And, insofar as my fiction has
been a product of anything, since the moment I realized that
my first novel could not be set in Arizona, it has been a product
of places that have, in turn, offered up people by the dozens.

Some years ago, at an East Coast writers residency, C.J. Hri-
bal, Michael Martone, and I were referred to by some as "the
corn boys," the result, I suppose, of our teaching in Midwestern
universities. It was odd for me to be referred to this way and I tried
to conceal my annoyance lest it be considered geographical snob-
bery. I don't, believe me, consider the small, shabby town in
upstate New York where I grew up to be superior to other places,
and if I'd grown up in Iowa, I doubt I would have minded
much being referred to as a "corn boy." I simply felt mislabeled,
and therefore misunderstood, in much the same way I feel now when
I'm referred to as a "Maine writer."

I may not be "the product" of upstate New York either, but
the link is there and I feel it profoundly. How else would I
explain the strange dreams I'm subject to for days before I visit
my remaining relatives in my hometown? How would I explain the irrational fears that descend upon me when I return,
primary among them the fear that I will be killed in an auto
accident during one of these quick visits? This was my grandfather's fear for me. We lived one house down from one of the
worse intersections in town, where local drivers routinely ignored a stop sign in plain view, bashing into each other and
narrowly missing small children who were crossing the intersec-

tion on errands to the corner market. My grandfather feared I'd be run down in sight of the front porch before I could make my mark on the world, and now, forty years later, I have inherited his fear.

How else would I explain the fact that when I pass by the open door of the worst dive in town, I sense that the empty barstool farthest from the light is really mine, that it's being saved for me, that perhaps in some alternate universe I'm already occupying it, that when the phone rings, I no longer even have to remind the bartender that I'm not there. What these irrational fears have in common is the sense that this place has a claim on me, a claim that may be presented at any time, a claim that seems less perilous to acknowledge than to ignore.

RICHARD RUSSO is the author of the novels *Empire Falls, Whore's Child and Other Stories, Straight Man, Nobody's Fool, Mohawk,* and *The Risk Pool.* He is the recipient of the 2002 Pulitzer Prize for *Empire Falls.*

Chapter 17

The More and Less of Writing Humorous Fiction

By Connie Willis

If you shy away from writing humorous stories, it's no wonder. They're tough to write. They're full of witty lines, sight gags, and wordplay, as well as plots, characters, settings, and everything else you're already struggling with.

And to top it off, no one will tell you how to write funny. "Humor is unanalyzable," the experts intone. And, "To dissect humor is to destroy it." Even Robert Benchley, a famous humorist who should have known better, declared, "Defining and analyzing humor is a pastime of humorless people."

The effect of all this is to surround humorous writing with a daunting air of mystery, to make you think it just comes naturally. Trust me. *No* writing comes naturally. And because it doesn't come naturally to you, *and* because Benchley said you're devoid of humor for even asking about it, you obviously have no business trying.

Balderdash! Humorous fiction has analyzable and learnable techniques. More than can be covered in a single chapter, in fact. But we can make a good start by looking at two of the most important techniques of humorous writing.

Exaggeration

To exaggerate is to enlarge or overstate the truth. It is the cornerstone of comedy, and so pervasive that stand-up comics can't get halfway through, "It was so hot last week," before the audience breaks in with, "*How hot was it?*"

Because of Johnny Carson and his peers, you might assume that exaggeration is a modern form of humor, but it's been around forever. Shakespeare called Bardolph's red nose a bonfire and said it was so bright it had saved "a thousand marks in lengths and torches." Samuel Coleridge described a night "so dark the cats ran against each other." And Americans have been telling tall tales for years about mosquitoes so big four of them could hold a man down, and places so cold that words freeze in midair and must be taken inside and thawed before you can hear them.

In *Roughing It*, Mark Twain, our national tall-tale teller, wrote about a horse so fast the wagon started thirty yards ahead of a cloudburst and made it home without getting a drop of rain on it: "But my dog was a-swimmin' behind the wagon all the way!" He also described the first time he ate a tamarind:

> They pursed up my lips, till they resembled the stem-
> end of a tomato, and I had to take my sustenance
> through a quill for twenty-four hours. They sharpened
> my teeth till I could have shaved with them, and
> gave them a "wire edge" that I was afraid would stay;
> but a citizen said, "no, it will come off when the
> enamel does"—which was comforting, at any rate.

Mark Twain called his exaggerations "stretchers," which is exactly the right word. Stretching the truth makes it funny, but don't yank it past the breaking point. Twain wouldn't have made his description of tamarinds funnier by writing, "And then they ate through my teeth and the insides of my mouth and my jawbone, and the whole lower half of my face fell off."

Those are definitely exaggerations, but not funny ones. It's not because we can't believe them—we don't believe Twain

had to eat through a straw, either. It's that they don't have anything to do with how eating a tamarind feels. Exaggerating the literal
truth, if it's done well, shows us the emotional truth of a
situation.

When Twain writes, "they sharpened my teeth till I could have
shaved with them," we laugh partly at the image it conjures,
but mostly because we've eaten fruit that felt exactly that sour.
The humor is already there. Exaggeration's purpose is to
bring out that humor. It's like turning the volume up so we can
hear better.

In the introduction to *Three Men in a Boat* (possibly the funni-
est book ever written and a required primer for anyone interested in writing humorous fiction), Jerome K. Jerome says the
book records "events that really happened. All that has been
done is to color them, and, for this, no extra charge has been
made." The events are all perfectly ordinary: trying to remember whether you packed your toothbrush, reading about diseases
and convincing yourself you have them all, trying to open a
can of pineapple when you forgot to bring the can opener:

> Then Harris tried to open the tin with a pocketknife,
> and broke the knife and cut himself badly; and
> George tried a pair of scissors, and the scissors flew
> up, and nearly put his eye out. While they were
> dressing their wounds, I tried to make a hole in the
> thing with the spiky end of the hitcher, and the
> hitcher slipped and jerked me out between the boat
> and the bank into two feet of muddy water, and
> the tin rolled over, uninjured, and broke a teacup.

This is exaggeration, but not by much. The truth has been
"colored" only a little. And it feels more like the truth than
a factual account of what happened. Jerome's exaggerations
bring out the emotional truth of the situation.

So you must start with the truth when you write humor. You must think about how sour the tamarinds in your life are and how ridiculous you feel trying to open your cans of pineapple, and build from there. And you must know when to stop, because bigger and wilder and more ridiculous aren't necessarily funnier.

A classic example is the tall tale about the place in Texas that was so dry that during Noah's flood. . . . You expect the punch line to be, "it didn't rain at all," which would be an exaggeration and fairly funny. But that's not how the story goes. It goes like this: "That part of Texas was so dry that during the flood it only got an inch and a half."

The story exaggerates well beyond the bounds of literal truth, but by stopping short, it somehow makes the whole thing seem almost plausible. (There *are* parts of Texas that seem that dry.) Sometimes less is definitely more.

Understatement

Understatement is less—much less. Instead of stretching or coloring the truth, understatement downplays it, describes it with restraint. Turns the volume down. Or off.

Mark Twain used understatement almost as much as exaggeration. "If at any time you find it necessary to correct your brother," he advised little girls, "do not correct him with mud." And he described an argument this way: "Then he rode over and began to rebuke the stranger with a six-shooter and the stranger began to explain with another." It's the exact opposite of exaggeration, and yet it makes you laugh because the description (or the language or the response) is so completely out of proportion to the situation. A gun battle becomes a "rebuke."

Don't get the idea you must choose one or the other. Humor is not a decision between More *or* Less. Twain often used understatement and exaggeration in the same sentence. After describing those tamarinds in hilarious overblown detail, he added laconically, "it seemed to me they were rather sour that year."

And Jerome combined exaggeration and understatement to wonderful effect in the episode of the pineapple:

> Then we all got mad. We took that tin out on the bank, and Harris went up into a field and got a big sharp stone, and I went back into the boat and brought out the mast, and George held the tin and Harris held the sharp end of his stone against the top of it, and I took the mast and poised it high up in the air, and gathered up all my strength and brought it down.

And just at the point when you're expecting Jerome to describe what happened in all its horrible, hilarious detail, he says instead:

> It was George's straw hat that saved his life that day. He keeps that hat now (what is left of it), and, on a winter's evening, when the pipes are lit and the boys are telling stretchers about the dangers they have passed through, George brings it down and shows it 'round, and the stirring tale is told anew, with fresh exaggerations every time.

But he doesn't tell us. All he says is, "Harris got off with merely a flesh wound." He leaves us to imagine the rest for ourselves, and the effect is funnier than anything he could have described.

Deciding when to use exaggeration and understatement is the problem, of course, and every author seems to have a different solution. Jerome sets up wildly slapstick situations and then, just at the critical moment, steps back and makes us imagine the outcome for ourselves. P.G. Wodehouse, on the other hand, never flinches at describing the ridiculous. It's his characters' responses that are understated, as in *The Return of Jeeves*. "Certainly a somewhat sharp crisis in our affairs would appear to have been precipitated, m'lord," Jeeves says when threatened with jail and a poke in the nose.

Twain uses understatement in his story of the ram standing at the top of a hill watching an old man bending down to pick up a dime. Since the outcome is inevitable, no one has to tell us what will happen. And James Thurber exaggerates the content of his stories, but writes in a cool, understated style. There's obviously no set rule.

The best answer involves reading lots of Twain and Jerome. And Thurber and Wodehouse. And Calvin Trillin and Erma Bombeck and whoever you think is funny. Reading humorous fiction and trying to analyze it (no matter what Benchley says) will not only help you learn how and when to use understatement and exaggeration, it will show you those other techniques authors use to produce their unique comic styles.

Then you must practice those techniques. And read some more. And practice some more. Because writing humorous fiction is hard. ("*How hard is it?*") But at least you don't have to *make* things funny. Things are already funny; you're simply using exaggeration and understatement and whatever else to bring out the humor that was already there.

And you'll be More or Less on your way to being able to write humorous stories.

CONNIE WILLIS is a multiple Hugo Award–and Nebula Award–winning writer of science fiction. Her work includes the novel *Doomsday Book* and her comic short stories, "Even the Queen" and "At the Rialto." Her most recent works include *Uncharted Territory* and *Passage*.

The Process

Chapter 18

How to Start

By Ann Collette

Humans are creatures who cling to ritual.

As a species, we hope that rituals enlighten us. We hope that rituals help us make the journey from one point to another easier somehow. We hope that rituals help us stay connected to what has come before and what may come in the future. Too, there's reassurance to be found in ritual, in repetition.

Writers know this. Every single author I talked to had an answer when I questioned them about their particular writing rituals. Each has some sort of talismanic behavior that gets them to where the words flow.

Maybe it's that we need to sneak up on writing: Why not adopt a ritual that allows you to limber up your mind before plunging in? You don't have to beat a drum, howl at the moon, or channel your spirit guide; your ritual may be as simple as checking your e-mail or cleaning the kitchen sink. Or, like many of the authors here, it may be as simple as having a cup of coffee.

So pour yourself a cup and come along as we discover how some of today's best authors attempt to demystify the creative process . . . through ritual.

•   •   •

What works best for me is to roll out of bed and down to my desk in the morning without quite waking up, to go from a night-dreaming state to a daydreaming state without any interruption. Too much consciousness gets in the way. The other thing that helps is iced coffee. It has to be iced, it has to be decaf, and it has to be hazelnut, or else the world just doesn't work right.

> Scott Campbell
> *Touched* (Bantam)

• • •

My aim is to get relaxed, so first I make sure that no major disaster, such as an exploding pressure cooker, can happen while I'm creating a masterpiece. Then I repeat these numbers: 30, 53, 57 (30 years between Homer's *The Odyssey* and *The Iliad*; 53 between Henry Roth's first and second books; and 57 is how old Cervantes was when he wrote the first, most sold and best novel in the history of Western literature, which makes fun of literature! So why get uptight?). Then I'm ready to burrow into my soft writing lounge and write away, still uptight.

> Elena Castedo
> *Paradise* (Grove/Atlantic)

• • •

I grab a book I love and saturate myself with someone else's amazing words. That usually serves as a springboard for my own writing.

> Elizabeth Graver
> *The Honey Thief* (Hyperion)

•   •   •

What it comes down to is looking more carefully, more attentively, at the people on the street from whom I usually turn my eyes, at photographs, especially old ones, into which I can place myself, looking back out.

John Hildebidle
Stubborness: A Field Guide
(Binghamton Press)

•   •   •

I'm very scatterbrained and what with my wife and I parenting two kids, my teaching in the evenings and freelance writing, it's difficult to keep a regular schedule. One thing that signals me to get back to where I was on a piece of writing is to play the same piece of solo piano music over and over again, particularly John Field's "Nocturnes." It helps slow my mind down, and because it has no language, I can hear the voices of my characters more clearly. I never listen to it when I'm not writing, though.

Richard Hoffman
Half the House (Harcourt,
Brace)

•   •   •

I use clothing to transport me to that place where I need to be to write. I have a black, wine, and magenta robe I call my writing robe (actually, I have two identical ones— one I keep in Cambridge and the other in Burgundy). Something about that robe imbues me with a little more energy, creativity, and magic than when I'm writing in a Yale T-shirt.

> Florence Ladd
> *Sarah's Psalm* (Scribner)

· · ·

I look at my ancestor wall, which has photos of all those folks in my family who were proud and reached high, whose tales I am in some way telling. I do household tasks, listen to music, read the newspaper. Sometimes I light candles and incense. Sometimes I plunder my journal. Anything that will make a bridge.

> Helen Elaine Lee
> *Water Marked* (Scribner)

· · ·

First I drive my son to school. Then I pour a cup of coffee, walk up to my study, and turn the computer on. I check my e-mail, then I either reread what I wrote the day before or the whole chapter I'm working on. Then I start.

> Elinor Lipman
> *The Inn at Lake Devine*
> (Random House)

· · ·

I rent a little office that's approximately the size of a small bathroom. The office is in a building of all shrinks, so I go there in the morning, press my ear against the wall, and listen to some stories, then try and write my own characters.

Stephen McCauley
The Man of the House
(Simon & Schuster)

• • •

The only time I clean my house is when I'm writing. I look around and see all this dust and can't sit down to write one word until things are clean. When I'm not writing, I don't care if the house is clean or not.

Mameve Medwed
Mail (Warner)

• • •

After I've finished the ritual of getting my daughter to school and have scanned *The New York Times*, I don't psyche myself to work as much as I create a barrier of order between myself and the real world. To do this I'll put the ingredients I'll later be using to prepare dinner on the kitchen counter. Then I walk, like a zombie, to my computer, delete junk messages from my e-mail, and begin to write.

Christine Palamidessi Moore
The Virgin Knows
(St. Martin's)

• • •

I have to send the kids out to daycare then drink a pot of

coffee and play my guitar until I get so disgusted with
myself that I have to write.

Tom Perrotta
Election (Putnam)

• • •

After squaring my three daughters away at school, I sit
down at my computer, milky coffee in hand, and dip
into my file. Face to face with the day-before's work, we
acknowledge one another, agree that the common goal
is progress. I type one line, maybe one phrase that's been
turning just so in my brain, yank out a comma, put it
back in. Having taken the upper hand, I get up once more
and trail the sunlight through my house, come back to
my chair and get to work.

Anne Whitney Pierce
Galaxy Girls: Wonder Women
(Helicon Nine)

• • •

I have no routine. I'm disorganized and undisciplined. I
don't do anything and resist writing as long as I can until
it takes over my life. Once it takes hold, everything else gets
pushed out of the way. Sleeping, eating—anything that's
pushable—is pushed right out of the way. Once it takes
over, I can write anywhere, as soon as I get to either a
piece of paper or a computer.

Lloyd Schwartz
Goodnight, Gracie (University
of Chicago Press)

• • •

I write in bed, in longhand. To get myself going, I read my drafts in whisper to my cat, who curls up in my lap in the deepest sleep. The combination of my whisper and his loud, rich purr makes even my most unpromising prose sound somehow sexy and intriguing. Before bouts of serious first-drafting, I fortify myself by eating Grape-Nuts, the best cereal for creative contemplation since it shuts out the world with its deafening crunch. I also find inspiration by raking leaves, taking showers, and rocking in place while staring fixedly at nothing. In their latter stages, my writing projects, like romances, always take on "a song." This I listen to incessantly as I rev myself up to work and rework my final drafts. For my first novel, *A Four-Sided Bed*, I needed a whole album, k.d. lang's "Absolute Torch and Twang."

Elizabeth Searle
A Four-Sided Bed (Graywolf Press)

• • •

I was a blocked writer for years and needed to build up the habit of writing every day. Once I realized I had a choice between being hard on myself or starting in a very small way, I made myself sit down for ten or fifteen minutes each day. The level of panic subsided because this daily ritual taught me you can get something done in small periods of time. It was sort of like physical therapy, where I had to build up my writing muscles. Now, I put in my contacts so I can't go back to sleep, make up the bed, have a second cup of coffee, and sit down at my desk by 9 A.M.

Marilyn Sides
The Genius of Affection (Harmony)

•   •   •

I get up really early, usually at a quarter to five in the morning. I drink a lot of strong coffee and then write until somebody else is awake.

Alice Hoffman
Here on Earth (Putnam)

•   •   •

Over the years, I've made peace with procrastination. I know that the sink has to be cleaned and toenails have to be clipped, so I don't beat myself up or suffer any guilt; instead, each day, I jump fully into that day's procrastination.

Pagan Kennedy
The Exes (Simon & Schuster)

•   •   •

I'm an everyday writer, a café-and-restaurant writer. I need food and coffee and conversation in the background and a street and people to look at. If things are too quiet, I can't concentrate.

Delia Sherman
The Porcelain Dove (Plume)

•   •   •

I have to check my e-mail and then get writing by 10 A.M. If I don't get focused by then, I won't have a good day. Even if I start by 10:30, it screws me up. Somehow the number ten has taken on a magical significance for me.

Arthur S. Golden
Memoirs of a Geisha (Knopf)

•　　•　　•

Get dressed (very important). Eat breakfast. Go to my desk and sit down at or before 9 A.M. There are no options about this, just as there are no options about going to work for someone else. Play one seven-minute game of computer Scrabble to warm up. Write until noon or shortly thereafter (with time-outs to load and/or unload the washing machine and dryer).

Anne Bernays
Professor Romeo (Weidenfeld & Nicholson)

•　　•　　•

When I'm home, my bed is nearby, tempting me to nap. If my writing needs a jog forward, a change of venue frequently helps; the Amtrak Metroliner from Boston down to New York is both scenic, and they have café service. A complete change in my environment like that usually helps.

Audrey Schulman
Swimming With Jonah (Avon)

ANN COLLETTE reviews fiction for *Publishers Weekly,* among many other things.

Chapter 19

The Use of the Journal in Writing a Novel

By Sue Grafton

The most valuable tool I employ while writing a novel is the working journal. The process is one I began in rudimentary form when I first started work on *"A" Is for Alibi*, though all I retain of that journal now are a few fragmentary notes. With *"B" Is for Burglar*, I began to refine the method and from *"C" Is for Corpse* on I've kept a daily log of work in progress. This notebook (usually four times longer than the novel itself) is like a letter to myself, detailing every idea that occurs to me as I proceed. Some ideas I incorporate, some I modify, many I discard. The journal is a record of my imagination at work, from the first spark of inspiration to the final manuscript. Here I record my worries and concerns, my dead ends, my occasional triumphs, all the difficulties I face as the narrative unfolds. The journal contains solutions to all the problems that arise in the course of the writing. Sometimes the breakthroughs are sudden; more often the answers are painstakingly arrived at through trial and error.

One of my theories about writing is that the process involves an ongoing interchange between Left Brain and Right. The journal provides a testing ground where the two can engage. Left Brain is analytical, linear, the timekeeper, the bean counter, the critic and editor, a valuable ally in the shaping of the mystery novel or any piece of writing for that matter. Right Brain is creative, spatial, playful, disorganized, dazzling, nonlinear, the source of the *Aha*! or imaginative leap. Without Right Brain, there would be no material for Left Brain to refine. Without Left Brain, the jumbled brilliance of Right Brain would never coalesce into a satisfactory whole.

In addition to the yin/yang of the bicameral brain, the process of writing is a constant struggle between the Ego and the Shadow, to borrow Jungian terms. Ego, as implied, is the public aspect of our personality, the carefully constructed personna, or mask, we present to the world as the "truth" about us. The Shadow is our Unconscious, the Dark Side—the dangerous, largely unacknowledged cauldron of "unacceptable" feelings and reactions that we'd prefer not to look at in ourselves and certainly hope to keep hidden from others. We spend the bulk of our lives perfecting our public image, trying to deny or eradicate the perceived evil in our nature.

For the writer, however, especially the mystery writer, the Shadow is crucial. The Shadow gives us access to our repressed rage, the murderous impulses that propel antisocial behavior whether we're inclined to act out or not. Without ingress to our own Shadow, we would have no way to delineate the nature of a fictional killer, no way to penetrate and depict the inner life of the villain in the novels we write. As mystery writers, we probe this emotional black swamp again and again, dredging in the muck for plot and character. As repelled as we may be by the Dark Side of our nature, we're drawn to its power, recognizing that the Shadow contains enormous energy if we can tap into it. The journal is the writer's invitation to the Shadow, a means of beckoning to the Unconscious, enticing it to yield its potent magic to the creative process.

What Goes Into the Journal and How Does It Work?

At the outset of each new novel, the first thing I do is open a document on my computer that I call "Notes" or "Notes-1." By the end of a book, I have four or five such documents, averaging fifty single-spaced pages apiece.

In my first act of the writing day, I log into my journal with the date. Usually I begin with a line about what's happening in my life. I make a note if I'm coming down with a cold, if my cat's run away, if I've got company coming in from out of town. Anything that specifically characterizes the day becomes part of the journal on the theory that exterior events have the potential to affect the day's work. If I have a bad day at work, I can sometimes track the problem to its source and try correcting it there. For instance, if I'm consistently distracted every time I'm scheduled for a speaking engagement, I can limit outside events until the book is done.

The second entry in the journal is a note about any idea that's occurred to me in the dead of night, when Shadow and Right Brain are most active. Often, I'm wakened by a nudge from Right Brain with some suggestion about where to go next in the narrative or offering a reminder of a beat I've missed. Sometimes, I'm awakened by emotion-filled dreams or the horror of a nightmare, either one of which can hold clues about the story I'm working on. It's my contention that our writing is a window to all of our internal attitudes and emotional states. If I sit down to write and I'm secretly worried about the progress I'm making, then that worry will infuse the very work itself. If I'm anxious about an upcoming scene, if I'm troubled by the pacing, if I suspect a plot is too convoluted or the identity of the killer is too transparent, then the same anxiety will inhibit the flow of words. Until I own my worries, I run the risk of self-sabotage or writer's block. The journal serves as a place to off-load anxiety, a verbal repair shop when my internal writing machine breaks down.

Generally, the next step in the journal is to lay out for myself where I am in the book. I talk to myself about the scene I'm working on, or the trouble spots as I see them. It's important to realize that the journal in progress is absolutely private—*for my eyes only*. This is not a literary *oeuvre* in which I preen and posture for some future biographer. This is a nuts-and-bolts format in which I think aloud, fret, whine, and wring my hands. There's nothing grand about it and it's certainly not meant to be great writing. Once a novel is finished and out on the shelves, the journal can be opened to public inspection if I so choose.

In the safety of the journal, I can play "Suppose . . ." and "What if . . ." creating an atmosphere of open debate where Ego and Shadow, Left Brain and Right, can all be heard. I write down all the story possibilities, all the pros and cons, and then check back a day or so later to see which prospects strike a chord. The journal is experimental. The journal functions as a playground for the mind, a haven where the imagination can cavort at will. While I'm working in the journal, I don't have to look good. I can be as dumb or goofy as I want. The journal provides a place where I can let my proverbial hair down and "dare to be stupid," as we used to say in Hollywood.

Using Your Journal as a Jump Start

The beauty of the journal entry is that before I know it, I'm sliding right into my writing for the day. Instead of feeling resistant or hesitant, the journal provides a jump start, a way to get the words moving.

To demonstrate the technique, I'll include a few sample pages from the journal I kept during the writing of *"G" Is for Gumshoe*. I do this without embarrassment (she said), though I warn you in advance that what you see is a fumbling process, my tortured mind at work.

"G" Is for Gumshoe is essentially a "road picture." In this seventh novel in the series, Kinsey Millhone discovers she's on Tyrone Patty's hit list, targeted for assassination in retaliation for her part in his arrest and conviction. The following passages of the journal begin some three chapters into the novel. Earlier notes, unfortunately, were lost to me in the transfer of the work from an old computer system to newly acquired

equipment. My intention here is not to try to dazzle you with my song-and-dance work, but to demonstrate the mundane level at which the journal actually functions.

1-2-89

Just checking in to have a little chat. I'm in Chapter 3 and feeling pretty good, but I'm wondering if I don't need some tension or suspense. We know there may be a hit man after her. She's currently on her way to the desert and everything seems really normal . . . nay, even dull. Do I need to pep it up a bit? She's almost at the Slabs. I've been doing a lot of description but maybe I need to weave it into the narrative better. Flipping back and forth from the external to the internal.

What other possibilities are there? I've noticed that with Dick Francis, sometimes when nothing's happening, you sit there expecting something anyway. I could use the external as a metaphor for the internal. I know I'll be doing that when Dietz enters the scene. What could Kinsey be thinking about while she drives down to the Slabs? She's talked briefly . . .

1-4-89

Can't remember what I meant to say in the paragraph above. I did some work last night that I'm really happy with. I'm using a little boy with a toy car at the rest stop. Added a father asleep on the bench. Later, he turns out to be one of the guys hired to kill her.

Want to remember to use a couple of things.

1. When the mother dies, Kinsey goes back down to the desert with Dietz. They search, finding nothing . . . maybe a few personal papers. What they come across, in an old cardboard box under the

trailer, is some objects . . . maybe just old cups &
saucers (which may trigger memories in Irene
Gersh . . .). But the newspapers in which these objects
are packed dated back to 1937 . . . Santa Teresa.
Obviously, the mother was there at some point.

When Kinsey checks into the mother's background,
she realizes Irene's birth certificate is a total fake.
The mother has whited out the real information, typed
over it, and has done a photocopy. All the information has been falsified. She's not who she says she was
during her lifetime . . . father's name is wrong . . .
I was thinking it might be Santa Teresa, but then Irene
would know at the outset she had some connection
with the town. Better she should think she was born
in Brawley or someplace like that.

Kinsey tries to track down the original in San
Diego . . . or wherever I decide to place the
original . . . no record of such a birth. Once Kinsey
finds the old newspapers, she decides to try Santa
Teresa records, using the certificate # which is the only
thing that hasn't been tampered with. Up comes
the true certificate.

Must remember that a social security card . . . first
three digits indicate where the card was issued.
That might be a clue.

Irene Gersh is floored. If mom isn't who she claims
she was, then who am I?

Must also remember that mom is frightened to
death. That would be a nice murder method.

Using Your Journal to Record Research

In addition to storyboarding ideas, I use my journal to record
notes for all the research I've done. I also make a note of any

question that occurs to me while I'm writing a scene. Instead of stopping the flow of words, I simply jot down a memo to myself for later action.

Journals often contain the ideas for scenes, characters, plot twists, or clever lines of dialogue that don't actually make it into the book I'm working on. Such literary detritus might provide the spark for the next book in the series.

Often, too, in the pages of a journal, I'll find Right Brain leaping ahead to a later scene in the book. Since I don't actually outline a novel in any formal or detailed way, the journal is a road map to the story I'm working on. If dialogue or a descriptive passage suddenly occurs to me, I'll tuck it in the journal and come back to it when I reach the chapter where the excerpt belongs. This way, I find I can do some of my writing in advance of myself. Right Brain, my creative part, really isn't interested in working line-by-line. Right Brain sees the whole picture, like the illustration on the box that contains a jigsaw puzzle. Left Brain might insist that we start at the beginning and proceed in an orderly fashion right through to the end, but Right Brain has its own way of going about its business. The journal is a place to honor Right Brain's ingenuity and nonconformity.

Sometimes I use the journal to write a note directly to Shadow or Right Brain, usually when I'm feeling blocked or stuck. These notes are like writer's prayers, and I'm always astonished at how quickly they're answered.

In the *"G" Is for Gumshoe* journal, you can see that by March, some three months later, the book has advanced almost magically. I'll do a hop, skip, and jump, picking up entries here and there.

3-12-89
Finally got Dietz & Kinsey on the road. They've stopped for lunch. She's asking him about his back-

ground & he's being good about that stuff. Want to keep them moving . . . let information surface while they're heading for Santa Teresa. Don't want the story to come to a screeching halt while they chit chat. Must keep defining his character through action . . . not just dialogue. Once I get the book on body-guarding techniques, I can fill in some technical information that will make him seem very knowledge-able. For now, I can do the small touches. At some point, he should give her some rules & regulations.

What else do I want to accomplish on the way up to Santa Teresa? Don't need any action at this point . . . don't need jeopardy per se. Must keep in mind that Dick Francis plays relationships very nicely without jamming incessant screams and chases into the narrative.

3-13-89

I wonder if chapter nine will last all the way to Santa Teresa. What does Kinsey do when she gets home? She'll call Irene to make sure Agnes has arrived, which she will very soon. She'll introduce Dietz to Henry Pitts who'll be briefed about the situation re: the hit man. Security measures (if I knew what they were . . .).

Want to dovetail "A" & "B" plots so both won't come to a ragged stop simultaneously.

Within a day, Agnes Grey will have disappeared from the nursing home.

Soon after, her body will be found.

Haven't quite solved the problem of how Kinsey gets hired to track down the killer.

Can't quite decide what the next beat is in the attempt on Kinsey's life. Dietz will get her a bulletproof vest. Does he jog with her? She won't really feel like it, and he'll advise against. He'll have her take a different route to the office & home every day . . . always in his company.

Maybe Dietz has to make a quick trip to Carson City . . . or someplace. Papa sick? Mama sick? An unavoidable personal emergency. If I played my cards right, his absence might coincide with Kinsey's second trip to the desert. I guess I'll map all this out as I get to it but it does feel like a tricky business to make the story move smoothly through here.

Why do I worry so much about boring the reader? I don't want it to look like I've sacrificed the mystery and the pace for mere romance.

And skipping ahead to August . . .

8-12-89

Trying not to panic here. In the dead of night, Right Brain suggested that maybe Kinsey gets locked in the very storage bin Agnes was locked in. Nice claustrophobic atmosphere.

As a reader, I don't object to being privy to the reasoning process a detective goes through as long as it makes sense to me and seems logical. When the leap comes too fast, then I object. I like for the detective to consider every possible alternative.

My problem here is one of transitions . . . forging the links between the scenes I know are coming up.

8-15-89

Book was due today but so be it. Just closed out Chapter 23 and opened 24. I'm going to write notes to myself for a while and then print pages 30-35 so I can have them handy.

Need to set up "It used to be Summer. . . ."

Maybe Kinsey & Dietz go back to Irene's & confront her with the true information on the birth certificate. If these aren't my parents, then who am I?

8-16-89

God, I'm tired today. I'd really love to sleep. Let's see what I can accomplish in a stupor. Can't wait for this book to be over and done.

Dear Right Brain,

Please be with me here and help me solve and resolve the remaining questions in the narrative. Help me to be resourceful, imaginative, energetic, inventive. And patient.

Look forward to hearing from you.

Sincerely,

Sue

I could pull up countless other samples, but you get the point I'm sure.

Looking Back

One comfort I take from my journals is that regardless of where I am in the current private eye novel, I can always peek back into the journals I've kept for previous books and discover I was just as confused and befuddled back *then* as I am today. Prior journals are reminders that regardless of past struggles, I did somehow manage to prevail. Having survived through two novels, or five, or even twelve, in my case, there's some reason to suppose I'll survive to write the next.

If you haven't already incorporated a journal or its equivalent into your current bag of writing tricks, you might try your hand at one and see how it works for you. Remember, it's your journal and you can do it any way you choose. If you don't use a computer, you can write yours in crayon on 10×14 sheets of newsprint. You can type it, write in longhand, use a code if you need to feel protected. You can log in every day or only once a week. You can use it as a launching pad and then abandon the practice, or use it as I do, as an emotional tether connecting me to each day's work.

To help you get started, I'll give you the first entry just to speed you on your way:

> Enter today's date.
> Just sitting down here to try my hand at this weird stuff Sue Grafton has been talking about. A lot of it sounds like California psychobabble, but if it helps with the writing, who really cares?
> In the book I'm working on, what worries me is. . . .

SUE GRAFTON is the author of the best-selling Kinsey Millhone series, the most recent of which is *"P" Is for Peril*. She is a past president of the Private Eye Writers of America and is the editor of *Writing Mysteries* (Writer's Digest Books).

Chapter 20

Pump Up Your Creativity

By Steven James

You slide behind the steering wheel, slip your key into the ignition and . . . nothing happens. You twist it back and forth, pound the dashboard a few times, and utter words that would make a nightclub comedian blush.

But still, nothing happens. The battery is dead. And you're not going anywhere until you get a jump start.

We all know what it takes to jump-start a car, but what do you do when you slide behind the computer, slip your fingers onto the keyboard, and nothing happens? You sweat and squirm, pound your desk and curse at the cursor, but it doesn't do any good. Your story is stalled out. How do you jump-start your brain?

Explore Your L.I.F.E.

When you don't know where else to turn, explore L.I.F.E., an acronym for Literature, Imagination, Folklore, and Experience. L.I.F.E. is a limitless well of ideas waiting to be tapped.

Coax new stories from classic plots by setting them in a different time and place; examine your imagination for themes that pique your interest; search through the timeless motifs of myth, fairy tale, and folklore; scour the expanses of your own experiences to spark new ideas. Let your memories come alive!

Some memories inspire us, others haunt us. Some memories cling to things we own, others hover around places we've been. Start with what you have, then nurture that fragment of memory: your teacher's face, the smell of your grandmother's cookies, the charming way your father used to whistle, the chill in your soul as you rushed to the hospital, the taste of salt spray that summer at the ocean, how it felt to hold your daughter's hand for the first time. Turn those memories over in your mind, flesh them out, allow them to breathe.

Change Your Perspective

Recently, while visiting a hotel in Denver, I noticed exit signs not only above the exit doors, but also at their base. "How odd!" I thought. "Only someone crawling on the floor would need a sign down there!"

Aha.

Whoever put those signs there had looked through the eyes of someone crawling for safety during a fire.

Creativity isn't seeing what no one else sees; it's seeing what anyone else would see—if only they were looking. Ideas come when we peer at the world through another set of eyes.

So, look at your story from another person's perspective. Step into the shoes of your main character and write a journal entry, a complaint letter, or a love note. Switch your point of view. Write a few paragraphs in first or third person. Think of how you would respond if you were in the story. Walk through the action, stand on your desk, crawl on the floor. And keep your eyes open for the doors no one else has noticed.

Let Serendipity Happen

In Horace Walpole's eighteenth-century Persian fairy tale *The Three Princes of Serendip*, the heroes discover new things again and again while looking for something else. From this we get the word *serendipity*, which Walpole defined as "the facility of making happy chance discoveries."

If you're drained of ideas, you might be trying too hard. You can't make happy chance discoveries until you step away and stop worrying. Relax. Worrying about problems is like looking at bacteria through a microscope—it doesn't help 'em go away, it only makes 'em look bigger.

So work smarter, not harder. Break your routine. Go to a movie. Have a cup of coffee. Abstain from octopus. Try writing in a different place or at a different time. Lift weights. Get up in the middle of the night. Place yourself in situations where you're not at ease—risking and responding to new challenges forces you to think creatively and opens the door for serendipity.

Set Boundaries

Photographers focus on a single event and snap the picture. Each photo reveals only a sliver of reality, yet that carefully framed sliver contains a world of meaning. A great photographer knows just what to leave out.

Writers don't have a viewfinder. The lens we look through is as large as our imagination. And when we can't think of what to write next, we often try generating more ideas when we really need to set more limits. Skilled photographers carefully frame their shots just right. Skilled writers carefully fence in their ideas.

Nothing stalls writing more effectively than lack of focus. Freedom to write anything usually ends up as an excuse for not writing anything.

What's your story really about? What's the theme? The deadline? The word count? If you weren't assigned any boundaries, set them yourself.

Look for Connections

Creativity occurs at the intersection of ideas, when two thoughts that seem to have nothing in common collide and form something new. Don't feel pressured to develop ideas from scratch. Look for ways of combining two or more familiar things into something novel and unique.

Do this by forcing yourself to make connections. Randomly choose any two objects in your home, combine them, and form something new: "carpet" + "lights" might become "carpight"—a soft, cushiony, glowing floor covering that turns on when you step on it.

See? Think metaphorically. For example, an idea is like a flame—it curls and leaps and has a mind of its own. It's unpredictable and uncontrollable. And it'll eventually burn out unless you feed it fresh materials. Give your ideas space and every once in a while, blow on them to keep the embers glowing and the flames sprouting up.

Look for parallels or connections between things that seem to have nothing in common. Let unexpected connections spark your writing.

Ask Stupid Questions

Don't be afraid to ask obvious, even stupid, questions.

Describe the finished story to someone. What has to happen before you get there? What does the reader need to know by the end? You may have left out a key thought, clue, or concept. Ask, "What's missing from my story? What have I left out? What would naturally come next?"

Use "What if?" questions to jar you toward a unique solution. "What if I started over from scratch? What if time wasn't a factor? Is time a factor? What if I made this a screenplay instead of a novel?"

Question Your Direction

A Jewish folk tale tells of a man searching for paradise. Every night he points his shoes toward his goal and goes to bed. Every morning he steps into his shoes and continues his journey. But one night, a mischievous imp turns the shoes around. The next day, the man thinks he's headed for paradise, but he's really walking back home. His problem had nothing to do with lack of effort or motivation. He even had a wonderful destination. He just never noticed he was walking in the wrong direction.

That same imp visits writers. He sneaks into our stories and points the plot in the wrong direction. And we keep plugging away, writing page after page of a story that's headed nowhere.

Sometimes we write ourselves into a corner. We try harder and harder to scale the walls we've erected without ever wondering, "Does this story even need that corner?"

Question where you're going. Don't assume that you're headed in the right direction just because you're picking up from where you left off yesterday.

Stay on track. Each day as you begin to write, make sure your shoes are pointing in the direction you wish to go.

STEVEN JAMES's stories and articles have appeared in *Guideposts for Teens, Breakaway, Brio,* and *Campus Life.*

Chapter 21

Breaking Through Writer's Block

By Octavia E. Butler

Writer's block is a deadness. Any writer who's had it knows what I mean. Writer's block is that feeling of dead emptiness and fear, that "can't write!" feeling that isn't quite on a par with "can't breathe!" but is almost as unnerving.

But the feeling is a lie. Can't write? Of course you can. Short of real physical or mental disability, you can research and write whatever you like. If you know your craft, you may even be able to write well in spite of writer's block. What's missing is not your ability to write, but your ability to feel any joy, any passion, any satisfaction in your writing.

But as writers, we should use everything that touches us. It's all ore to be refined into story. I'm more aware of that now than ever before because I've just spent almost ten years alternately fighting and using writer's block while working on books called *Parable of the Sower* and *Parable of the Talents*. I've never before written so slowly. The two books stalled and stalled and stalled. Each time I thought I had found a way to tell the story that I wanted to tell, I would hit another wall—or the same wall. And usually that was because I was unknowingly trying to do something that was wrong for the story.

The books are the near-future story of one woman's obsessive struggle to spread a belief system—a religion—that she feels will focus humanity on a specific, constructive goal and turn it away from the chaos into which it has descended.

Knowing that much, at least, I knew that I had a story. I had a character—sometimes homeless, sometimes a community leader, sometimes on the run—who, against all likelihood and common sense, was trying to do something she believed in while her world took casual, lethal swipes at her.

So if I had a story to tell and a passion to tell it, where were the blocks? They were near the beginnings of each book. As I began *Parable of the Sower*, I found it difficult to develop any empathy with my main character. I didn't like her. I didn't like the fact that to do what she wanted to do, she had to be a kind of power-seeker.

Changing POV and Other Tricks

I've written much about power in my earlier novels. It fascinates me—what it does to people, what they do with it. I've had characters inherit power or get handed power in the shape of heavy responsibility, but before the Parable books, I had never written about a powerless person who sought great power. I discovered that I found such a person morally questionable at best. Without realizing it, I had bought into the idea that any-one who wanted power probably shouldn't have it.

On an intellectual level, I realized that power was just one of humankind's many tools, like education, like technology, like money, like a lawn mower for goodness' sake. Power is a tool. It's what we do with it that's good or bad. But knowing this didn't change my feelings—thus the block.

I tried distancing myself from the character by writing about her from the point of view of first one, then another of her relatives. But each of these efforts dragged, then died. So I tried telling her story from an omniscient point of view, another way of not getting too close. When this failed, I froze.

Desperately, I tried some of my favorite block-breaking

tricks—writing at different locations, for instance (at the library, on long bus rides, at the beach). I tried taking a break from my writing and reading other people's work. I read several best-selling novels and some fiction and nonfiction from that ever-growing stack of books that I had always meant to read. That was good. And I tried writing as my main character, writing for practice, not for publication in my character's voice. I tried to force myself into her skin. This works most of the time. It feels mechanical and artificial at first, but after a while it gets easier, more natural.

Not this time.

Finally, I began to write bits from my character's religious book so that I could quote them in the novels. I didn't know at that point that I would begin each chapter with such quotes. And I was surprised to find myself writing in verse. I realized that the research I had done was beginning to kick in.

A Poetic Lift

There comes a time for me within each of my novels when what I know from research becomes such a natural part of the story that I forget that I haven't always known it. In this case, I had been glancing through books of a number of actual religions. I needed a form for my character's religious book and I worried about making her religion too much like one of the existing religions. I found that I liked the form of the Tao Te Ching—a slender little book of brief, seemingly simple verses. I began to write my own, quite different, quiet little verses. I'd written no poetry of any kind since I was in school, and even then, I only wrote it under duress. But time seems to have eased my resistance. The stuff I came up with at first was terrible, but it was fun to write, then to rework into something less terrible.

The change of genre helped me to break my block. Suddenly

I was working on the novel in a whole different way, and it was intriguing.

One of my early inspirations helped move me along too: the news. The ugly things in the novels happened because today's dangers—drug use, the popularity of building prisons coupled with the unpopularity of building and maintaining schools and libraries, and the yawning rich-poor gap—grow up to be tomorrow's disasters.

At last, I began to write more successfully as my character— to write in her voice. But it was her voice as a young girl. When we meet her in *Parable of the Sower*, she has already come up with some of her religious ideas, but she's just a kid at home with her family. She isn't a power-seeker yet. She hasn't done anything questionable and nothing terrible has happened to her. Yet.

Terrible things do happen to her, though, and she must respond to them.

Eventually she is stripped of home, of family, of everything except her beliefs. She rebuilds her life and begins a community several hundred miles north of where she grew up. She turns a horrible situation into a hopeful one. She begins to attract people to her beliefs. And that's where *Parable of the Sower* ends. I thought I was rolling. I really did know the story I wanted to tell, and I didn't expect to have any trouble finishing it in *Parable of the Talents*. I did a publicity tour with *Sower*, and wrote an introduction and several afterwords for *Bloodchild*, my short story collection. Then I began to work seriously on *Parable of the Talents*. I had already written a few chapters. Now, working steadily, I wrote about 150 pages. Then I realized I was going wrong. Normally, I don't rewrite whole novels. I don't do a rough draft, second draft, third draft, and so on. I do one complete draft. Then I do line corrections. This works for me because I can't go on writing when I know something's wrong. I've got to fix the problem as soon as I realize it's there. If that means I have to dump sixty or eighty pages, so be it. I've learned the hard way that I lose interest in a novel if I write the whole thing and then go back to try to fix things.

So after I'd written the first 150 pages and realized that there was a problem, I had to go back and try to fix it. Eventually, I had to go all the way back to the beginning. The problem was this: My plot and my character were going nowhere near where they should go. In fact, they went nowhere at all. No doubt this had something to do with the fact that I felt, at this point, exactly the opposite of the way I'd felt when I began *Sower*. I had gone from not liking my character at all and trying to distance myself from her, to liking her far too much. I identified with her. And I didn't want to hurt her anymore. Character in conflict is the essence of story, but liking a character too much to give him or her trouble is one of the most ordinary hazards of writing. It was the cause of a serious block. I knew what I needed to do, but every time I tried to do it, I failed somehow. The story slipped away from me and went wrong. And when it did, I couldn't go on. I wrote the first 150 pages over and over and over again, getting nowhere. I had never done that before. The worst thing was that with each repetition, I proved to myself that I couldn't get it right. It was impossible. I couldn't do it. It was as though I had forgotten how to write. Very scary. And yet, I couldn't let the novel go.

If there's any single talent a writer needs, it's persistence. If you can keep at your writing and you can learn as you write, you can tell any story you want to tell. I used to say this before I began the Parable books, and I say it now that they're written, but there were times while I was writing them when I wasn't sure it was true.

Diversionary Breakthrough

Years passed. My life changed. I bought a house. I finally broke down and bought a computer. I'd written eleven books on manual typewriters and they were high-tech enough for me. But my editor didn't much like them, and I was beginning to feel left behind by the world in general. As soon as I began to use the computer, it became a nastier enemy than the novel had ever been. In fact, the computer made me forget how impossible the novel was. And, nastily, I found that giving my character trouble got easier since I was getting so much trouble myself. Again, learning to do something new helped me break the block. My unconscious mind needed the vacation from the novel—or needed the new and different opponent. Once it had both, the block was broken.

Writer's block, then, has been a guide and a goad to me. It's stopped me from writing badly. Like power, it's been a tool. It isn't a tool that I would want to use, but writers can't always be choosers. And if we're serious, we do use everything.

OCTAVIA E. BUTLER has won Hugo and Nebula awards for her science fiction writing. She recently was named one of the one hundred best writers of the twentieth century by Writer's Digest readers, editors, and advisory board members.

Chapter 22

"Murder Your Darlings"

By James Patrick Kelly

It's in our nature to fall in love with words, particularly our own. Clever turns of phrases excite us; we beam like proud parents when our protagonists take on lives of their own; a shapely plot twist can turn our heads. There's nothing wrong with indulging in the occasional fling, as long as it ends before your final draft. When the time comes to make that last revision, you must harden your heart, sharpen the ax, and murder your darlings.

Well, maybe not all of them. Just the shiftless ones, those previous freeloaders who are too busy looking good to do any work. Once you learn how to spot them, you'll see them everywhere, in unpublishable manuscripts and in award-winning stories, in my work and hers and yours.

Some writers like to fix problems by adding rather than subtracting. First, they layer in just a little more complexity to develop a rounder Aunt Penelope. Then they expand the garage scene to foreshadow the car chase. Last, they have Biff's lawyer explain the rules of evidence to his secretary after the trial so slow readers will understand the end. If these writers worry about wordiness at all, they might tighten a few lines here and there. Drop a *he said* on page two. But major surgery is for beginners, right?

What many writers don't realize is that muscular prose alone can't lift a narrative. Any sentence, no matter how powerful, that serves no story purpose is nothing more than wasted words. Obviously, adjective pileups and unnecessary clauses and clunky diction must go. However, effective cutting involves more than line editing. You can also strike whole paragraphs—pages, even! For example, toss out that extra twist and the plot might become clear. Rather than reconstructing the pyramids in five paragraphs (despite that week you spent cruising the Nile last summer), pick the two best and let readers supply some of their own building materials.

Routine Surgery

Although I'll offer specific suggestions for what to excise, please don't memorize my list. These skills are most useful when used intuitively, not consciously. The best way to prevent verbosity is to develop an instinct for cutting, which means you should practice every day. I know enough writers to realize there's no universal technique for getting words on (or off!) paper. But here's the routine that works for me.

I write at the computer, the greatest advance in literary technology since the eraser. I spend the first hour or so paring and revising the previous day's work. This not only promotes the proper mind-set, but it also helps me reenter the world of the story. I'm rarely stuck because I always begin with these editorial warm-ups—much easier than a first draft, in my opinion. In the middle part of the day, I compose as carefully as I can. Later, however, I may let standards slip to fill my daily complement of screens. This admittedly sloppier work will either be cleaned up or pruned first thing the next morning, as the process begins again.

Although I edit daily, I rarely attempt major cuts until I finish a working draft. I like to split production of a finished manuscript into two stages: revision and deletion. In the revision stage, I make sure I've given my readers enough of everything: plot, character, setting, theme. I search for logic flaws and continuity breaks;

I run my spellchecker. Revision ends once I'm satisfied the manuscript is as complete and coherent as I can make it. Only then do I go through it one last time, with an itchy finger on the delete key.

Major Surgery

How much to trim at this point? Based on extensive reading, I estimate the current rate of literary inflation is about 10 percent. If my revision draft is twenty pages, I aim for a finished manuscript of eighteen.

Two pages! How can you carve two pages of living prose from a story without killing it? Here are some things to look for:

• **Adjectival and adverbial leeches.** Start at the sentence level, hunting for the unnecessary modifiers that drain the life from prose. Strong verbs are the key to taut writing. Rather than "The ungainly triceratops walked slowly away," try "The triceratops lumbered away."

• **Clumsy entrances and exits.** Don't waste time moving people around. Too many doors open and close in fiction. If you want the UPS man to deliver a mysterious parcel, he doesn't need to knock, come in, and ask Reggie to sign for it. When Janet screams at Bob that she's sick of his catting around and wants a divorce, why must she also stalk from the house to her car and peel out of the driveway? It's not crucial that you punctuate emotional scenes with histrionic exits. If the scene isn't angry enough, fix it. Don't take the easy way out by slamming the door.

• **Unnecessary scene or time switches.** Aristotle was wrong about physics, but he was right to recommend unity of time and place. Before you board a cruise ship or skip ahead three weeks, always ask: Is this trip unnecessary? When you change venues or let time fly, you create an extra narrative burden. You must describe the new setting or explain what happened in the interim. Compressing these story elements can save words while maintaining the focus on character and action.

• **Overpopulation.** In the attempt to re-create the sweep and richness of life, some writers keep cramming characters into a story until it resembles the Marx Brothers' stateroom in *A Night at the Opera*. The people you want readers to care about will be lost in a mob scene, so keep the cast to a minimum. Name as few characters as you can; describe even fewer. If you can combine two characters into one, you probably should.

• **Overdramatization.** "Show, don't tell," can be a dangerous policy. Wordy writers think they must dramatize everything. But a story isn't a game of charades; come right out and tell readers what's what. Do you really need a rhapsodic paragraph about Amanda's aquiline nose and alabaster skin and piercing blue eyes and tawny mane, when all you wanted to say was that George was attracted to her? When necessary, tell—don't show.

• **Arriving early and staying late.** All stories do not start on page one—only the good ones. If you're the first at the party, there's usually nothing to do until the other guests arrive except to stand around and admire the furniture. Writers who start their stories too early have the same problem. They waste time describing the china on the breakfast table or the daisies nodding in the garden. Or they deliver a weather report. Yet the same people who chuckle at the howler "It was a dark and stormy night" don't hesitate to play meteorologist in opening paragraphs of their own fiction. Similarly, when the story is over, stop writing. There's no need to explain what became of everyone and how they all felt and what it all meant. Memorable fiction rarely ends with the last line. By leaving some things unwritten, you empower readers to imagine what happens next. It is one skill to recognize potential cuts, another to make the right ones. A strategy I've developed is to read my work aloud in draft. Try it and listen carefully to the expression in your voice. You may actually hear your interest level peaking and dipping.

For those who just can't bring themselves to operate on their own fiction, get a second opinion. Almost anyone can help, even your mom. In fact, if you're dissatisfied with the criticism she's been giving you lately, don't ask for it next time. Instead, just hand her the manuscript and a blue pencil and tell her to prune 10 percent. While Mom may not have been an English major, she'll know when she's bored. Easier for her to remove the slow bits than to critique your subtext.

Unfortunately, the craft of cutting is undervalued in a world where writers are paid by the word. And it shows; you don't have to look hard to find padded work in print. Yet clearly it is precision that separates the journeyman from the master. Perhaps the way to grow as a writer is to shrink your manuscripts. As Sir Arthur Quiller-Couch so memorably put it, "Whenever you feel an impulse to perpetrate a piece of exceptionally fine writing, obey it—wholeheartedly—and delete it before sending your manuscripts to press." Or, better still, *murder your darlings.*

JAMES PATRICK KELLY's works include *Look Into the Sun, Planet of Whispers,* and *Wildlife.* He has also published more than thirty short stories in science fiction magazines.

Chapter 23

A Four-Step Plan for Revision

By Raymond Obstfeld

Revising can be daunting. There's so much to look for—pacing, characterization, plot, theme, style. When I sit down to write the first few
versions of a chapter, the jumble of clumsy words appearing on the
screen is a far cry from the perfect passages I'm imagining in my mind.

Early drafts lay down the basic story and characters while the
final drafts fine-tune what's already there. In the early stages of writing and revising, you're more daring because the area is still uncharted. But once you've charted it—that is, once you have the characters you want, doing and saying the things you want, in the order
you want—now you're ready for the final draft.

Ground Rules

First, compartmentalize your approach. The strength of the following four-step method of revision is that by doing only one step
at a time, you're fully focused on that one area. Don't give in to
the temptation to fix something that's not part of the step you're
pursuing. Keep in mind that each step has an ultimate goal, and
achieving that goal is the whole point of a particular revision.

Second, apply this process only in short, self-contained sections. If you're revising a long story or novel, use this method
on scenes or chapters. I strongly discourage writing the full draft

and then going back to revise. That's because the act of revising sometimes involves rethinking what you're writing about, what you want to say, whom these characters are, where you're going with the story. Sometimes you only discover the answers to these questions during a rewrite. There's usually a reason you get stuck in a particular place: You realize something is wrong with what you've written or intend to write. You just don't yet know what that something is. You need to take the time to figure out the exact element that's bothering you to know what comes next.

Step One: Structure

Goal: Develop a clear and compelling plot.

Look for: Too passive, talking-head characters; no plot buildup/anticlimactic action.

How to fix: Basically, you're looking to see that events are in the right order and that, if they are, the scene builds toward a satisfying climactic payoff.

The passive/talking-heads scene occurs when characters are sitting around yammering back and forth without any tension to the scene. They're called talking heads because what they're saying seems removed from any sense of characterization. It's as if they are puppets speaking the author's words rather than real people speaking their own minds.

One simple way to fix this is to change the setting so the scene is more active. Instead of a husband and wife sitting in the airport waiting for his mother to arrive and discussing how horrible she is, put them in a car stuck in horrendous airport traffic that may make them late. This additional element shifts the readers' focus to the urgency of the couple being late, which makes the readers anxious and therefore more apt to pay attention to the dialogue. Also, it gives the couple more to talk about (the awful traffic, his or her awful driving) so the conversation seems less contrived and more natural. And it gives a concrete focus to the mother's character by introducing the fact that she hates it when people are late; this shows us who she is and replaces long descriptions of how controlling she is.

Each scene is like a ministry: It has a beginning, middle, and end. The beginning introduces the conflict of the scene, the middle complicates it, and the end resolves it. That means every scene has to have a "hot spot," a point in which the action and/or emotions reach an apex. When revising for structure, make sure you locate the hot spot and make sure it generates enough heat to justify the scene. One of the main reasons scenes weaken here is that writers end the scene too early, as if it were a TV show and they were breaking for a commercial. An argument doesn't end when someone makes a witty or stinging comment; it keeps on going to the point where people are uncomfortable, frustrated, at a loss for words. So must the scene.

So far, I've discussed revising structure within a scene or chapter. However, once the whole story is completed, you must also revise the structure of the larger work. This means making sure all the scenes are in the best order. Before moving scenes around, I suggest you create note cards for each scene or chapter. Record who is in the scene, what happens in it, and how many pages it is. Tack them up in order on a bulletin board. Do you have too many passive scenes together? Are the settings too similar? By studying the cards, you can sometimes discover structure problems. Move the cards around; see if changing the order helps. Or perhaps you'll find you need an additional scene between a couple characters.

Step Two: Texture

Goal: Sharpen descriptive passages to make characters, setting, and action more vivid.

Look for: Too much or too little description, research "info dump," too many adjectives, information in wrong place.

How to fix: This step has a lot to do with defining your own style.

Some writers use a lot of description, others use very little. There's no right way. But when there's so much description that the story's momentum bogs down, that's too much. Or if there's so little that the characters or settings are bland and nonmemorable, that's too little. Most writers, myself included, have many descriptive passages that they love but that must go because they call too much attention to themselves and detract from the story. Anytime you see a passage of description that is so poetic and involving that the reader stops to admire the author, cut it. Save all those wonderful passages you cut in a folder; you may be able to use them in another story.

Telling the reader too little can be equally annoying. Even though the writer may tell us the scene takes place in an alley, if the reader emerges from the scene and still doesn't have a feel for the setting, then the reader never experiences the alley and therefore is never fully involved.

Directly related to this is the dreaded "info dump." This is where the writer decides to stop the story cold to give a lot of details about the history of the house that the characters live in or how to pilot a plane. Yes, sometimes those details are important to your story and add a level of credibility. But novice writers either include too much information or too many such passages. One of my students is writing a novel that involves sailing a yacht. This author has sailing expertise, so he includes page after page of description about the technical aspects of sailing. Workshop reaction to these scenes is always the same: There's so much technical information that the readers get lost and no longer care about what's happening to the characters. However, there's another student in the same class who is also an expert sailor and writing a novel about sailing, but reaction to his work is always enthusiastic because we get just enough information to accept the realism of the scene, but not so much as to numb us.

Aside from adjusting length, writers can vastly improve the impact of the texture by concentrating on word choices. Read through the manuscript once and circle words that could be stronger. Then go back and take your time replacing them. Don't rely on a thesaurus; many times you'll just trade one dull word for a more complex and even duller word. The word you're looking for often isn't a synonym; it's just something richer, more evocative.

A common reason that passages can bog down or lose their snap is that the writer has burdened them with too many adjectives. Most of the time when there are several adjectives together, at least two of them have the same meaning. For example: "She was a quiet, introspective, shy girl." Think of every adjective as a one hundred dollar bill and spend wisely.

Step Three: Dialogue

Goal: Elicit character personality through conversation.

Look for: Too many tag lines, too few tag lines, tag lines in the wrong place, bland or melodramatic lines.

How to fix: Tag lines are the "he said" and "she said" parts of dialogue. If there are only two speakers, several lines can go on without telling us who the speaker is; the reader already knows.

To add tag lines in such a situation is really nothing more than a crutch to avoid making the characters' voices so individual that the reader can recognize their cadence and tone without being told.

Yet there are times when the reader does have to be told who is speaking. This can be because there are several speakers, or the dialogue is interspersed with action or interior monologues, or it's needed for the sake of the rhythm. The following are several examples of the same line of dialogue:

> "Hi," she said, moving toward me.
> "Hi," she said. She moved toward me.
> She moved toward me. "Hi."
> "Hi." She moved toward me.

The first two examples are friendlier because the "she said" slows the pace, taking away some of the energy from her act of moving. The second two examples are more dramatic because they present just the dialogue and the action, which now seems more deliberate and aggressive.

Where the tag line goes affects the emphasis on the dialogue. Look at the following variations. Which has more impact?

> "This is yours. That is not," he said.
> "This is yours," he said. "That is not."

The second version is stronger because the emphasis is now on "That is not." Placing the emphasis there adds an ominous tone. The first version has the lines together, which doesn't emphasize either and makes the dialogue seem breezier.

Sometimes you need to identify the speaker, but you don't want to use the word *said* for the millionth time. You can substitute an action instead:

> "You always do this to me," I said.
> I said, "You always do this to me."
> I shook my head. "You always do this to me."

Don't overdo this technique, otherwise every line of dialogue will have a gesture attached and the characters will all seem like they're on a caffeine buzz.

Finally, keep your tags simple. The more complex the tag line, the more it detracts from the actual dialogue. Avoid adverbs (e.g., she said angrily).

One of the things I do before editing my own dialogue is to read a passage by someone whose dialogue I admire (Elmore Leonard, Ross Thomas, Lorrie Moore, Jane Smiley, Peter De Vries). Which writer I choose to read depends on the tone I want to achieve. If the scene calls for fast-paced, edgy dialogue, I may read Leonard. If I want playful and desperate, I may read playwright David Mamet. Read the dialogue passages until you have a feel for the language, then go right back to your work and start editing.

Step Four: Editing

Goal: Tighten pace and continuity.
Look for: Repetition through implication, slow passages.
How to fix: Cut. Cut. Cut.

This is often the hardest part for writers because they've worked so hard on every word. But this final step is the one that gives the work its final shape. Much of what you will cut is repetition, words that repeat what the reader already knows because it's been directly said or implied elsewhere.

Once you've finished editing your manuscript, go through again to make sure that there are clear transitions bridging your cuts.

A Final Word on Final Drafts

Although the phrase "final draft" suggests the last time you'll revise, that really isn't the case. Final draft really refers to the final process of revising. It's when you're satisfied with the basics, but want to erase any persistent flaws.

However, there is a point at which every manuscript must be abandoned, sent out to publishers, and the next work begun. This four-step revision method will allow you to reach that "final" draft more comfortably because you will know you have examined every aspect of the work possible. But if you've completed these four steps and you still feel the work needs something, begin again with step one.

RAYMOND OBSTFELD received an Edgar nomination for his novel *Dead Heat*. He has also written the Writer's Digest titles *The Novelist's Essential Guide to Crafting Scenes, Fiction First Aid, Careers for Your Characters,* and the "Fundamentals of Fiction Writing" for Writer's Digest's WritersOnlineWorkshop.com.

Chapter 24

Twenty-One Tweaks to a Better Tale

By James Plath

During the sixteen years that I edited *Clockwatch Review*, I often found myself wishing that every writer could work as an editor for a year. After all, it's impossible to read sixty-plus manuscripts daily and not develop a pretty fair sense of what makes a short story work.

While editors learn a lot about fiction, writers, unfortunately, are left only with cryptic rejection slips that say things like "sorry," "try us again," or "this came close." But the high volume of submissions makes it impossible for most editors to explain what revisions a writer might undertake. That's probably one of the most frustrating aspects of editing, because I often think to myself that a tweak here or there would make a huge difference in a rejected story. Here are twenty-one tweaks you can consider when trying to revive a rejected story:

1. Could It Use a New Beginning?

Lead with a powerful scene, a witty exchange, or a dazzling description that's now buried. Or, try X-ing out paragraph one, then two, and so on, until you get to something that includes more action, interest, or contrast than your original beginning. You'll find that what you had may have been only throat-clearing, rather than saying something necessary to the overall story.

2. Does the Ending Point Toward a Deeper Story?

The best endings resonate because they echo a word, phrase, or image from earlier in the story, and the reader is prompted to think back to that reference and speculate on a deeper meaning.

3. Is There a Dominant Visual Image?

With the movie *Deliverance*, it's the "Squeal like a pig" mountain rape scene; with *Pulp Fiction*, it's the needle thrust into the heart of a woman who had overdosed. Strong central images such as these anchor the story in our memories.

4. Is the Right Person Telling the Story?

I vividly remember a Kurt Vonnegut story of a broken relationship, told not by one of the participants, but by a plumber wedged underneath a kitchen sink whom the couple seems to have forgotten. Speculation on the part of a narrator is sometimes more interesting than exposition.

5. Is There Enough Interior Monologue . . . or Too Much?

It's amazing how many writers tell a story from a certain point of view, but don't spend much time inside that character's head. Without internal thoughts, which can serve as a counterplot to the physical action, a story will be less complex. But pick your moments. Characters should reflect during pauses in the action, not during physical action scenes.

6. Are There Too Many Minor Characters . . . or Too Few?

There are no hard-and-fast rules, but short stories can't hold too many characters (or proper names). If characters aren't absolutely necessary, get rid of them—or at least don't give them names. Call them by their occupation, function, or dress, like "the grocer," "the girl who kept staring at him," or "the man in the blue shirt."

7. Are There Enough Scenes, Too Many, or the Wrong Ones?

A scene should reveal something about the character, advance the plot in a significant way, provide insight into the "theme," or, as Eudora Welty suggested, do all three. Too few scenes can make a story seem like little more than a sketch; too many scenes can dilute a story to the point where important scenes can lose their power; and dramatizing the wrong moments is like highlighting the wrong passages in a novel for the next reader to find.

8. Why Are You Telling Me This?

The movie *Stand by Me* is a tale of twelve-year-olds framed by a beginning where a writer is seen contemplating a headline about a local attorney's murder, and an ending where we see that writer finding inspiration from his son and a playmate to end his story. The frame gives the story an immediate context and anticipates the "why" question.

9. Do You Appeal to a Reader's Senses?

The world around us is made "real" by our senses: touch, smell, taste, sight, and hearing. Stories that lack a convincing sense of reality often lack imagery that appeals to a reader's senses. A writer once told me that he strives to include five sensory details on every page. In retrospect, that seems like overkill, but you can make a fictional world come alive for readers by making it first come alive for your characters.

10. Do You Appeal to a Sense of Place?

Many stories exist in a vacuum, where lines are spoken without any description of an interior or exterior setting. That's like going to the theater and having the house lights never come on, or having characters stand there and deliver lines without any stage action.

11. Do Your Characters Have Sufficient Motivation?

What drives them to do the things they do? Do we know what they want?

12. Could You Make the Time Frame More Interesting?

Too many stories revolve around a single incident covering one to three hours. Could your current story really be a scene within a larger story? What if the story was stretched, like an image stamped in Silly Putty, until it became distorted and possibly more interesting?

13. Could You Add Texture to Your Story With Echoes, Allusions, and Metaphors?

The fiction studied in college—Literature with a capital "L"—is rich with figurative language and echoes. Figurative language includes metaphors and similes ("he had teeth like an alligator"), symbols and allusions ("someone had arranged the leaves on his lawn in the shape of a cross"), while echoes work by repeating key phrases or words within the story so that they have a cumulative effect on the reader.

14. What If Your Narrator Was Unreliable?

Would your story be more interesting if we were led to believe that your narrator wasn't telling the whole truth, or if we perceived something different from what the narrator seemed to perceive?

15. Do You Give Readers Enough Trivia Information and "Deep Thoughts"?

If your character is a bricklayer, then readers want to learn more about a bricklayer's world—the technical aspects of the job, as well as the mindset of a mason.

16. Will Lyrics, Letters, or Lists Add Interest?

These details double as plot devices. Consider what the "Sheik of Araby" lyrics add to F. Scott Fitzgerald's *The Great Gatsby*, or the letter that turns to pulp in Daisy's hand, or the list of socialites who frequent Gatsby's parties.

17. What About Coincidence and Irony?

These literary conventions add considerable interest. Say you have a story about a divorced parent who contracts AIDS, where the focus is on her first finding out and then wondering how to make provisions for her children. If you make her ex-husband the one in the relationship who was promiscuous or a drug abuser, it establishes an irony that sets up an emotional response in the reader.

18. Does the Story Have Enough Contrast?

Too many stories focus on a cast of characters who look, talk, and act alike. If your characters are similar, try introducing quirks, interests, speech patterns, expressions, physical traits, or emotional responses that will set them apart from others. When you walk down the street, what do you notice in a sea of people: two men of the same race and height, or members of the opposite sex who are dressed radically different or have dramatic height contrasts?

19. How Lively Is Your Dialogue?

Friends of Tennessee Williams said that they often thought the author had a whole house full of people, because there were all sorts of voices in varying tones and volumes coming from his writing room. That's because Williams acted out his scenes while he wrote, trying to get each character right. You can try that trick, but if your dialogue still doesn't ring true, perhaps it's what your characters are saying rather than how they're saying it. What's more interesting? Overheard conversations at the beginning or end of a date, party, or gathering of friends, or conversations from the middle?

20. Can You Up the Ante?

The simplest fictional formula is situation, complication, and (ir)resolution. Many times we get stories where the complication feels like part of an emerging problem the character must face, rather than an additional factor that will make a resolution tougher. Other times the complication just isn't complicated enough, or there isn't enough at stake. Try intensifying an existing complication, or toss in one or two more for good measure!

21. When All Else Fails, Why Not Try a "Sidecar" Approach?

So many of the stories we saw felt like theme park rides where the car follows a predictable route and can never leave the track. A boy breaks his mother's priceless vase, and the story follows the external action of his attempts to repair it and the internal action of him trying to decide whether (or how) to tell his mother about it. But what if that boy was in junior high and had just hooked up with his first serious girlfriend, and the story's focus is instead on their relationship? The vase could become a subplot, which could complicate things if the girlfriend thinks he should do something different from what he's inclined to do.

•   •   •

Greater complexity means greater reader interest. So tweak away!

JAMES PLATH has taught creative writing on the college level and edited and published *Clockwatch Review*.

Chapter 25

What to Do About Criticism

By Laura Hendrie

I'm sitting at a bar with a young man who's recently taken to calling himself a writer. After throwing back a shot of whiskey, he turns to me and says, "I think the greatest thing about writing is the honesty of the response you get back. Nobody hedges. Nobody tries to be polite. It's exhilarating. Know what I mean?"

I look at him with curiosity. We've just spent an hour together in a class where he was told by several writers, including me, that his novel—despite interesting characters, sharp-paced dialogue, and a real eye-opener of a plot—doesn't work. As far as I could tell from his reaction at the time, he wasn't all *that* thrilled by honesty, and now, though he smiles warmly at me before he turns to motion for another drink, I notice a tic in the muscle at the side of his neck.

A negative response from your readers—especially when they've taken the time to be conscientious about it—is always a shock. It's like getting kicked in the behind while bending over to pick up the penny. It's not the kick that hurts, it's the humiliation of having bent over for the penny. True, your voice may not quiver when you're thanking them for their honesty. Your hands may be steady when you're opening that letter of advice from the editor you've always admired. You may even be able to agree with your favorite author when he tells you that he thinks your new book isn't half as interesting as the last one you wrote. But your whole face is on fire, there's a roaring in your ears, and behind that pleasant, puppet-strung "uh-huh" of yours stands an infuriated, tic-faced little dictator demanding to know this instant one of three things: (1) how you could allow these half-wits near your best work; (2) why you *ever* thought you could get away with calling yourself a writer; or (3) how you're ever going to write again. And this may be where you stop. But it shouldn't be. In fact, the difference between the writer who's going to add up to something in a few years and the writer who's not may have less to do with the quality of the work than with the way each one handles criticism.

Using Criticism to Your Advantage

Some writers *use* criticism. Experienced writers do it all the time. They selectively choose whom to listen to, selectively listen for what they need to hear, and selectively use the information they're given. They do this with the same skill and concentration they use in their writing. Some writers will panic and toss out everything readers didn't like while embalming for worship everything they praised. Either that or balk at the very idea of changing a word or comma. A successful writer will panic, too, but then he will flounder onward, pondering this criticism and sweating out that compliment, trying all the wrong advice and being thoroughly disgusted with himself when he can't seem to make it work, until somewhere along the line, if he's open enough, he turns almost by accident to the advice he needed to hear in the first place—the advice he was too biased or nervous or green to understand before—and wham! He's invented something new. Not only that, but he's learned things *not* to invent along the way as well.

Writers who realize that feedback can be a valuable tool use it often and with growing dexterity and gratitude. And why not? Writing is a lonely enough experience without summarily refusing all help and input from outsiders. To do so simply because the reader may be wrong, the advice might upset you, or you don't like to be told what you didn't think up yourself is not only stubborn, but ultimately foolhardy.

If you're thinking, "Yes, but writers who can jump at a chance to receive feedback don't get the kind of feedback I get; they don't have to put up with the grunting manuscript-eaters I've got to deal with," you're wrong. Everybody gets their share of negative feedback and everybody gets their share of nonobjective, incompetent criticism. So don't think you're being unfairly picked on when even the most unskilled reader you know calls to tell you how to fix your story or poem, when even the silliest little free pamphlet-magazine sends you a rejection. It comes with the territory.

Writers who use critical feedback are not less egocentric or thicker-skinned or more flexible than writers who can't. Writers are by definition egocentric, thin-skinned, and highly sensitive to criticism. They write to be understood and when they are not, no matter how they may try to hide it, it hurts.

But while one writer may walk off from a negative response to his work looking like a suicide headed for the bridge, another writer can leave the same situation with a sense of excitement, even eagerness. Why? Not because he enjoys humiliation. And not because he is, in John Wayne's words, a damn fool. He just hasn't lost sight of his priority in the process. His priority is and always should be, even at the cost of pride and temporary pleasures, *to improve the writing*.

Okay, so you want to improve your writing, too. So you want to be able to learn from readers even when they start sucking the air out of the room. How do you manage it?

Step One: Ask Yourself Why

The way to handle criticism is to know *why* you're asking for it. You should know the answer to this *before* you ever send out a piece of work to be read.

This is not as easy as you might first suppose. Writers may be notoriously honest, but when it comes to the question of why they're sending out their work to be read, they tend to hold their hands over their mouths when they speak. Or as Logan Pearshall Smith explained it: "Every author, however modest, keeps a most outrageous vanity chained like a madman in the padded cell of his breast."

So the first question you should answer has two parts, one for the writer in you and one for the madman: (1) What do you think you want? and (2) What do you *really* want? "I know!" you chirp like the good child. *"To improve the writing!"* But to do that you must be as honest about your weaknesses as you are about your strengths. This can be extremely difficult when your weaknesses are being pointed out to you by someone else. Honest readers know this. That's why there are so few of them. They know how likely it is that when you say you want honesty, your preference is praise. Yet the irony is, you know you have to have that dose of honesty once in a while. You can't live without it, not if you're to become any sort of "real" writer.

The best way to get honesty from your readers is by asking for honesty from yourself. This is why *before* I send off a story or poem, I clear a place on my desk and sit down with a clean sheet of paper and a thick, black felt-tip pen to work out the reasons *why* I'm about to send out my work to whatever reader(s) I've chosen. I start at the top with the word:

Priorities

Some days, this in itself is enough to make me feel virtuous. Below that, I write:

Why do I need to send out this piece?

Priorities are more like eternal laws than personal decisions. They do not change much and they are as easy to remember as the memory of your mother's voice telling you to sit up straight or that brussels sprouts are good for you. I have two priorities: "To improve the writing" and "to get honest feedback." My only other priority is when I'm sending my manuscript out to be published, and then I'll naturally include, "to have the story published."

Notice how I avoid using personal pronouns in priorities. I like to keep them sounding as noble and unselfish and thoroughly martyred for the sake of the writing as the mother who offers to crawl to Bethlehem for the sake of her children.

When I'm done with that, I move down to the middle of the page. There I draw a heavy black line similar to the River Styx and below that I take a breath and write:

Preferences

Then, I write:

What else do I want?

This is where it gets tricky. You'll do anything but admit what you *really* want, right? To get around this, write your answers in the form of questions.

What else do I want?

To show my readers that:

- *I'm a living treasure?*
- *I've led a fascinating life? (had fascinating parents? children? dogs?)*
- *I'm not afraid of a little criticism?*
- *I should be published soon in some magazine their mother works for?*
- *I'm nothing like them?*
- *I'm just as good as them?*
- *I'm ten times better than them?*

I try to put the preferences that sound most vulgar right at the top of the list. That way I offer myself the chance to be honest from the start. I also think it's helpful to go over each item and ask yourself, "If I could ever be *so* grossly self-centered as to want that and then the opposite actually happened, I wonder how I'd feel?"

Then close your eyes and imagine it. If you feel anything like nausea or dizziness, you're probably close to the truth. Keep going. When it comes to preferences, i.e., vanity-driven motives that have absolutely nothing to do with good writing, still waters run deep. And what do you do with all this truth? Examine your options:

- Forget about sending out the story.
- Forget about getting honest feedback and send the story to your aunt who "always loves anything" you write.
- Send it out to honest readers but ask them to read only for grammar and spelling errors. Or better yet, tell them to read it "only for enjoyment." (Don't worry; they'll get the point.)
- Send it out and prepare yourself for the possibility of seeing every one of your preferences shot for the sake of improving the work.

If you choose the last option, remember two things. One is that the reason you're asking for feedback is that you are still learning to write. (If you're smart, you'll spend your entire life learning and still never be able to admit you know how.) The other is Marcus Aurelius's quote: "It is not death that a man should fear, but he should fear never beginning to live." Which in my neck of the woods translates to mean that if I'm fully prepared to get bucked off my horse in a negative critique and then I actually get bucked off, I'm a lot less stunned about it than if I assumed my horse wasn't the bucking type. Plus I'll be able to get back on faster and decide which direction to go in next with a great deal more clarity and eagerness.

The surprising thing is this little pregame self-exam can make a big difference. Let's say, for example, that I've given my fiction to my most honest reader, who then informs me that she thinks the main character is insipid. If I'm not aware of my preferences, if I've deluded myself into thinking that honest feedback was my *only* expectation, I may get the desire to, let's say, snap off her head at the neck. Why? Because the story was so *obviously* all about me and my incredible childhood! Granted, I *called* it fiction instead of autobiography, granted I *asked* for her honest opinion—but *really*!

But if, on the other hand, after admitting to myself that my desire to send out my poem about Miami was influenced not only by my desire to improve the work but also because the reader I chose just happens to edit a magazine called *Miami Monthly*, I can't be all that upset with her if she spends her time talking about the heavy-handedness of the setting. After all, she's kept her priorities straight—to give honest feedback. I'm the one who bent the rules, who tried to submit to her magazine without her realizing it. But I can forgive myself—wanting love is only human, right? I'll look at the poem some more, try to see what she saw, maybe even change the setting to something I know more about. And in the meantime, I've discovered a gem: The reader who insists on being honest.

Step Two: Ask Your Readers Questions

Contrary to what many people believe, giving a manuscript to readers for a critical discussion does not mean the writer gives up control of it. Far from it. In most cases, readers look to the writer for direction. If they sense the writer's priority is to improve the work, they'll try to deliver; but if they sense the writer is fishing for compliments or expecting a browbeating, they're likely to do that, too. It's hard not to. So if you don't want to leave your next critique feeling duped, take charge. Teach your readers how to teach you.

One way to do this is to come to the discussion with a carefully planned set of what I call writing-oriented questions about your work. Asking writing-oriented questions accomplishes several things. It makes you an active participant in the feedback process, provides a framework for you and your readers to address particular concerns about the work, and helps organize your readers' discussion into themes that are easier for you to grasp, understand, and use later.

But most important, writing-oriented questions clarify for everyone concerned why the critique is taking place. Not because the writer is hoping to be coddled and not because the readers want to toot their horns about how much they know. No, this discussion is taking place for one reason and one reason only: *To improve the writing.* Most readers appreciate being reminded of this.

Which is why, if you want your questions to be writing-oriented instead of self-oriented, they should be written down *before* you enter the critique, before that little madman imprisoned in your breast—your ego—starts shrieking and rattling his chains too loudly for you to think.

A writing-oriented question sounds exactly like what it is. It's the same kind of open-ended question English teachers pose for their students on a piece of literature, and it demands the same sort of response from readers, i.e.:

- Clearly stated ideas about the piece backed by concrete examples;
- Objectivity in arguments;
- A strong sense of respect for and deference to the work (i.e., a writing-oriented question asks the reader for a clear description of what *is* on the page, not a prescription of what to put there next);
- Examination based on two bigger issues: What works? What doesn't work?

Now let's put this to the test. Suppose that as the author, you're curious to know if the complexity of your main character translates onto the page. If you ask something like, "Did you like the main character?" or "Didn't you think that ending was confusing?" the reader feels trapped. The questions are close-ended and ego-oriented. They plead not for an honest response from the reader, but an ego-mollifying, uninformed, and uninformative, knee-jerk response like "yeah" or "sure."

A writing-oriented question, however, might be, "Can you describe the kind of person the main character is?" Now you are asking an open-ended question that demands objective information based not on opinion but on what is on the page. *You* as author know the answer. You know it because it's your work, but see if your readers know it, too. If they don't, and you know they're careful readers, then the character is obviously not as fully realized on paper as he is in your head.

Here are some other examples of writing-oriented questions:

- Can you tell me why the man does what he does?
- Can you tell me why or why not the point of view (the pace/voice/setting/dialogue/whatever you're concerned about) works for this particular piece?
- Can you tell me what the strongest images were in the piece and why? The weakest? Why?
- Can you explain why I changed from third person to first at the end?

Adapt questions to your specific needs, your specific style, and your specific readers. Then make sure to open your ears. Good listening begins with respect. Write down everything, even if you don't agree with it. [If your critique occurs through the mail, copy down the comments from your reader(s) in your own hand.] Listen not only to what is said, but also to what is not said. Be courteous. Be sure you understand. Encourage them if you think they are holding back. And *never* argue. You are there to improve the writing, and no matter how far off the mark they are in this regard, they are trying to help. Remember this: The more you're able to hear what they're saying and why they're saying it, the more you'll understand the worth of it later.

Step Three: What to Do With Feedback

After you come out of a critique of your work, you've got, as you know, several choices. If you don't believe what you hear, you can throw a fit and send the story to someone else. If you believe it, you can throw a fit and destroy the piece. Or you can throw a fit and then hide the piece in the back of your closet for a while.

But most writers—even the ones who don't throw fits—end up wanting to rewrite. The question is how to do it when every voice is yammering at you except the original one that told you to write the piece in the first place. Here are some methods that have helped me:

Pace problems: I learned this method from Andre Dubus and I still use it, especially when I think my work may need to be heavily edited. I clear out the furniture in my living room and then lay out my manuscript, page by page, on the floor, like tiles. I then get down on my hands and knees and, starting at page one, skim the content and then paraphrase it in one short sentence. I do this with every page, using ditto marks and arrows where the idea doesn't change from one page to the next. It is much like dismantling and cataloging a skeleton, studying the shape and weight of each bone so as to better understand the body and how it works. When I'm done, my list can tell me how much space each idea/character/scene takes up and how they fit and move (or don't fit and move) together. This has, at times, clearly mirrored for me what my manuscript as a whole needs in terms of trimming here and fattening there.

Story development problems: I prefer free-form writing. The purpose is to suspend critical judgment by writing down whatever comes into your head, whether it's related to the subject or not. Be silly. Be crazy. Write fast and judge nothing. This can lead you to stumble over your subconscious memory and onto the missing key, which will once again unlock the sound of the story you want.

Character development problems: Any long-married person will tell you that after you've grown accustomed to someone, no matter how much you love them, you can sometimes lose sight of who they are until you take a break from your regular surroundings, when that person becomes suddenly strange and wonderful all over again. Therefore, if you're having trouble getting interested in or understanding one of your characters after a critique, remove the character from the situation you had him in and try him out in something else. Describe him in front of the mirror brushing his teeth. Put him to bed, or if he's already there, put him in the kitchen in his pajamas staring into the refrigerator for something to eat. Use any small, mundane act (new action is not what you're looking for, it's new insight into personality) and see how he does it. Study movements, look for revealing details, listen to what he thinks. Whole new personality quirks for characters have come to me in this way, sometimes even whole new characters. And even when they don't, it's a good exercise anyway.

Morale problems in general: When I get so bogged down by negative feedback that I don't know where to begin, I sometimes give myself an absolute three-week deadline to finish the story *and* an absolute order to stop writing anything but random notes to myself for a week.

This may sound crazy and it certainly can make you feel crazy, but it's like turning on the heat under a pot of water and then putting a tight lid on it so the pressure builds, making the water boil faster. In my case, it makes me both acutely aware of and eager to foster the idea that everything I do and see and feel is related to what I'm going to write, whether or not I'm writing it at the time. What I see happening around me, what I read, the way I talk, what I eat, what people say to me, sometimes even what I dream—if I believe all of it holds messages for my writing in all sorts of mysterious and coincidental ways, when I am truly focused on that, it works. I'll pick up a magazine

245

in the local laundry with a quote in it that is exactly what I was trying to get at; I'll hear a conversation at the store that is stunningly like what my fictional character wants to say; I'll sit down to write a letter to the editor of a newspaper and suddenly know how the story, which is in my bottom drawer, will end.

The more aware I can make myself of the possibility of the answer coming to me unannounced, the more it does. This is not magic. It has nothing to do with New Age affirmations. It is simply allowing the mind to imagine what it wants while keeping tabs on the priority of improving the writing.

You'll have more success with a holistic, work-oriented approach to rewriting than the simplistic types of problem-shooting the how-to books suggest. A story is a living, breathing organism with all kinds of angles and textures and private, changeable moods to it, and it should be viewed as such, from a cubist's vision, seeing all different sides at once. This doesn't apply just to writing it. You can dictate it to a tape recorder. Read it in a voice other than your own. Shout it at the wall. Whisper it to your cat. Make it into a poem. Draw a picture of it if you can. Anything, anything that will *let the story speak*.

Because in the end, that is exactly what will happen. The story will speak. It will make your decisions for you, either by becoming too awful to work on another moment or by becoming too interesting not to. You can count on it. No matter how badly it's written in its first draft, no matter how much negative and/or uninformed criticism it gets buried under, no matter how cruel and barbaric your ego behaves when left alone to rewrite it, if the story has something worthwhile in it, it is indestructible. Throw a good idea away and it will emerge in the next story you write. Hide a good character in your closet and sooner or later you will hear him telling you to take him out again, whether you want to or not. You can't stop it.

Writers in the critiquing process too often forget this. They think they're in charge of the story or the readers are in charge of the story, but the truth is, *the writing is in charge.* It is the top priority. Treat it as such, listen to it as such, honor it as such, and from the day you get back the results of your first critique to the day you sit down to rework the final draft, you will be better able to make wise decisions.

LAURA HENDRIE's work has appeared in *The Missouri Review, Taos Review, Writers' Forum,* and in various anthologies including *The Best of the West I* and *III, Into the Silence,* and *Ten American Signatures.* Her latest work is the novel *Remember Me* (Picador). Hendrie lives in Maine.

The Genres

Chapter 26

Literary or Commercial?

By Nancy Kress

As the Bard told us, "All the world's a stage," and that includes your work of fiction. The parallels between a stage and a book are compelling. You, like all authors, create "characters" in a "setting" who speak "dialogue" encased in "scenes." Most importantly, you, like the playwright, have an "audience." His audience views the story from in front of the footlights, gathered into a large mass; yours views the story from a chair or bed, one at a time.

As you write, how aware should you be of your audience? How much should you be shaping your material to please that audience? And what do those people out there want, anyway?

What's the Difference?

In general, fiction is divided into literary fiction and commercial fiction. Nobody can definitively say what separates one from the other, but that doesn't stop everybody (including me) from trying. Your book probably will be perceived as one or the other and that will affect how it is read, packaged, and marketed.

Literary fiction pays more attention to style than does commercial fiction. Usually, it also probes characterization more deeply. It's often slower paced than commercial fiction because added description and character development take up many words.

The typical worldview implied by literary fiction is complex and ambiguous, trying to be faithful to the complexity and ambiguity of life. A traditional "happy ending" is possible, but not usual. Its themes are timeless. Ezra Pound defined literature as "news that STAYS news."

Toni Morrison writes literary fiction. So do John Updike, Paule Marshall, Anne Tyler, Dan McCall, Alice Hoffman, and most of the short story writers published in *The New Yorker*. Literary fiction usually is published in hardcover and/or "trade paper"—those oversized paperbacks with tasteful covers. Editors who buy it have definite, often idiosyncratic ideas of what constitutes "quality writing."

Commercial fiction can be just as well written, but in an entirely different way. It's usually faster paced, with a "stronger" plot line: more events, higher stakes, more danger. Characterization can range from good to practically nonexistent. The style is usually "transparent," which means the writer wants to tell the story in words that don't call attention to themselves, so the story itself—and not the style—receives the attention.

What makes commercial fiction "commercial" is that editors expect to make a profit from selling it (not always true of literary fiction). The larger the audience, the better. And audiences for commercial fiction are larger than those for literary fiction. (As Mickey Spillane pointed out, "Those big-shot writers . . . could never dig the fact that there are more salted peanuts consumed than caviar.") Commercial fiction is usually hardcover and/or mass-market paperbacks, with covers designed to attract browsers. Editors look for strong story lines that they believe will attract the "average reader." Commercial fiction writers include Tom Clancy, Stephen King, Danielle Steel, Judith Krantz, and John Grisham.

Just to complicate matters further, there also exists "genre fiction," which may be literary or commercial. Genres include romance, science fiction, fantasy, Westerns, and mystery. These are invented marketing categories that once didn't exist. George Orwell's *1984* wasn't marketed as "science fiction"; it was just another novel.

For commercial books in a genre, readers' and editors' expectations may be fairly rigid. Some romance lines, for instance, issue fairly detailed writers' guidelines explaining exactly what must happen in a book they publish (and what must not). Other commercial genres have their own expectations: a case successfully solved, a slain outlaw, a human triumph over a sudden alien invasion.

Literary genre books, in contrast, have more in common with the characteristics of literary fiction as described above. Some examples: Ursula K. Le Guin writes literary science fiction; Larry McMurtry writes (among other things) literary Westerns; P.D. James writes literary mysteries.

Thus, your first step in considering your audience is to define what sort of book you're writing. Why? Because the answer will determine what your book must include to sell it to an editor. It may be a graceful style, or penetrating character insights, or a happy ending, or detailed and accurate descriptions of police work. You discover what your kind of fiction requires by reading it. A lot of it. Constantly. With interest and—one hopes—some amount of appreciation.

Suppose your book falls between genres—a sort of historical mystery, say. Should you still write it? Yes, if it's the story you really want to tell. Just be aware that marketing it may be much more difficult—not because the book isn't good, but because of the way the publishing world is structured.

Who Reads What?

Now that you know your general audience, it can be helpful to picture the specific audience for whom you're writing. Many authors say that writing to someone specific helps them better focus on what to say, in what order, and with what effect.

Who should you imagine reading your words? Some writers picture a specific market segment, a faceless mass made up of certain readers. Narrowing your imaginary readership to a specific group—women, or ten-year-olds, or sophisticated mystery lovers—also may help you get a feel for what will make your novel work.

A perverse but effective-if-you-can-pull-it-off variation on this is to picture your audience, decide what they want . . . and then write something else. Umberto Eco, author of such erudite mysteries as *The Name of the Rose*, claims to do this. According to *The Writer's Quotation Book: A Literary Companion*, Eco has said,

> Usually the recipe for a bestseller is to give people what they want. My challenge is and was: Give them what they do not expect. Be severe with them. The world of media is full of easy answers, wash-and-wear philosophies, instant ecstasies, what-me-worry Epiphanies. Probably readers want a little more.

Do you think they want a little more? If so, picture a group of sophisticated readers who like to be surprised and challenged, and write for them.

Other authors imagine not a group of readers, but one specific, fictional individual and write for him or her. Also from *The Writer's Quotation Book*, John Updike, author of *Rabbit, Run* and *Couples*, says he pictures his ideal reader in quite specific detail:

> When I write, I aim in my mind not toward New York but a vague spot a little east of Kansas. I think of the books on library shelves, without their jackets,

years old, and a countryish teen-aged boy finding
them, and having them speak to him. The reviews, the
stacks in Brentano's, are just hurdles to get over,
to place the books on that shelf.

Who is your ideal writer? Does it help you focus if you describe
him or her to yourself and then write to please that person?
Try it and see. Or try John Steinbeck's (*Of Mice and Men*) trickier
variation: writing to please a specific real person you know.
Pick this person carefully. Make sure your reading tastes match
before you begin mentally addressing your fiction in that specific direction.

Finally, there are writers who picture their audience as a clone
of themselves—someone identical to their own selves, but un-
acquainted with the book. Would their other self like it? If so,
such writers reason, so will other readers. This group includes
John D. MacDonald, Marianne Moore, and Stephen King.

What Works for You?

All this advice can be applied in two ways. First, you may be one
of those writers who holds a dual image of what you're writing as you write it. Part of the dual-image writer's mind is always
immersed in the story, living and breathing and feeling it along with
the characters.

The other part holds itself back a bit, looking at the words on
the screen from a distance, weighing and judging. If you are
this sort of writer, it may indeed be helpful to assign the
weighing-and-judging to a definite image of your audience.
Let him/her/them decide what to keep in, what to delete, in what
direction to move the plot.

If you're a different sort of writer, however, don't split yourself
in two while writing. Every atom of your being is involved
in the story, and trying to please an imaginary onlooker only

paralyzes the creative flow. Forget the audience while you write your first draft. Evoke that audience when you go through the second draft, revising and polishing. After all, an audience may be more welcome at a dress rehearsal rather than a first readthrough.

All right, everybody, places . . . open the curtain.

Writing the World of Fantasy

By Terry Brooks

I remember vividly, twenty years later, what Lester del Rey repeatedly used to tell me about writing fantasy. Lester was a longtime writer, critic, and editor in the fantasy/science fiction field, and I was fortunate enough to be able to work with him during the first fifteen years of my professional career. Most of what I learned about being a commercial fiction writer, for better or worse, I learned from Lester. Lester used to say that it was harder to write good fantasy than any other form of fiction. Why? Because a writer of fantasy is free to invent anything, unfettered by the laws and dictates of this world and limited only by the depth of imagination and willingness to dream. The temptation to free-fall through a story chock full of incredible images and wondrous beings can be irresistible—but, when not resisted, almost invariably disastrous.

What he was telling me was that in creating a world populated by monsters and other strange life forms, reliant on uses of magic and shimmering with images of childhood tales, legends, and myths, a writer runs the risk of losing touch with reality entirely. Given the parameters of the world and characters that the writer has created, something of that world and those characters must speak to what we, as readers, know to be true about the human condition. If nothing corresponds to what we know about our own lives, then everything becomes unbelievable. Even the most ridiculous farce must resonate in some identifiable way with truths we have discovered about ourselves. Even the darkest sword and sorcery epic must speak to us of our own harsh experience.

Achieving this end as a fantasy writer demands mastery of a certain skill, one not uncommon with that required of a ship's captain charting a course at sea. When putting together a fantasy tale, a writer must navigate a treacherous passage that bears neither too hard to starboard nor too far to port in order to avoid arriving at an unforseen destination or, worse, ending up on the rocks. Fantasy writing must be grounded in both truth and live experience if it is to work. It can be as inventive and creative as the writer can make it, a whirlwind of images and plot twists, but it cannot be built on a foundation of air. The world must be identifiable with our own, must offer us a frame of reference we can recognize. The characters must behave in ways that we believe reasonable and expected. The magic must work in a consistent and balanced manner. The book must leave us with a feeling of comprehension and satisfaction at having spent time turning its pages to discover its end.

How does a writer accomplish this? Fantasy stories work because the writer has interwoven bits and pieces of reality with imagination to form a personal vision. Understanding the possibilities is a requirement to making choices. Those choices might include various forms of magic, types of weapons and armor, fantasy races and creatures, and ancient societies on which speculative fictional worlds and characters can be based. Each writer must choose the ones that work and make them the building blocks of a story's foundation.

Description lends weight and substance to ideas, and nowhere is that more important than in a world that doesn't exist—at least outside the pages of the writer's story. So giving the reader an understanding of how a world looks, tastes, smells, sounds, and feels is crucial. In fantasy, more than in any other form of fiction, the reader must feel transported to the world being created, while at the same time readily comprehending what it is he is experiencing. When an otherwordly character is introduced, the reader must be made to see the differences, but must recognize the similarities as well. Details ground the story's larger images and keep the reader engaged.

I happen to favor rather strongly the practice of outlining a book before trying to write it, and I would recommend it to beginning writers, in particular, for two reasons. First, it requires thinking the story through, which eliminates a lot of wasted time chasing bad ideas. Second, it provides a blueprint to which the writer can refer while working on a story over the course of months or even years. Use of an outline is not a popular practice because it is hard work. It isn't easy thinking a story through from start to finish. But writing a hundred pages that have to be discarded because they don't lead anywhere is a whole lot more unpleasant. Moreover, outlining gives a writer a chance to add to the details of the book, to pen notes in the margins, to decide how all those bits and pieces of reality I mentioned earlier will fit with those grand landscapes of imagination.

This seems a good place to stress the importance of "dream time" in the creative process. All good fantasy requires a certain amount of gestation, a period before pen is set to paper or fingers to keyboard, in which a writer simply gives free rein to imagination and waits to see where it will go. After a path reveals itself, a writer should start to map that path, carefully noting which side roads are offered, what travelers await, where dangers might lurk, and how lessons could be learned. If the writer is patient enough, eventually a story will present itself. If it is the right story, it will demand to be written. It simply won't stand to be cooped up. But this is a process that is difficult to rush and one in which the writer must trust. It sounds a bit mystical, but it really isn't. It's puzzle building without a box cover. It's outlining in your mind.

There is one final lesson Lester taught me that I want to pass on before I end this. Some years back, I was fussing to him about finding an idea for a story that hadn't been used before. I wanted something new and original. He gave me one of his patented smiles—the ones that always made him look like a cross between your kindly uncle and Jack Nicholson in *The Shining*—and told me in no uncertain terms that new ideas did not come along that often and that when they did, they came in disguise. It was better to take old, established ideas and just turn them over and over in your mind until you found a new way to look at them. Then write about what you saw.

It was good advice then. It's good advice now. Go forth, and write something magical.

TERRY BROOKS has more than fifteen million books in print worldwide. He published his first novel, *The Sword of Shannara*, in 1977. His most recent novel is *Antrax*.

Chapter 28

Once Upon a Character

By J.V. Jones

So, you're ready to start writing that huge, multivolume fantasy epic that's going to give Tolkien a run for his money. You've done your research on Tartar horsemen and Icelandic death ballads. You've drawn your map, complete with rocky shallows called the Teeth of Dragons and a mysterious dark mountain called the Dread Peak. You've recovered from the wounds incurred teaching yourself how to use a forty-inch longsword (so you can really nail those sword fights!). Now, having raked the white pages for character names, you're finally ready to write.

You begin typing: "Rob Rye was riding down a leafy lane when he was jumped by a band of evil dwarves." At this point you know that Rob (our hero) will acquit himself splendidly, demonstrating pluck and tenacity in the face of the evil dwarves, who thereby gain respect for him, lay down their weapons, and let him live. One of their party (Gonk, the least evil of their band) decides he will leave his dwarven brethren and ride with Rob for a while. Thereby begins the most important element in epic fantasy: the bringing together of the companions.

These companions are always a mixed bunch. There's usually a princess in disguise as a beggar girl, a smart-talking dwarf, a scarred and bitter sorcerer (who may or may not see visions), a silent and smoldering swordsman with a past, and, of course your hero, Rob.

Here's where the challenge begins: These fantasy archetypes can be lifeless carbon copies of every other fantasy you've ever read. Or you can make them truly your own.

Writing complex, surprising, unforgettable characters should be our goal whether we're writing Westerns, romances, hard science fiction, or epic fantasy. Readers are attracted to a particular genre because of the formulas and traditions it follows, but they fall in love with an individual book because of the characters.

Characters in genre fiction can be especially hard to write, as it's easy to fall into stereotypes. Take epic fantasy, for example: Elves are mysterious beings, long-lived and enigmatic. Dwarves like beer and are obsessive about family lineage. And everyone knows that giants are slow-witted and untrusting, but once their loyalty is won, they'll fight at your side until the bitter end.

So how do you make your characters stand out, while still respecting the traditions of the genre?

Playing the Name Game

The first thing is names. Whenever I introduce a new character, he or she doesn't begin to take on life for me until I find a name that really fits. In fantasy, it's tempting to choose names that are unpronounceable and full of apostrophes. Names such as "Shaer'laegh ab'Nhah" may look good, but they throw little light on the character who owns them. It's a missed opportunity. Say our Shaer'laegh ab'Nhah is an evil sorceress from a long and noble line of Sorcerer Queens. Wouldn't it be better to reflect some of that history, regalness, and evil in her name? What if we named her "Isane Rune" instead? Then we've got the "is" sound working for us, like a snake hiss, and the second name is strong and short, suggesting old myths. And most of us can actually pronounce "Isane Rune."

A well-chosen name can evoke images and feelings in readers' minds before the character even walks on stage. Tolkien knew this. Doesn't "Sauron" sound a bit like "Satan"? And doesn't "Frodo" remind us of that rotund, slow-moving, extinct bird, the dodo?

You also need to help readers keep your characters straight. Here again, epic fantasy presents a particular challenge: By definition, it requires a cast of hundreds, perhaps thousands. The easy road to take is differentiating characters by their appearance: Isane Rune is tall and willowy, with long silvery hair; heroic Rob is sandy-haired and muscular; Gonk, our once-evil dwarf, has arms the size and color of whole hams. The trouble is, this doesn't give readers the kind of information that sticks in their minds and won't let go. After they've met a dozen evil dwarves with arms like hams, it's going to be difficult to tell Gonk apart from his evil band.

So, how do we make physical traits and appearances memorable? In my novel *A Cavern of Black Ice,* I had to introduce a secondary character named Duff. Even though Duff doesn't have a great bearing on the overall story, he plays a vital role in one scene, and it was important that he be both likable and physically strong. I knew it wouldn't be enough just to tell readers this, so I endowed him with a peculiar talent:

> Duff had a bit of every clan in him, at least that was what he claimed. He was the hairiest man Raif had ever seen, and in his youth he had been famous for his teeth. Logs, barges, carts, carrion and sleds: with a rope between his teeth, Duff had hauled them all. His teeth were still splendid to this day, and as he brought over a tray steaming with hot shammies, hot beer and hot meat, he grinned broadly, revealing surprisingly small but perfectly even teeth. Raif remembered Tem asking Duff once how he had got his teeth so strong. "I used to crush pond ice with them," he had said.

Claiming Duff pulls great weights with his teeth not only lets readers know he's a big strong guy without actually coming out and saying so, but it also gives them a mental image of him. Next time they encounter Duff, they should say to themselves, "Here's that guy Duff—the one who hauls things with his teeth." And that's the main aim of any physical description: giving readers a little bit of information to associate with a character's name.

The Dwarf Is in the Details

Descriptions of physical characteristics are useful, but if you have a lot of characters to describe and introduce, you'll need to vary your technique. Often, the most distinguishing feature of a character isn't physical; perhaps they're of high social standing and proud of it, or absentminded and bookish, or, like Isane Rune, have a talent for seduction.

Here's where epic fantasy comes into its own. We're writing in a world of our own invention and so are free to conjure up the most enticing and exotic details at will. We need only describe Isane Rune's clothes to give a fully fleshed description of the woman. She's rich, evil, and seductive, so let's clothe her in "layer upon layer of shadowsilk, heavy as the gold that went into its weaving, transparent as the shadows that gave it its name." With Gonk, we need only describe his weapon: "a three-foot hammer with a head of black iron, much bashed and much repaired, balanced by a handle carved from wood so dense that no oil could find purchase in the grain." We're not only describing clothing and possessions here, but also the people who own them.

Fantasy gives us a lot of leeway with characterization. Like clothing and weaponry, we can invent manners of speaking and peculiarities of dialect that shed light on a character, his upbringing, and origins. Perhaps our hero comes from a remote mountain village and he calls all sorcery "magics." Then, a few chapters later, when we introduce a new character who uses the same plural form of "magic," readers will be alerted that this new character hails from the same region as our hero.

Careful use of such details encourages readers to become actively involved in the characterization process. Instead of telling them that this new character comes from such-and-such a place, we can give them the clues to work it out for themselves.

Playing Against Archetype

The most direct form of characterization takes place when we're inside a character's head, seeing the world from her point of view. As writers, this is our best chance to show all the subtlety and contradictions that go in to making a character work. For genre writers, especially writers of epic fantasy, this is where we have to be wary of making our heroes too heroic and our villains too evil for words.

Yes, we know that ultimately Rob is going to spurn Isane Rune's seductive machinations, but wouldn't it make him more believable if the temptation were real and it cost him dear to reject it? Young men are hormone factories. When Rob sees Isane dressed in her shadowsilks, with her pale flesh peeking through, his first thought isn't going to be, "Uh-oh. An evil sorceress. I must avoid her at all costs." More than likely he'll be thinking a whole range of things, one of which may very well be, "I wonder what she looks like naked." Similarly, Isane Rune may consider herself to be evil incarnate, but perhaps she surprises herself with a flash of jealously when our beggar princess lays a protective hand on Rob's well-muscled shoulder. A character capable of feeling jealously may or may not be evil, but she is human. And readers can identify with that.

When writing archetypes—the evil overlord who schemes to take over the world, the kindly and absentminded wizard,

Twelve Character-Driven Fantasies

- *The Tombs of Atuan* by Ursula K. Le Guin

- *Reaper Man* by Terry Pratchett

- *The Dragonriders of Pern* by Anne McCaffrey

- *The Deed of Paksenarrion* by Elizabeth Moon

- *Assassin's Apprentice* by Robin Hobb

- *The Once And Future King* by T.H. White

- *Ill Met in Lankhmar* by Fritz Leiber

- *Lyonesse* by Jack Vance

- *Nine Princes in Amber* by Roger Zelazny

- *Witch World* by Andre Norton

- *The Baker's Boy* by J.V. Jones

- *Tigana* by Guy Gavriel Kay

the enfeebled king incapable of ruling his country—we must be careful to present these characters as human beings. They must surprise us from time to time. Even the most kindly and absentminded wizard should have some prejudices and irrational fears. Give him something to hate (besides the evil overlord). Faultless characters are irritating. And villains without any redeeming qualities stop being human and become card-board cutouts instead.

One of the best ways to create memorable characters is to play against these archetypes. If Rob encounters a fumbling, white-haired wizard in a tall hat, readers will assume the wizard is a good guy. Imagine the surprise when the wizard turns out to be keeping the souls of dead children in a jar! Such juxta-positions have to be lightly done or you risk plunging your dramatic novel into parody, but every epic fantasy should con-tain at least one character who flouts traditions: an intelligent and highly literate giant, a dwarf who's never been near a ham-mer in his life, or a beautiful and mysterious beggar girl who's nothing more than she seems.

A Good First Impression

Now that we've chosen a name for our character, and provided him with distinguishing characteristics and enough contradic-tions in his personality to make him appear real, we have the next obstacle to overcome: the first appearance. The first ap-pearance is crucial. If Isane Rune doesn't make an impact the first time readers encounter her, they'll forget her. Then, two chapters down the road, when they encounter her again, they'll think, "Was she in that scene earlier, with Rob? Or was that some other witch woman?" When they should be thinking, "There's that Isane Rune again. What a bitch! I wonder how she's going to knife Rob in the back this time."

The most important thing about a first appearance is that readers come away with a strong impression of the new char-acter. This impression can be anything. We could have our char-acter eating something especially nasty, such as raw kidneys leaking blood, or he could be rebandaging an old war wound that refuses to heal, or perhaps she's wearing stout workboots under her gown of lace and silk.

In *A Cavern of Black Ice*, when I introduced a female assassin named Magdalena Crouch, I was anxious that she be like no other female assassin I'd ever read about. This meant she couldn't be some devastatingly beautiful charmer, luring men to their deaths with promises of sex. Her first appearance was vital to this goal. I asked myself, "How can I present her in such a way as to make her interesting?" I began by giving her a nickname:

> The Crouching Maiden, as she was known to the very few people in the Northern Territories who could afford to deal death at the rate of one hundred golds a head, waited for Penthero Iss to speak. She was perhaps 20, no 30, no 40 years of age, with hair that may have been either brown, red, or golden depending on the vagaries of light. Her eyes he had given up hope on. Looking straight into them when he had opened the door, he had seen nothing but his own reflection staring back.

If readers come away with no other information from this scene than the idea that Magdalena Crouch is difficult to see, I've done my job. A first appearance should whet readers' appetites, leave them wanting to read more about a character and her deeds.

Another way to make a strong first impression with a character is to give her some good lines to say. It's not enough that Isane Rune be evil; she must *sound* evil as well. Writers of epic fantasy have a rare opportunity to write dramatic and unusual dialogue for their characters. Patterns of ordinary speech can be modified, replaced with the rhythms of Chaucerian English, Celtic myth, or Germanic romances. Take our once-evil dwarf, Gonk. He's mountain-bred, tough as nails, and been immersed in Dwarven culture all his life. In our opening scene,

when Rob battles the evil dwarves, Gonk is the first of his
band to realize that Rob is more than just a boy with a sword.
We could have him cry out to his brethren, "Let's lay down
our weapons and let the boy live, as he's surely more than he
seems." Or we could say, "Hold your hammers, men. Hold them!
The Tall One has more than metal in his sword. I taste the First
Mountain in the air today."

Who knows what the First Mountain is? (The mythical home
of one of the Dwarven gods?) That isn't the point. Right from
the first line of dialogue he utters, Gonk is speaking in an idiosyncratic way, lacing his speech with "dwarfisms" such as Tall
One and First Mountain. The process of characterization has
begun.

Of course, dramatic dialogue shouldn't be limited to opening
lines, but you get the idea: All words you put into your characters'
mouths should sing of their eccentricities as well as forward the
plot.

Actions Speak Louder . . .

Our character is now fully fleshed, complete with name, faults,
irrational fears, and idiosyncrasies of speech. We've introduced him in such a way as to make him memorable to readers.
That leaves just one thing: his actions.

All the above advice isn't enough to create unforgettable characters unless we give them something remarkable to do. Who
can forget the time Frodo slipped on his ring in a tavern full of
people? Or the artful way Corwin hid his memory loss from
his siblings in Roger Zelazny's *Nine Princes in Amber*?

The truth of a character lies in his actions. If our hero is so
terrified of the Dark Lord that his hands tremble at the sound
of his name, if he swears to himself that he'll never stand against
him, and if all he wants is to live peacefully with his true love

Welcome to Clichéville

Banish these too-familiar characters from your fiction:

• The fire-breathing religious leader determined to squelch new ideas

• The evil corporate chief who cares nothing for the environment/his employees/the inhabitants of the nearest star system

• The scientist who can't see the danger his project poses

• The brave but mysterious adventurer who turns out to be a long-lost noble

• The misunderstood visitor who needs help to return home

• The bloodthirsty military leader for whom the ends justify the means

• The especially stupid authority figure who will not listen to reason and will botch every decision, thereby causing all the problems of the story

• The thoughtless "good" king/leader who listens to stupid authority figures

• The evil overlord who is pure evil

• The has-a-good-heart-and-knows-what's-right-but-is-sadly-misunderstood younger sibling

• Anyone astoundingly beautiful

and herd goats, think how effective it will be when the final battle is joined and he draws his blade regardless.

That is the essence of a memorable character: Human fears and human longings, and actions that rise above both.

J.V. JONES is the best-selling author of five fantasy novels. Her fifth book, *A Cavern of Black Ice*, is the first of an epic fantasy series.

Chapter 29

Innovation in Horror

Jeanne Cavelos

When I teach creative writing and ask my students what they believe their strengths and weaknesses are, almost all of them include creativity as a strength; almost none include it as a weakness.

As a result, few developing writers spend a lot of time and energy on *making* their work creative. They feel, by the very act of typing in words, they already are being "creative." After all, they are creating something new.

But there's the rub: How *new* is it?

Horror is a genre, a type of literature that has certain identifiable characteristics. When people who enjoy horror read your story, they are not reading it in a vacuum. They are reading it as part of a genre, constantly comparing your story to other horror stories they have read. If I have never read Edgar Allan Poe's "The Tell-Tale Heart" and I write a story very much like "The Tell-Tale Heart," readers who know Poe's story may not be as thrilled with my Big! Surprise! Ending! as I had hoped. To them, it's no surprise. They've read it before and they've read it better (you can't beat Poe).

To be a creative, innovative horror writer, you must read a lot of *everything*, and a lot of that everything must be horror. You may be thinking, *How can I be creative and original with all those other authors' ideas floating around in my head*? But this is critical: The sheer amount of material floating around in your head will prevent you from copying any one author.

Instead you will find a tiny piece of character from this book, a tiny piece of plot from that book, a certain stylistic technique from that other, which you will combine into something totally new. It is the writer who reads only Stephen King who will turn out stories that sound like Stephen King—on a very, very bad day.

If you can accept the need to know the horror writing that has gone before, you might still have difficulty with the idea of extensive reading *outside* the field. Simply by the law of averages, more great writing has been done outside the field of horror than within it. Another law of averages. The more great writing you read, the more will rub off on you. Read works from different periods of history, from different cultures. Read fiction and nonfiction. Many innovations arise from taking ideas outside the genre and bringing them in. Some of our favorite stories even mix genres.

When a story is innovative, it brings fresh ideas and techniques to the genre. It helps enlarge the genre and renew it. It helps keep the genre exciting and alive for future generations of readers. And it creates one hell of a great story.

Innovate or Imitate?

Why do so many people think John Carpenter's *Halloween* is a great movie? (I'm using a movie rather than a novel as an example because I think more of you will be familiar with a particular movie than a particular novel. But my point holds equally true for novels and stories.) If you watch it now, it may seem a rather tame and predictable slasher movie. But when it came out, nothing quite like it had ever been done before. It was intense, tightly plotted (the whole story takes place in one night), concerned itself very little with explanation (we have no idea why the killer goes after Jamie Lee Curtis with such determination), and had an incredible amount of suspense (every scene either had the killer in it or had in it evidence of something the killer had done, like a dead body). It didn't spend half of its length building up to killings, as so many movies of the day did. A murder occurs in the first five minutes. Each of these elements was not new, but this combination of them was, and it was very powerful, touching off a whole series of sequels and imitators. *Halloween* expanded and renewed the genre.

Stephen King has had a similar effect. He combined elements in a totally new way. Never before had classic horror arche-types, like the vampire (*Salem's Lot*) or the haunted house (*The Shining*), seemed so possible in our mundane, middle-class world. He brought these horrors down to earth, making them not the province of unstable minds and rarefied atmospheres, but of Anytown, U.S.A., in the plumber's house, the son's room, right under the bed. In the early 1980s, King had a huge impact on the genre, expanding and renewing it and spawning hordes of imitators. Even today his influence is strong on many developing horror writers; there are more than a few who believe that to write horror is to write "Stephen King horror"—since they've never read anything else they've liked.

The question is, do you want to be an innovator or an imita-tor? It's normal for young writers to be inspired by books or movies and to begin writing by emulating those sources. But horror that simply reflects the source that inspired it is not going to be rich and powerful; it's going to be a pale reflection of its source. A writer must take various sources of inspiration and filter them through his own unique sensibilities.

There are, of course, an infinite number of ways you can make your story innovative. Writing is a layered and complex pro-cess, and each story combines multiple elements. In creating new combinations and new patterns, you are innovating.

Innovative Plotting

What will the plot of your story be? What fear will it focus on? Many writers choose a plot by choosing a horror archetype to write about. Maybe you decide to write a vampire story, or a ghost story, or a serial killer story, or a zombie story. That's okay. These archetypes have developed and persisted over the years because they tap into our fears and have a strong, resonant effect on us. But they also present a serious challenge to today's writer: What is *your* vampire story going to do that no other vampire story has done before? (This is quite a question, considering how much material has been written about vampires.) What unique sensibility do you bring to a vampire story? If you don't have a powerful, significant difference to offer in your story, then you probably shouldn't write it.

Maybe you decide to center your plot around a specific fear—one of *your* specific fears. This can be a wonderful technique, because if you are afraid of "it," chances are you can also make the reader afraid of it. But when I ask writers what they are afraid of, they usually come back with answers like "cockroaches." That's a perfectly valid answer, and if you are truly afraid of cockroaches, perhaps that can play a part in a story sometime.

But that's not a very deep-rooted fear. What I want to know is what frightens you at all levels, not only at the surface but at the deepest levels. That way, perhaps cockroaches cannot only be scary and gross, but can symbolize a deep fear, the fear, perhaps, of chaos, of forces beyond your control. Most of us fear this a lot more than we fear cockroaches. Don't just throw a ton of cockroaches in a story and assume your reader will be horrified (how many cockroaches are in a ton, anyway?). The cockroaches need to tie into a deeper fear: *Why* do they scare you so much? Becoming aware of the unique way that you see things and writing a story that reflects your unique sensibility is the key to writing innovative horror.

Once you have a basic concept for your story, you need to develop it into a plot. Now, the great thing about the horror genre is that, unlike other genres, it allows infinite possibilities.

The horror genre has only one requirement for membership: The story must make the reader feel . . . *horrified*. Many writers don't realize how revolutionary this is. In other genres, a fairly strict plot is imposed. In a mystery, a crime must occur, usually a murder, which must then be solved by the end of the story. In a romance, two people must meet and fall in love. But the plot of a horror story can be anything, as long as it makes the reader feel horror. So why is it that the plot of so many horror novels can be summarized like this?

> *Prologue:* Evil creature is awakened and kills one or more victims in spectacularly gruesome fashion.
>
> *Chapter 1:* Introduction of thirty-something family man (often a writer) who's carrying around a problem from his past.
>
> *Chapters 2–15:* Evil creature creeps into life of family man, killing numerous other victims on its way (in spectacularly gruesome fashion) and threatening members of the family man's family. The family's pet usually gets it at this point. Family man continues to suffer over problem from his past.
>
> *Chapters 16–19:* Family man recognizes the threat of the evil creature, fights the evil creature, figures out the secret to killing it and triumphs, killing the creature in spectacularly gruesome fashion and simultaneously resolving his problem from the past.
>
> *Chapter 20:* Family man and his family (minus pet) live happily ever after. Creature is dead (or is it . . ?).

If horror, as I said, puts no constraints on plot, why does this darned thing sound so familiar? As an editor, I have read this plot more times than I can count and many more than I want to remember. These days, any horror manuscript with a prologue makes an editor sigh in despair. Reading a lot in the field will help these old, tired patterns become more apparent to you. Then as a writer, you can decide to avoid them, or you can play off them, beginning your novel in a way that makes us think we know exactly what is going to happen and then surprising us by taking the plot in a totally different direction.

Innovative Style

So one important method of innovating comes from choosing and developing your plot, in deciding *what you are going to say*. The other method arises from deciding *how you are going to say it*. Your writing style, or your voice, reflects your personality, your beliefs, your concerns. In writing, you are commenting on life, the human condition. What do you believe? What do you want to say?

Just as each person has a distinctive speaking voice, a distinctive tone and timbre, a distinctive way of putting words together and certain preferred words, so do we each have a distinctive writing voice. This is often more difficult to develop. Beginning writers tend to write like the authors they have read. One of my students told me she would write like Stephen King when she was reading King, like Harlan Ellison when she was reading Ellison, and on and on. She had no style or voice of her own. And truth to tell, she wasn't really writing in King's style one week and Ellison's style the next (a writer could have worse problems). She was writing in a style that was a pale, inferior reflection of King's style, or Ellison's style, or. . . . She could never write King's style as well as King, because King's style reflects who he is, how he thinks, and how he expresses himself. Your style, if it is to be *your* style, must do the same for you.

How you say something is just as important as *what* you say. Critics today bemoan the elevation of style over substance, but style is critically important in powerful and innovative writing. In fact, much of the innovation in horror in recent years has come in the area of style. While Stephen King introduced a style that was immediate, concrete, accessible, and down-to-earth, post-King authors are introducing literary, postmodern, experimental styles.

Perhaps you don't understand what I mean when I say style. In the following two passages, the plot is the same, but the style is very different. In other words, *what* is said remains the same, but *how* it is said changes drastically. Here's an example of a very familiar, overused style of horror writing:

> Colin stared at the razor, shiny and sharp, that Robert held above him. *OH MY GOD*, Colin thought. *HE'S GOING TO KILL ME!* The hairs on the back of his neck prickled.
>
> Robert prodded the knife into his neck. "I will kill you. I will leave no one alive to talk about me after I'm gone."
>
> Colin's brain sent an urgent message—*Push Robert out of the way! Scream! Do something!* But shock had frozen him still.
>
> Robert laughed, his breath an execrable stench hanging in the air like a cloud of corruption. He fixed Colin in his hypnotic gaze, the twin black orbs holding him immobile.
>
> Colin realized sickeningly that he was helpless. *I'm going to die (oh God please help me God). I'm going to die! And when they're finished with me, they'll kill my beloved Mary!*
>
> With a snarl of rage, his lips drawn back from his teeth, Robert brought the razor down across Colin's throat. He let out a demonic yell.
>
> Colin's world went black.

I'm afraid I don't have the space here to tell you all that's weak and derivative and clichéd in the previous example, which I wrote myself, but if you've read a fair amount of horror, this probably sounds about as familiar to you as the plot outline I gave earlier. If something sounds quite familiar, then you know it's not innovative. Many developing writers, having grown up on the horror of the 1980s, think that this is the *only* way horror can be written.

Let me give you another example, this one by the fine author Ian McEwan from *The Comfort of Strangers*:

> Mary was watching the object Robert clasped in his hand. Suddenly it was twice its length, and she saw it clearly, and though every muscle in her body tightened, only the fingers of her right hand clenched softly. She shouted, and shouted again, and all that left her was a whispering exhalation.
>
> "I'll do whatever you want," Colin said, the level tone all lost now at the sound, his voice rising in panic. "But please get a doctor for Mary."
>
> "Very well," Robert said and reached for Colin's arm, and turned his palm upward. "See how easy it is," he said, perhaps to himself, as he drew the razor lightly, almost playfully, across Colin's wrist, opening wide the artery. His arm jerked forward, and the rope he cast, orange in this light, fell short of Mary's lap by several inches.
>
> Mary's eyes closed. When she opened them Colin was sitting on the floor, against the wall, his legs splayed before him. Curiously, his canvas beach shoes were soaked, stained scarlet. His head swayed upon his shoulders, but his eyes were steady and pure, and blazed at her across the room in disbelief.

"Mary?" he said anxiously, like someone calling in a dark room.

"Mary? Mary?"

"I'm coming," Mary said. "I'm over here."

The main difference here, for the purposes of our discussion, is that the first author is trying to emulate the voices of other authors she has read; the second author is trying to reproduce his vision of life—and has developed his own voice to do so.

To get a better idea of the possibilities for innovation in horror, read these genre-stretching works: Patrick McCabe's *The Butcher's Boy*, Jennifer Lynch's *The Secret Diary of Laura Palmer*, Ian McEwan's *The Comfort of Strangers*, or Tim Lucas's *Throat Sprockets*.

Innovation is a critical component in any strong work of horror, and it does not come easily or automatically to us "creative" souls who write. Strive for innovation in your writing and never give up. If you can express what concerns you in a way that reflects your own unique sensibility, then you are being truly innovative, and the horror you create will be truly special.

JEANNE CAVELOS was a senior editor at Bantam Doubleday Dell, where she ran the Abyss horror imprint and edited a wide range of fiction and nonfiction. Jeanne left New York to pursue her own writing career and is the author of the bestselling *Passing of the Techno-Mages* trilogy, set in the *Babylon 5* universe, as well as the highly praised *The Science of Star Wars* and *The Science of the X-Files*. Since she loves working with developing writers, Jeanne created and serves as director of Odyssey, an annual six-week summer workshop for writers of fantasy, science fiction, and horror held at Southern New Hampshire University (www.sff.net/people/jcavelos).

Chapter 30

The Who in Whodunits

By J.A. Jance

Even though I was never allowed in a college-level creative writing class, I did pick up that age-old golden rule of writing: Write what you know. So how does someone who has never been a cop or a lawyer know enough to write murder mysteries?

Part of the answer, of course, lies in doing research—in talking to law-enforcement officers, reading law-enforcement manuals, and keeping up with current events. (For example, I discovered that Freon smuggling is big business on the U.S./Mexico border by reading about it in *The Wall Street Journal*.)

Doing that kind of research, however, is only part of the answer—the easy part. The rest of it comes from living life. True, my characters Sheriff Joanna Brady and Detective J. P. Beaumont are both law-enforcement officers, but they're people first. In order to make my characters seem like living, breathing people, it's my job—the author's job—to know everything about them.

I'll be the first to admit that my characters are an outgrowth of everything I am and everything I've done. I learned to be a detective by having a houseful of adolescent children. My working career may not have included any stints in law enforcement, but I have been a teacher, a librarian, an insurance agent, and a mother. All of those occupations require people skills, and knowing how people think and work is essential to creating believable characters. After all, characters are people, too. At least they should be.

People Into Plot

When it's time for me to start a book, the first thing I have to come to terms with are the people involved in the story. Once I know who they are and what made them that way, then I'm able to place them in fictional situations, all the while understanding how and why the characters behave as they do. For me, plot evolves from character, not the other way around.

With Joanna Brady, for example, in writing *Desert Heat*, I found myself launching a new series having already written nine Detective Beaumont books. I met Joanna at the same place my readers did, having a conversation with her daughter. Joanna and Jenny are sitting in the breakfast nook of their cozy ranch house, waiting for Joanna's husband to come home and take Joanna out for their tenth-anniversary dinner. Jenny, a precocious nine and a half, asks her mother whether or not she was a preemie since the required nine months between her parents' wedding and Jenny's birthday had been shortened to six. Faced with this disturbing question, Joanna has no choice but to answer truthfully, and she does.

That conversation told me several things about Joanna Brady, the most important of which was that she wasn't perfect. Headstrong and opinionated, she and Andy are still living with their small-town lives tainted by the shame of having had a shotgun wedding. The fact that Joanna doesn't dodge the issue let me know that she was a good mother, one who cared enough and had the moral fortitude to tell the truth even when the truth made her uncomfortable.

All those traits taken together—Joanna's everyday honesty, her straightforward way of looking at life, her willingness to acknowledge her own infallibility, her resilience—serve her in good stead in the hours and days ahead when Andy's shooting and eventual death plunge her into an entirely different life. Even so, several chapters into the book, I was still struggling to understand her when I came upon a pivotal scene.

Joanna and her best friend, Marianne Maculyea, are in a hospital waiting room where they have just been told that Joanna's wounded husband has pulled through surgery but is still in critical condition. The doctor suggests the two women go somewhere to sleep. Refusing to leave the hospital, Joanna and Marianne prepare to bed down for the night in the hospital waiting room. Struggling with her own fear, Joanna asks Marianne to pray for her. Marianne does so, reciting the words of comfort found in a simple childhood prayer.

Those words appeared through a veil of tears. In that moment, I realized that I really knew who those two women were. I understood what made the two of them tick as well as the depth of their friendship. Six books later, I'm confident that I still do.

When I sit down to write a Joanna Brady book, I have to think about what's happened to her in the previous books and how those events may have changed and influenced her. I also have to know about her life prior to the books. I think part of what makes Joanna believable and likable is the fact that she doesn't remain static. She changes from book to book. She learns from her mistakes even as she makes new ones. After all, learning from mistakes is part of what makes people human.

Straw Into Fictional Gold

For me, in order to create believable characters, I need to feel strongly about them one way or the other. While attending the University of Arizona in 1964, the creative writing professor wouldn't allow me in any of his classes because I was a girl. I've never forgotten what he told me: "Girls become teachers or nurses. Boys become writers."

Those words had a profound effect on my life. When that professor walked into one of my books nearly twenty years later, it's hardly surprising that it was in the guise of Andrew Philip Carlisle, the crazed killer in my psychological thriller,

Hour of the Hunter. Carlisle, a former creative writing professor from the University of Arizona, returns to Tucson looking for the two women who sent him to prison six years earlier. As a writer, it was easy for me to turn my old nemesis into a terrifying character—easy and gratifying both.

The same thing could be said for the dead dentist in Beaumont number five, *Improbable Cause*. He's dead on the first page for no other reason than the fact that one of the few dentists in my hometown didn't believe in using Novocain.

In the early seventies, my life was touched and changed by a chance encounter with a real-life serial killer. Over a period of several months, I watched a Pima County homicide detective grab hold of that case with a such a fierce tenacity and concentration that even his twenty-year marriage couldn't compete and survive. When it came time to write my first mystery, I used that detective as a model for J.P. Beaumont.

Beau first walked into my books in *Until Proven Guilty* to investigate the death of a child. Angel Barstogi had been strangled and her remains tossed into an overgrown blackberry bramble in Seattle's Discovery Park. By the time readers first meet Beau, his marriage has already fallen victim to both his job and to his ongoing love affair with booze. As he follows the case to its conclusion, Beau is drawn into the orbit of the haunting and mysterious Anne Corley, whose profound impact on his life changes everything that happens to him after that—in thirteen books and counting.

Like Joanna Brady, J.P. Beaumont isn't static. He, too, changes over time and from book to book. His battle with the bottle, his difficulties with keeping and losing partners, his disdain for the "brass" upstairs, along with his gradual reconciliation with his family all serve to make him seem "real" both to me and to readers.

In writing about Joanna Brady, it helps that I know what it's like to be a struggling single mother. With J.P. Beaumont, I write with the dubious benefit of having spent eighteen years of my life living with a man who subsequently died of chronic alcoholism at age forty-two. For Diana Ladd in *Hour of the Hunter*, I drew on my frustration at being cornered into teaching school when what I really wanted to do with my life was write.

Seeing how those realities turn up in my books makes me feel a bit like Rumplestiltskin: I take the straw from my life and spin it into gold—gold with a very strong basis in reality. And the truth is, that reality is important to me. If it doesn't seem "real" to me, I can't write it.

Caring About Your Characters

I once read a series of unpublished manuscripts for a writers' conference. In one of the manuscripts—purportedly an intergalactic murder mystery—none of the ethnic-sounding names given to the characters seemed to jibe with who they were or how they behaved. When I questioned the author about this, he told me, quite seriously, that he'd written the story using words like *Protagonist* and *Villain* and *Officers One, Two, and Three*, then went back and used his computer's search-and-replace command to name the characters.

I tried to explain to him that it hadn't worked. I wanted him to understand that, as the author, it was his responsibility to know everything about his characters before he started to write. He needed to know about their favorite foods, their relationships with their parents and siblings, where they went to school, and whether or not they attended Boy Scouts or CYO when they were kids. I hope the young writer heard what I was telling him, but I doubt it. His next question was, "But is it still publishable?" The truth is, his story wasn't publishable—far from it.

The author's responsibility goes far beyond simply naming. Caring is also essential, and that goes for minor characters every bit as much as it does for major ones. Several years ago, a good friend of mine was killed by a drunk driver. After years of effort, her husband finally saw to it that her killer was sentenced to prison—for a total of sixteen months, with time off for good behavior. At the time, I was getting ready to write Joanna Brady number four, *Dead to Rights*. The real-life situation so offended me that I had to put a drunk driver who gets a judicial slap on the wrist into my book. What happens in the story isn't exactly what happened to my friends, but it's close enough that I'm moved to tears by it, and so are my readers. It's hardly surprising that when we next see the drunk driver, he's back at home and getting on with his life. It's also not surprising that he doesn't make it through the second chapter of the book.

The lesson I learned from that situation is that, as a writer, I may have an obligation to "care" about my victims, but I sure as hell don't have to like them. Once the drunk driver was dead, then it was simply a matter of choosing the right killer from among the several people who, justifiably or not, wanted the man dead.

From Writer to Detective

Some writers begin their books by doing detailed outlines of all the action. If that works for them, fine, but it doesn't work for me. I've never mastered the art of outlining, perhaps because I have an abiding distrust of Roman numerals. I usually start with some-one dead and then try to get a grip on the various people involved in the story. That goes for the killers and victims as much as it does for the detectives investigating the case. I can't write believably about a murderer until I understand that person's motivation for taking the life of another human being.

Sometimes while I'm writing, the story will grind to a halt partway through. I sometimes refer to this phenomenon as my "Chapter Eleven Wall." Over the years, I've come to under-stand that if a story stops and won't move beyond a certain point, it probably means I have a problem with one or more of my characters' motivations. Once I go back and tweak the motivations, or look around and find the character who "really" did it, then the story gets back on track.

How does one go about "tweaking" a character? You think about him, day and night. Sometimes for hours on end. That kind of concentrated and specific thinking counts as some of the hardest work I do in the job because often it requires me to do the unthinkable—to change my mind. Revising text is child's play compared with the hard work of rethinking, but that's how I sometimes arrive at the conclusion that the person I originally thought was the killer didn't do it.

When that happens, I have my own opportunity to play detective. I look through my cast of characters. Finding the real culprit gives me an essential "eureka!" experience. Maybe people who do detailed outlines have those same exhilarating moments of discovery, but it seems to me they would be harder to come by if the writer knew in advance everything that was going to happen.

With no formal training in writing but with an extensive background in reading and a good foundation in grammar and spelling, I started my writing career in March 1982. My first book never saw the light of day. My second book was accepted and published by the second editor who saw it. *Rattlesnake Crossing*, published in July 1998, was my twentieth book. Three more are written and not yet published with six more under contract beyond that. This far into my career, I have some confidence that once I start a book, I will be able to finish it. Part of that confidence comes from what I now regard as the Amended Golden Rule of Writing: Write what you know, and know your characters best of all.

J.A. JANCE's newest books are *Birds of Prey* and *Paradise Lost.*

Chapter 31

Writing Suspense That'll "Kill" Your Readers

By Carol Davis Luce

You're about to begin a scene in your story that you hope will set your readers' hearts racing. This scene takes special care to execute. This is a . . . *suspense scene.*

By the time readers get to this scene, you've already laid the groundwork for conflict (you'd better have, anyway). Through dialogue, narrative, and actions, readers have been primed to expect a confrontation of some kind, somewhere. And now it's time to deliver. You want to do it right. You want to pull it off. Want to know how? I won't keep you in suspense.

Tension Comprehension

Tension is the act of building or prolonging a crisis. It's the bump in the night, the ticking bomb; it's making readers aware of peril. (A baby strays from its mother and toddles onto the railroad tracks. *Tension* begins when, in the distance, a train whistle is heard. *High-tension* occurs when the baby plops down in the center of the tracks and begins to play.)

To write effective suspense, you need not see menace in every corner. But you must be aware of the potential threat of menace. You—and, through you, your readers—must feel the tension. As you set the scene, sense the danger, and anticipate the perilous outcome.

Use the following techniques to set your scenes aquiver.

The "Big Bang" Technique

One way to write a dramatic, tension-filled scene is with the element of surprise. The Big Bang is just that. The scene appears innocuous: Our protagonist is enjoying a pleasant walk in the woods when BANG! Disaster strikes. Both protagonist and reader are jolted by the sudden attack. With the Big Bang, the big moment begins and ends with the bang. This type of scene lacks genuine suspense, which is best built slowly. It is, however, extremely effective when used sparingly. Use it too much and readers won't be shocked for long—they'll feel cheated. And they'll come to expect these explosions, which is certain death when trying to lay the ground work for suspense. In fact, I'm mentioning it first here so we can get it out of the way and move to much more effective techniques.

The "Jack-in-the-Box" Technique

I prefer to take readers slowly and steadily along the dark and sinister path of suspense, allowing them to experience first-hand the sights, sounds, smells, and pending peril. The jack-in-the-box technique beats the bang because it builds suspense. To maximize the suspense you must emphasize the tension (bring it to a higher level); you must stretch readers' stress and emotions.

It's those critical moments before Jack the clown springs from the box that generate high tension. We turn the crank, the music plays, we know he's coming . . . we just don't know when. Think of building suspense this way: Blow up a balloon in front of some friends. Inflating it is a simple, nonthreatening action—

anyone can do it. But when the balloon appears to be fully inflated, keep on going. Now, in a deliberate manner, you've taken it beyond a nonthreatening act, and those watching will begin to feel a sense of uneasiness. Apprehension. Tension. With each breath, their tension increases. Bracing for the inevitable does no good, for when the bang finally comes, everyone jumps. And once it's over, the relief is obvious. The tension has burst along with the balloon.

Although the balloon was filled with nothing more than hot air, it's the premeditation, along with the obvious intent to inflict a certain amount of suffering, that makes for high tension. Fill your balloon with trepidation and you will turn something that bobs merrily in the wind into something that grabs you by the throat and won't let go.

In a suspense novel, stretch these jack-in-the-box scenes to different degrees. Do this by varying the pace. The suspense can be quick or it can be drawn out, depending on how fast or slow you want the crank to turn. Too quick and the tension is gone before it even begins. Too drawn out and the tension dissipates through sheer tedium. If too much time passes from the point when you first introduce the threat to the actual execution of that threat, readers may simply forget about the initial threat, thus destroying the dramatic tension.

And sometimes attempts at generating suspense fall apart completely. In my novel *Skin Deep*, I wrote a scene where a killer with a straight razor, wearing a ski mask and gloves, breaks into the heroine's apartment and hides in her bedroom closet. The heroine, true to the story line, comes home and soon enters the bedroom (the tension builds; readers know he's behind that door, waiting to pounce). She begins to unbutton her blouse as she moves toward the closet. She reaches out, places her hand on the knob and. . . .

In an early draft of this scene, I had my heroine abruptly turn and leave the room, leave the apartment even, to visit a friend downstairs. Still in the closet, our killer sweats it out in his wool ski mask and thick leather gloves until she finally returns some time later to begin the chain of events all over again. The only death here was the death of any suspense I'd started to build.

The scene was changed in the final draft to let the action flow uninterrupted. Also, to further enhance the suspense, I had the heroine's "peril detector" kick in just as she reaches for the doorknob. Something (a gut feeling, perhaps) tells her she is in danger. Readers experience first her trepidation, then her terror, as she turns to run.

And that "peril detector" is important. In another novel (not mine, this time) a killer stakes out the heroine's nightly route and waits in the shadows for his chance. On three occasions (three times!) the heroine strolls within several yards of her attacker-to-be yet manages to avoid any confrontation. Each time she comes a little closer, but one thing or another keeps her out of harm's way.

The serious suspense flaw here lies not only with repetition without repercussion, but that the heroine never sensed she was in any danger. It made her appear too lucky for words and made the killer appear foolish and inept. Too-lucky heroines and too-inept killers will have readers reaching for the light switch.

Remember, you might get away with something like this once, possibly twice, but never three times.

The "Shifty Eyes" Techniques

Shifting from scene to scene and from viewpoint to viewpoint often increases tension. Switching from the antagonist (the bad guy) to the protagonist (the good guy) can effectively set up the forthcoming conflict. It works best if the scenes are kept short. This technique should be used only in setting up the conflict, such as bringing the two 'tagonists together in a direct confrontation. Here's how it works:

Scene A: The protagonist is in her car, driving home.

Scene B: The antagonist breaks into the protagonist's house. (You can show his sinister intent through an action, such as his killing a pet or breaking a cherished antique.)

Scene C: The protagonist arrives home and enters her house.

At this point, the remaining action is carried out in one scene, one viewpoint, preferably the protagonist's.

Early in my novel *Night Stalker*, heroine Alex Carlson is aware that she's being stalked (anonymous calls, a break-in, threats, and so on) by a psychopath. She lives alone in a secluded hillside house, and to make matters worse, she's afraid of the dark. The scene played out like this:

Antagonist's point of view:

> He worked the glove off his right hand with his teeth, then pulled the butane lighter from his pants pocket. . . . The phone rang. . . . Between the first and second ring he heard her key in the lock. He stepped back into the dim recesses of Alex Carlson's painting alcove.

Protagonist's point of view:

> Alex shifted the grocery bag to her left hip and opened the door. The telephone rang again as she hurried downstairs to the study. . . . [Following a brief telephone conversation, Alex hears a soft click on the line after her friend hangs up.] Goose bumps rose along her arms. Standing at the desk, the grocery bag clasped tightly to her chest, she shivered. The click on the line, she tried to assure herself, had been Greg's secretary—nothing more.

The "Through Your Eyes Only" Technique

If you're using a strict first-person viewpoint, you can build suspense by planting "clues" through your protagonist. It can be as simple as hearing a click on the line, as Alex did, and going from there. Suppose that after hanging up the phone, Alex feels a chilling breeze at her back. She notices an open window that she was certain she'd closed before going out. On the table by the window, a small potted plant lies on its side. The wind? The cat? Alex's "peril detector" begins to kick in. She remembers that Greg's secretary is out of town; if someone picked up the line, it had to be someone in her own house. On the floor above she hears footsteps, followed by the soft thunk of the dead bolt on the front door being engaged. And then the lights go out. . . .

Alex's own trepidation fuels the tension for the scene. Her ensuing terror after the lights go out (she knows now the killer is in the house with her) will propel the tension to its climactic end.

Study scenes in suspense movies, too. In *Sleeping With the Enemy*, protagonist Sara Burney, an abused wife, has staged her own death to escape from her deranged husband. She changes her identity and moves to a small town to start over. But she can't stop looking over her shoulder. We watch as the husband gets closer and closer, wreaking havoc as he goes. And just when Sara begins to feel safe, he finds her. Remember the chilling scene where Sara is reclining in the bathtub, all bad thoughts cleared from her mind by thoughts of her new love? That's when suddenly she notices that all the towels and washcloths (her husband was phobic about neatness and order) are in perfect alignment. Her worst fears are confirmed when she sees all the canned goods in the kitchen are similarly arranged. He knows she is alive. He knows where she lives. He's been in her house. Where is he now?

Even animals can be utilized to convey a sense of doom. Here's the protagonist's cat in *Night Stalker*.

Alone in the house now, Blackie paced fitfully, his tail twitching in spasmodic bursts. He jumped onto the counter, jumped down. He scratched at the glass of the slider, meowing. Suddenly he stopped, his body stiff. With ears pointed and alert, he looked upward, listening. His tail bristled. Then, even more agitated, he resumed his scratching at the glass door.

Cats, killers in closets, and balloons stretching to bursting. Suspense is a state of mind. How you build that suspense can make the difference between your readers chucking your book for a good night's sleep or nudging their spouse to say, "the suspense is killing me."

CAROL DAVIS LUCE has published a number of suspense novels with Zebra Books. Her latest is *Night Passage*.

Keeping Them in Suspense

By William J. Reynolds

I've gotta know.

That's what keeps your readers turning the pages into the wee hours when sensible folk have gone to sleep, or long after the time when they really should have started supper or tackled that briefcase: *They've gotta know what happens next!*

That *I've gotta know* is the essence of suspense. No matter your genre, the length of your story, or the medium in which it appears, you can't build a page-turner without suspense. Of course, genre fiction requires the same ingredients as all fiction: compelling characters we can identify with, a plausible plot and intriguing subplots, richly evoked settings, appealing writing. But a romance, mystery, science fiction, fantasy, Western, or other genre or subgenre yarn without suspense is like coffee without caffeine—no kick and not very addicting.

Yet "suspense" is one of those tricky words that covers an awful lot of real estate. Suspense in a Tom Clancy technothriller is an entirely different animal than in a LaVyrle Spencer romance.

Can I Super-Size That for You?

So, to start building your own page-turners, the first thing you need to remember is that there are different types of suspense. I think of suspense as coming in three sizes, like soft drinks:

small, medium, and large. Most stories—except perhaps the very shortest of short fiction—will feature all three sizes at different intervals.

Dashiell Hammett's masterpiece *The Maltese Falcon*, for example, begins with what I call "small" suspense, in the more leisurely style of 1930s writing: Sam Spade and his partner, Miles Archer, are enlisted by a Miss Wonderly to find her sister, whom she's tracked to San Francisco. Spade and Archer—and we—know the whole thing's fishy: the woman's story doesn't quite hang together, she offers much too big of a retainer, and so on. So far it's not so much an *I've gotta know* as an *I wonder what* . . . . We keep turning the pages for much the same reason that Spade and Archer take the case: to see what's really going on.

We come out of it better than Archer, who gets whacked a few pages later. Now Hammett has bumped us up to medium-sized suspense; the addition of mortal danger has changed our almost-idle curiosity into the beginnings of that *I've gotta know*: Is Spade next? Or is Spade the killer? And what about this Miss Wonderly? Later, as the mysterious Joel Cairo enters the story, Hammett hands us the large-sized suspense: Who is this sinister yet comic little man? What does he want with Spade? Is he the killer? Finally, at the conclusion, Hammett slips us the extra-large size, as we wonder whose side Spade is really on and what he'll do now that the "black bird" is in hand. (Keep it for himself? Betray "Miss Wonderly"—really Brigid O'Shaughnessy, with whom Spade now has a romantic relationship—and throw in with the bad guys? Or turn the lot of them over to the cops?)

We've gotta know.

Planning a Roller-Coaster Ride

That brief synopsis gives us a second inkling of the nature of suspense: There are waves of suspense.

And thank goodness! Can you imagine how exhausting it would be to read a novel that maintained "large suspense" at a fever pitch from beginning to end? Even if it were possible to write such a thing, no one would have the stamina to finish reading it, and so it wouldn't exactly fit the definition of a page-turner, would it?

Yet a novel that kept a constant medium- or small-sized suspense going wouldn't carry many readers past the midpoint, either. Every so often, you need to turn up the juice. Think of a roller coaster: Usually the ride starts off slowly, building to a peak; then there's a sudden drop, a quick ascent to another peak; then another drop, perhaps around a curve; then a brief level interval; and so on.

Just as the roller-coaster ride offers interludes of relative calm, so too must fiction give the reader a bit of a breather now and then, an interval of release. A suspenseful episode must be resolved, at least for the time being, and the reader must be given time to recover before the next ascent begins.

Look at how the master of suspense, Alfred Hitchcock, handles it in *North by Northwest*. Hitchcock delivers the suspense in carefully measured waves, each slightly higher than the last, each independently resolved (at least temporarily), and separated by "breathing space," usually in the form of the interplay between Cary Grant and Eva Marie Saint, later in a few clever scenes between Grant and Leo G. Carroll. None of those intervals is extraneous, however. Each pushes the story forward. For instance, the romantic interlude on board the train doesn't just mark time, like the "romantic" interludes in, say, a James Bond movie. Hitchcock uses this "down time" to define the characters while skillfully foreshadowing the next episode of suspense: We come to realize that Saint is not necessarily what she seems. Grant knows this, too. So even before the train reaches the station, we've begun to wonder what will happen when it does. Will she betray him? What's her game? Whose side is she on?

We've gotta know.

Sources of Suspense

Okay, so suspense comes in different sizes and gets delivered in waves. But where does it come from?

The most obvious source of suspense is plot—indeed, in genre fiction especially, it's nearly impossible to separate the two. Consider *North by Northwest* again and its mistaken-identity plot: A bunch of obviously sinister characters are convinced that Cary Grant is somebody they've been pursuing for some time and for some unsavory purpose. Grant, naturally, tries to elude them. They, also naturally, don't want him to. You can scribble that on the back of a cocktail napkin and immediately see all sorts of suspenseful threads come curling out of it. Who are these bad apples? What do they want with whoever they think Grant is? How will Grant give them the slip? How will they seek to get him back? Who will help or hinder him? And we haven't even gotten to Mount Rushmore yet!

Suspense grows easily out of your characters, too. Once you've begun to establish the plot and started to move characters around, their actions and reactions will provide suspenseful episodes within the framework of the plot. From almost the first page of *The Maltese Falcon*, Hammett shows us that Sam Spade is at best amoral. Not especially bad, but no saint, either. He's been fooling around with his partner's wife for some time, but when that partner is murdered, Spade commits himself to finding the killer. Knowing that Spade is neither black nor white, we *don't* know for sure how he'll act or react. We don't know if he'll angle to keep the falcon for himself. We don't know if he'll throw in with the bad guys (whose own alliances, springing from their own characters, keep shifting and reforming). We don't even know whether Spade himself killed Archer—even Archer's widow, Spade's lover, doesn't put it past him.

So suspenseful elements in the plot generate suspenseful episodes that grow out of the characters' personalities. And how the characters respond or react drives forward the plot, generating new suspenseful episodes to which our characters must react. We've built a perpetual-motion machine!

Suspense also derives from place (an alien world subject to unpredictable seismic disturbances; a downtrodden border town tyrannized by bandits; a lonely and desolate coastal village) and even meteorology. I set my Nebraska detective series in and around my hometown of Omaha, not an obviously suspenseful locale. But I've made use of the unpredictable nature of Midwestern weather to augment suspense. The onset of a summer storm foreshadows the climax of *Money Trouble*, giving my private investigator (known only as "Nebraska" for reasons too numerous and tedious to relate) that inexplicable yet undeniable feeling that something is about to happen. The gray, joyless days of deep winter in Omaha have also helped build suspense. I began my fourth novel, *Things Invisible*, with a character observing, "Days like this remind you that you're going to die."

Pacing Yourself

Finally, suspense springs from your style of writing, the viewpoint you select, the words you choose, and the way you employ them—particularly the way you order and pace your words. Remember that roller-coaster ride? It works for pacing your writing as well as your scenes. Generally, a suspenseful episode will be introduced with a longish, somewhat leisurely passage, just as a roller-coaster ride begins slowly. As the episode reaches its crest, the sentences become terse, telegraphic. Things are happening now.

Sentences are short.

Paragraphs too.

Maybe there isn't even time to—

You get the picture?

See how this works in a scene near the conclusion of my latest detective novel, *Drive-By*. The good guys have cornered the bad guy, a gang leader, in a scene purposely evocative of an Old West showdown. However, the appearance of a young woman who was involved with the gang but who's now on the side of the angels—maybe—has thrown the heroes' plan off the rails:

> Like most people who were alive in the '60s, I carry in my head an indelible picture of the assassination of Lee Harvey Oswald. There is Jack Ruby, the back of his head, the extended gun arm. There is Oswald, collapsing in on himself, his face distorted in pain. And there is the unlucky escort, the cop in the light-colored suit and hat, his eyes and face wide in the surprised realization of what is happening right before him, right beside him, and which, proximity notwithstanding, he is powerless to prevent.
>
> Now I felt the way the cop in that picture looks.
>
> Gerard Jones had been smiling at Elmo. He turned back to give Yoli some of the same. Her right hand came out of her jacket pocket, where it had been all along. There was a flat .22 in her hand. Its chrome plating caught a stray particle of light from somewhere and threw it across Elmo's left sleeve.
>
> She emptied the gun into Gerard Jones's midsection.
>
> He caved in on himself and fell back.
>
> I caught him. He didn't care.
>
> I put him down on the cold ground, groping for the

pulse I knew would be dropping off. His blood was hot on my hand and face.

I looked over my shoulder. Elmo had taken the .22 from Yoli. She offered no resistance. She looked down at Gerard like he was just another body on the six o'clock news.

Here's what I tried to do: First, an introspective, almost chatty lead paragraph to draw the reader into the episode. (Remember, this is pulled from a longer scene, so presumably the reader is already primed to wonder how it's all going to play out.) Then a series of quick, short, even single-sentence paragraphs to convey the impression that whatever happens is happening quickly and unexpectedly, like the on-camera murder of Oswald. The last two paragraphs wind things down. They're a little bit longer, and the sentences are returning to a more natural flow.

Turning the Last Page

Believe it or not, that scene is not the end of *Drive-By*—close, of course, but not quite—and that fact serves to point up that the resolution of your story is in itself an important element of suspense. I'm not saying you should leave the reader hanging; in fact, you should not, unless you're writing a soap opera. You must resolve events in a satisfactory manner. But that doesn't mean you need to elaborately bundle everything into a tidy package, as in a Sherlock Holmes story. Think about it this way: Suspense is a roller-coaster ride, right? Highs and lows, fast and slow, curves and straightaways, all designed to thrill the rider. At the end of this fabulous, heart-pounding ride, will you want to stand around for ten minutes while the operator explains *how the ride works*?

My point: The words "The End" should come as quickly as possible after the final climax. Avoid the long valedictory exposition; it deadens the suspense you've carefully crafted and sustained. (Mysteries are especially prone to this disease, but no genre fiction is immune.)

Hammett perfectly illustrates the proper say-what-you-have-to-say-and-get-out-of-Dodge style at the end of *The Maltese Falcon*. We've followed along as Spade picks his way through the complexities of the case, using his nemeses' greedy, double-crossing natures to play them against one another until, finally, he turns them all over to the cops. Then come thirteen concise paragraphs, none longer than about forty words, that serve not to explain the denouement but rather only to close the story and give us one final look into Spade's character. There are one or two loose ends—not the least being the whereabouts of the title falcon—but who cares? Miles Archer's killer is captured, and that was Spade's real interest. The conclusion is satisfactory, logical, and perfectly in keeping with all that's gone before. It caps off a suspenseful story; it doesn't blunt it.

Most important, we've finally found out what we've gotta know.

Me, Myself, and I: Suspense in the First Person

Aside from *Sunset Boulevard*, it's tough to think of any first-person stories where the narrator dies—for obvious reasons. Who then would tell the rest of the story?

That's only the most extreme example of the special problems of creating suspense when the story's told by "I." You can't even really put your first-person protagonist in mortal danger. Sure, she can get into a mighty tight corner, and you can have us believe this could be the final curtain. But in the end, we all know that it can't be.

One trick that's worked for me (my "Nebraska" detective novels are told in the first person) is to plot the story so the hero isn't alone in peril. This shifts the focus from him trying to save his own neck (which the astute reader knows is going to be saved anyway) to trying to save his and someone else's. Now the question isn't just how he'll get out of the bind, but also whether he'll be able to save the other character. Sometimes he does and sometimes he doesn't.

The other problem I've wrestled with in first-person storytelling is more general, but one that significantly affects the suspense. In the mystery genre, we're burdened with this ridiculous notion of "playing fair with the reader." The idea is that it isn't "fair" to have Perry Mason, on the last page of the book, explain that he cracked the case by virtue of being the only one—including the reader—who knew that the defendant and the deceased were third cousins twice removed.

Obviously, an author who pulls that sort of stunt won't be invited back to pull it again, so, clearly, there is something to be said for "playing fair." But when your protagonist is telling the story, presumably at some point after the fact, your suspense could seem artificial, even underhanded. After all, the narrator knows what happened next!

So it becomes even more imperative in a first-person tale to make sure the suspense is natural, organic, flowing logically from what we know about the characters, the plot (so far), and so on. Here's what I mean:

> I knew from the moment I awoke that something was wrong. But what? I showered, dressed, and made breakfast, all under an oppressive cloud of nameless dread. Finally, when I sat uneasily at the table and opened the newspaper, my premonition was realized.

Melodramatic, but you get the idea. Sure, there's suspense at work there, but it's artificial, imposed on the scene rather than springing naturally from it or any other aspect of the story. Compare to this version:

Nothing seemed out of the ordinary when I first woke. I showered, dressed, and made breakfast, all in the usual fashion. I sat down at the table and opened the newspaper. Suddenly I wasn't hungry anymore.

You see? The suspense flows more naturally. The very fact that our narrator bothers to limn a perfectly ordinary, mundane morning already sets us on edge, because we just know something's going to happen. (Admittedly, there's a hint of if-I-knew-then-what-I-know-now—also deadly in a first-person narrative—but so slight a hint that it smacks more of foreshadowing than of a smug I-know-something-you-don't-know.)

WILLIAM J. REYNOLDS is the author of detective novels, including the Shamus Award–nominated *The Nebraska Quotient*, two nonfiction books, and scores of short stories and magazine articles.

Chapter 33

Inside Christian Fiction

By Penelope J. Stokes

"Jesus," Madeleine L'Engle says in *Walking on Water*, "was not a theologian. He was God who told stories."

And good stories they were, too—stories that shook the religious status quo to its foundations, stories that made people think, that made them wonder and question and reevaluate their own relationships with God. Sometimes they were stories that made his listeners angry. Stories about death and rebirth, about sin and redemption, about a God who cares enough to go after one wandering sheep or to search the entire house for a single lost coin. Stories about an outcast who becomes a model of godliness by helping a wounded enemy. Stories about a father who forgives even before his wayward son has repented. Intriguing stories. Disturbing stories. Stories that comforted the afflicted—and afflicted the comfortable.

If you don't believe stories have power, watch what happens in your church on some sleepy Sunday morning. The pastor drones on about justification and sanctification and nearly every other religious term you can think of, and then suddenly says, "Let me tell you a story." Heads pop up, spines straighten, and eyes open. Ah, here it is. Not doctrine or law or history, but a story. We can relate to a story. We can hear it, glean its meaning, and make our own applications. We can find our own truth in its words—truth that may have more influence for change than all the shoulds in Christendom.

Making It in Christian Fiction

Writers who hope to succeed as novelists in the Christian market
need to understand how the CBA (formerly known as the
Christian Booksellers Association market; see page 308) works,
and to take into account a number of primary considerations
before attempting to sell a proposal.

Like any other marketplace, the Christian publishing market
has its benefits as well as its limitations. For the Christian
who wants to write high-quality moral fiction, CBA publishers
offer the opportunity to publish in an environment open to
spiritual truth, and to reach an audience hungry for that truth.
In most cases, a writer does not need to have an agent to get
a reading from a CBA editor, although many Christian writers
these days are opting to ally themselves with literary agents
who specialize in marketing to CBA publishers. Many Christian
publishers are smaller than the New York megahouses; thus,
a writer may find that the atmosphere in a Christian publishing
company is warmer and more intimate, and that Christian
companies tend to give more attention to their writers. In general,
Christian publishers are a bit more open to untested writers
and more willing to take a chance on a new writer if the author's
work shows promise.

The limitations of publishing with a CBA house relate primarily to theological and financial issues. Theologically, the more
conservative publishers expect fiction to have a strong evangelical content and an overt moral lesson or spiritual "take-away
value." Other less conservative companies emphasize quality of
writing and development of plot and character, but still demand a
certain level of theological rectitude: characters who are identifi-
ably Christian (or who come to Christian faith during the
course of the story), a biblically based representation of God,
and a worldview that reflects the justice and mercy of God,
where the good get rewarded and the evil get punished.

In financial terms, many of the smaller evangelical publishers do not have sufficient working capital to invest enormous amounts of money in marketing and advertising. Advances, particularly for new writers, are generally minimal, and first print runs tend to be small. But the larger, more profitable big-name companies in the CBA are beginning to match some of the New York houses, offering substantial advances, good royalty schedules, and excellent marketing.

Distinctive Features

A writer who wants to publish novels in the religious market-place needs to have a clear idea of the distinctive features that separate Christian or evangelical fiction from general-market fiction. In general, the Christian market is geared toward the conservative end of the evangelical spectrum. Readers, booksellers, editors, and publishers expect a certain level of conservative Christian theology. This perspective does not always have to appear in the form of decisions for Christ, sermons, or prayers, but it must be visible in some form.

Some Christian publishers provide a detailed doctrinal perspective for potential writers in their writers guidelines; others require the use of specific Bible translations for any Scripture passages that may be used. And almost all publishers are looking for particular kinds of books that fit into their publishing grid. In addition to genres that fit the specific niche of each evangelical publisher, most CBA publishing houses will be looking for the following issues in the novels they acquire.

• **A clearly articulated Christian worldview.** A Christian worldview is based on the assumption that God is in control of the universe, and that true meaning and fulfillment in life are based on a relationship with the Almighty. This does not mean that bad things never happen, but that evil will be punished in the end and good will prevail—either in this world or in the world to come. A Christian worldview offers a perspective of a universe that includes spiritual vision, order, and moral resolution. Christian writers do not have to blind themselves to reality, but their writing must hold out the possibility of hope.

• **A familiar but intriguing setting and/or time frame.** According to a survey conducted by a major CBA publisher, readers are most often drawn to settings they feel comfortable with or that are familiar: American rural/small-town environments (as in Janette Oke's nostalgia novels), and well-known historical time frames such as World War II, the Civil War, or Victorian England. These settings and time frames attract audiences because readers feel they already know something about the era and the environment.

• **Universal themes and subject matter.** Novels usually work best in the CBA market when they connect with some issue of current interest or universal appeal: love, suffering, injustice, moral challenges, or family relationships. Contemporary novels often approach controversial issues directly (abortion, for example), but these issues must also be approached carefully lest they become extended sermons.

• **Action orientation.** Action-oriented books that include intrigue, movement, suspense, danger, and ultimate resolution usually work best in the CBA market. This general principle does not eliminate the value of character-oriented books, but it's a good idea to steer clear of psychological novels comprised mostly of self-awareness, internal insights, or relationships. Something has to happen for a book to be successful in the Christian market.

• **Viable Christian characters.** Conservative Christian readers look for characters they can relate to—"good Christian people." Characters do not have to be perfect (who is, after all?), but main characters—heroes and heroines—are generally most acceptable when they have a clearly identifiable evangelical faith, along with some kind of memorable "conversion" in their history. Most Christian readers are looking for a conflict of good versus evil, one of the universal themes described previously. At the very least, the central character must have redeeming faith values, an intrinsic goodness or nobility—perhaps a "lapsed Christian" with a background of faith that ultimately leads to recommitment. Some of the more conservative Christian publishers tend to be wary of characters who are too Catholic in their expressions of faith.

• **Series plans or potential.** Although some companies are now successfully publishing stand-alone novels, many publishers have found that a series is more marketable than a single novel, particularly with historical fiction.

Compelling characters or intriguing plots lead the reader to anticipate the next book, and the series creates its own natural marketing momentum. Plans for a trilogy, a four- or five-book series, or even a single sequel can be a major selling point for a proposal.

• **Strong evangelical perspectives.** Certain Christian publishers insist on a strong conservative perspective that goes beyond a basic Christian worldview. These publishers will respond positively to characters who pray and see obvious answers to their prayers, who make decisions based on Scripture, and who have significant changes wrought in their lives and attitudes by the power of God working in difficult circumstances. Most CBA publishers expect their authors to refrain from writing scenes that include gratuitous sex or overt sensuality, obscenity and profanity, humanistic philosophy, or excessive violence (particularly toward women).

Acceptable Compromises

Some of these limitations present significant problems for novelists in the Christian market. Since real life contains violence, sex, and profanity, how do you write "real" fiction and create "real" characters under such constraints? Perhaps the key to that dilemma lies in the Christian novelist's perceptions—that Christian worldview. The fact is, spiritual growth and the search for truth are also integral issues in human life, issues that are sometimes ignored altogether in general-market fiction.

When personal religious compromises are necessary, they should be evaluated on the basis of the author's own belief system. Some issues can simply be soft-pedaled, as Jan Karon

About the CBA

The CBA, formerly known as the Christian Booksellers Association, serves more than 3,500 member retail stores in more than forty countries, including 2,500 stores in the United States. Some 625 product suppliers, including publishers, are members.

The CBA's annual international convention draws more than 12,000 people and more than 400 exhibitors.

Published writers are eligible for CBA membership if they are active in the business of writing product for resale through the Christian retail stores, working at least thirty hours per week in this field. Membership is $150 annually; benefits include the CBA membership directory, suppliers directory, a monthly association magazine, and reduced prices on products and convention registration. Be aware, however, that the vast majority of CBA members are retail stores or suppliers. For more information, contact CBA at 9240 Explorer Drive, P.O. Box 62000, Colorado Springs, Colorado 80962-2000; phone: (800) 252-1950; fax: (719) 272-3510; Web site: www.cbaonline.org.

has done so well in the Mitford books; others can be addressed head-on through characters who exhibit growth and change as the novel progresses. I would never advise authors to try to write something that is in direct contradiction to their personal values, but I often encourage authors to find the common ground between their own beliefs and the perspectives of their readers.

The challenge to the Christian writer, then, is to create fascinating, memorable characters and gripping plots, and still represent the validity of Christian faith in human life. Writers who employ sound principles of good fiction can find ways to communicate a clear Christian worldview without compromising the artistic and literary demands of high-quality fiction.

Jesus was "God who told stories." And we, as writers who bear Christ's name, have the same calling: to tell our stories with skill and craft and passion, and to allow God to use our words in the lives of others.

It is a gift and a calling. But it is also a job.

Work hard. Listen. Learn. Grow.

God is in charge of the outcome.

PENELOPE J. STOKES holds a Ph.D. in Renaissance Literature and has taught literature and writing at the college level. She is the author of numerous novels and nonfiction books, including *The Complete Guide to Writing & Selling the Christian Novel* (Writer's Digest Books), from which this article was adapted.

Chapter 34

The Basics of Romance

by Rita Clay Estrada and Rita Gallagher

What Is Romance?

Let's start from the beginning. What is a romance? With all the books out there, why is one called a *romance* while another is labeled *women's fiction* or *Western* or *science fiction* or *mystery* or *techno-thriller* or . . . well, you get the point.

It's so simple, and so very complicated. A romance is present in every book that has a man and woman falling in love, but all of those books are not part of the romance genre. A story is only a romance when the main theme of that book is romance!

In other words, it doesn't matter whether it's a Western, mystery, or science fiction as long as the main theme is romance. Then, and only then, can it be called a romance.

> *The expanding marketplace for romances has allowed the genre to evolve into formula fiction without the formula.*
>
> —Debbie Macomber

What Is Not a Romance?

If the main theme of a story is a man and woman fighting for their lives against the Mafia as they fall in love with each other, it's probably a thriller. If the man and woman fight *each other* as they try to flee the Mafia, it's probably a romance.

See the difference?

Whatever the emphasis is, that's what the book is. Think of movies: *Star Wars* was a science fiction story with a romance growing between the action. *Pretty Woman* was a romance set in the powerful elite of the corporate world. The basic rule is that for a book to be a romance, the romance must be the most important element in the story.

Now, to throw in a monkey wrench.

Danielle Steel-types of books aren't romances. They're known as *soaps.* Why? Because they're problematic—one heart-kicking dilemma after another. One life-threatening quandary after another. One tear-jerking, emotional death and divorce after another. The romance is secondary to the problems, growth, and tears of the heroine. That's a soap. Danielle Steel created the written form and made it her genre. Many have followed, but few have had the success she has.

Maeve Binchy and others have created another genre . . . and you guessed it, these books are not romances either. This genre deals with women—the problems and quiet realities of their lives. These women experience growth, new beginnings, raising children alone and doing it to the best of their ability, leaving husbands and winning the economic war, going back to school, opening businesses and going to work for the first time. Through all of this, they make a success of their lives. This genre is called *women's fiction.*

In an equal, more knowledgeable world, this would all be called just good plain fiction. It used to be, but not now.

The publishing industry has an odd view of fiction sales. If you took away genre and subgenre fictions, what would you have? You'd have what the market supports today: general fiction and women's fiction. The reasoning is that general fiction is anything written by a male that both men and women read. Women's fiction can be written by men or women, but is usually aimed at women, since most American men don't (yes, you may read "won't" here) read women fiction writers unless it's in a genre they can publicly relate to—a genre like mystery (Sue Grafton, Agatha Christie, Mary Higgins Clark, and so on).

All methods of writing can be applied to any type of fiction writing. Good plot and good writing span all kinds of storytelling.

We hope we can explain all about the romance genre by starting at the heart of romance. And that place is called *category romance*, a good place to study the genre in a form that's pure.

Category—The Heart of Romance

Category books are produced in *lines*. Lines come out with new titles monthly, and a set amount of books are usually published each month. All books in a line carry the same theme. They also have a set word count and topic, and each line has a very personal tone. Each line is different, although sometimes the differences are subtle. Any books published in the Harlequin lines (Temptation, American, Presents, Romance, etc.) or Silhouette lines (Desire, Romance, Intimate Moments, etc.) are category books. Also, almost all category lines are contemporary romances, and most have word counts of 75,000 words or less. Therefore, category romance is often referred to as "short contemporary" romance.

Categories are very important for the romance genre. They not only have very loyal fans, but they introduce new trends in fiction that are exploding or sneaking in the back door. What you see now in the microcosm of category romance, you can bet you'll see in stand-alone books in the near future.

Any story where the main theme is love between a man and a woman is a romance.

Basic Plot of Romance

In a romance, there is One True Love for the heroine, and once he comes on the scene early in the book, there are no other men for her—just as, from that point on, there are no other women for him (especially in category romances). The hero doesn't cheat on the heroine, and although there are times he may want to throttle her, he never, ever lays a hand on her. That's the basic backdrop for the plot.

For every rule we've just stated, you can find an exception in the nearest bookstore. However, those writers have already sold their work. The very word *exception* tells you how hard it would be to sell an out-of-the-mainstream story until you sell your first. Then, when you have a book or two under your belt and your editor wants another, you can try something out of the ordinary. It's easier to slip a foot in the publishing door when it doesn't have a ten-ton ball and chain attached.

Now, when we say middle-of-the-road story, we certainly don't mean middle-of-the-road characters. They need to be original and spicy, with distinct personalities. Characterization is where you can get creative and really show your style.

Let's face it. You need two main things to write a good story: a tight plot and realistic characters who live on after the book is put down. It can be 60–40 or 40–60, but it's best when it's 100–100.

By the way, a lot of good published stories have had better characters than plots, but no one cared because the characters *were* so good that the reader suspended disbelief.

A romance novel is . . .

• about a woman trying to achieve her heart's desire, facing and fighting obstacles to reach it—and succeeding in the end.

• about a woman learning who she is, finding her place in the world, then fighting to gain (or keep) it.

• about the uncertain and confusing feelings that go with that most important part of women's emotions—*love!*

• about the irresistible physical and emotional attraction between male and female. Some lines (such as Harlequin Romance or Steeple Hill) deal subtly with this aspect of romance. Others, such as Harlequin Temptation and Silhouette Desire, are more descriptive about sexual attraction—and about sex. However, whether subtle or descriptive, romance with all its joys and many-faceted complications is what makes the world go around.

> *My first editor, Vivian Stephens, once told me, "When you get the world's attention, you'd better have something good to say." That has stuck with me to this day, twenty years later. A writer's priority must be the book. Invariably, other publishing idiosyncrasies— poor distribution, lousy covers, sloppy editing, promotion or the lack thereof, scathing reviews—become distracting factors. But the writer's primary focus must forever and always be the manuscript. If it's not good, nothing else matters.*
>
> —Sandra Brown

A romance novel, like any other kind of book, should have a *wow* start, something that instantly pulls the reader into the story. The first sentence should make the reader care about what's going to happen and curious enough to race through the pages to satisfy that curiosity.

From Root Ideas to Character Growth

So far we've given you a general idea of what a romance novel is all about. Now let's go a little deeper. What follows is an overview of what it takes to actually write a romance novel.

Writing a Story With Purpose

The first thing to think about it is, what is my story about? *Theme. Root idea. Premise.* What do those words mean? They mean there must be a reason or purpose for your story. If you know what you're trying to prove when you write your romance novel, the words will flow easier, your characters will respond better, and the entire design of the book will fall into place. Are you trying to prove that a woman who once loved and lost can love again? Or that a woman who loves her own child enough to kidnap her isn't really a criminal?

No matter what your purpose, jump into the middle of the problem. Then, after briefly sketching the back story, show step-by-step why (as in the first example) a woman *can* love again. Or why the kidnapping mom *isn't* a criminal.

As you proceed, don't forget that this is a *romance* novel. The hero must be introduced almost immediately, and he should complicate things for the heroine, not make them easier. Ultimately, the heroine has to solve her problems for herself and reconcile her attraction to this man who is making her goal more difficult. And since love, though sometimes difficult, is balanced with joy, your character's perspective will change during your story; she will be able to resolve her problem on her own, strengthened by the hero's love.

How she responds to this change in her life—how, because of love, her focus changes, converges, then tries to readjust—is the heart of your story.

Premise Is the First Step to Plotting

The plot is the map or the blueprint of your book. Knowing your premise and sticking to it will keep your story from losing energy and direction. Premise will keep your story on what editors call "the main thrust" and help each step, incident, and reaction evolve logically. Although the reader doesn't know where you're heading, you need to know at all times. Sometimes that's easier said than done, like when you're in the middle of a great scene and the dialogue gets away from you, but it's worth the effort in a well-plotted story.

The Rules of Sexual Awareness/Tension

A romance novel has two more important ingredients:

- sexual awareness
- sexual tension

Rule One: From the first time they meet, the hero and heroine are deeply aware of each other. They don't have to like each other instantly, but they do have to be aware. This awareness escalates, changes, and rearranges throughout the story and culminates in the resolution.

Rule Two: The hero and heroine should be together as much as possible. In scenes where they are necessarily apart, the absent one should be kept in the reader's mind through memories, yearnings, and so on.

Rule Three: Each time they are together, their feelings should take on another aspect. Their emotions will strengthen, shake, threaten, and, as the book progresses, solidify the relationship.

Rule Four: The senses of hero and heroine are sharpened when they are together. Whether they are fighting or on the verge of making love, sexual tension escalates with each scene.

Conflict

A woman betrayed by love decides to give up all men for the rest of her life. Then, having charted her course, she is suddenly confronted with the hero, who shatters all her previous conceptions about the opposite sex. Both inner and outer conflict will appear here. And again, senses, feelings, and emotions are the three parts of the engine propelling the story to a satisfactory conclusion.

Conflict is the engine that moves the story forward. There is no story without it. Conflict forces the characters to modify their different traits and perspectives. It forces the hero and heroine to rise above the situation, to become strong, to find themselves and their self-esteem. In a romance, just like in any other well-written novel, conflict is the crux of the story.

A romance novel is about two very different people who meet and, despite differing perspectives, fall in love. Throughout the book, they overcome their differences, learn from each other, and draw closer together.

A romance novel is about two halves becoming a whole—then joining forces to become two joined wholes. (This is our personal philosophy, but history has proven that every well-received book holds the same premise.)

Why? Because one of the things we've learned over the years is that the best romance novels are not about codependence; they are about finding love in equality. The female has problems to work out and a process to learn from. She will make him fall in love with her and help teach him his own lesson. Now that's a *woman*—not a dainty flower or a codependent wimp who can't live without a man to guide her!

Hey, I've been rejected by some of the best.

—Jo Beverley

That is one of the most important points we can make to you. These female characters are stronger than they know, are more inventive than they give themselves credit for, and are number one survivors. The man is the extra. He is not the only way to go.

And we don't believe that one character flaw should be used to illustrate the fullness of true love. It's not the right image to demonstrate in this form of print. We said image because we think romances help strengthen minds and resolves, defining what is right and good about men *and* women.

Characters Make the Conflict

Before writing about your characters, get to know them. Give them opposite backgrounds, personalities, and traits. For example: A fragile, gentle woman owns a china shop. She falls in love with a muscle-bound, former football player who doesn't know Limoges from Wedgewood. Each time he enters the shop, he creates disaster. But when he takes her in his arms for a passionate kiss, she is treated like rare porcelain.

He is a hamburger and beer man; she is a caviar and champagne lady.

Result—conflict!

She loves the symphony and ballet; he finds them terribly boring. She loves attending theater parties on opening night; he hates to wear a tux. In every aspect of her life (except for her choice in a man), she is rigidly formal.

Result—conflict!

What does he have to learn from her?

What does she have to learn from him?

If you know the personality of the heroine and hero, you will know which traits will draw them together and which traits will create conflict between them.

With some skill and thought, you can even turn these character tags around and still have a strong story.

Expressing Character Through Point of View

Point of view (POV) is the person who's telling the story. If it's the female, then you're writing as if you're in her head, thinking her thoughts, and feeling her desires, needs, and wants. You do the same thing if it's the male point of view.

A long time ago, writers (especially new writers) were told to stay in one viewpoint forever: the female point of view. Now editors and readers alike want to see both sides of the main characters.

Note: This does not mean that you skip from one head to another to another and then back again. For reader identification and ease, stay in one mind for each scene.

Because women relate best to basic female emotions, the heroine's viewpoint is usually presented. Every woman understands the pain of lost love or betrayal, whether or not she has experienced it. Women also understand the determination to seek a goal and the joy of achieving it, regardless of whether the goal is fame, fortune, or a man.

In a romance novel, another key word is *man*. If a woman thinks that all she wants is fame, fortune, and a career, a man will usually pop up to complicate her life and give her more than she bargained for. That's what a romance novel is all about: Goal (whatever she wants or strives for) = achievement and love.

Now let's talk about the male point of view.

Writing is an action verb. Do it, don't just talk about it.

—Marie Ferrarella

What is important about the hero? The hero is the catalyst for the heroine. Like a powerful magnet, he enters her life and creates physical and emotional chaos. (So what's the difference in real life? Not much!) The heroine is drawn to him, and all her prior ideas about life and love are turned topsy-turvy. How she deals with this hero and her own private, conflicting emotions are what the story is all about.

There is another reason for explaining the thought processes of the hero in a romance novel. Within those pages, a reader finds the hero of her dreams: the man that she married or wants to marry. Not that he's perfect—he can't be perfect, and neither can the heroine. But the interaction and growth they experience, no matter how abrasive at the beginning, brings out the best in each of them by the story's end.

The greatest joy women find in the hero's role is seeing what makes him tick. For years, men were seen as gods, strong and virile. They ruled the woman's world and many women were intimidated by their power. In romance novels, the reader is given a peek inside those Lords of the Realm. Many female souls rejoice when they see that men are also vulnerable. Men can be hurt, they can yearn, suffer, and even cry. And miracle of miracles, when true love takes over a man's heart, he can change. He can grow and become as strong as the women we admire. The heroine he loves can smooth his rough edges. She can teach tenderness where there was insensitivity, compassion where there was heartlessness, and selflessness where there was selfishness. She can show him the strength in being vulnerable. And the reader identifies.

> *Romance heroines aren't "women who love too much," nor are they perfect. They tackle their problems head-on and stand by their convictions. These are women of courage, risk-takers. Women as real as you and me.*
>
> —Debbie Macomber

Prevailing Over Conflict!

By their very natures, your characters create story energy through conflict.

What she wants isn't what he wants.

What he thinks isn't what she thinks.

He disagrees with what she does and vice versa.

With all that conflict, what, you ask, could possibly hold these two people together?

Answer: These five points:

1. A strong physical (chemical) attraction.

2. The fact that opposites attract.

3. The hero's surprise to find a woman who isn't so blinded by his charm that she keeps her opinions to herself.

4. Or, though intrigued by the hero, the heroine fights being told what to do, when to do it, how to think, and so on.

5. Committed love! All the push/pull of likes, dislikes, fights, and make-ups forces both hero and heroine to look, not only at each other, but at themselves.

Because the heroine is a strong and worthy adversary, the hero grows strong and worthy, too. You can also reverse the theory, but we like it this way best.

What do these five points accomplish? Character growth.

What Is Character Growth?

With every painful hit life hands us, we adjust and grow, change our perspective, and try to avoid making that same hurtful mistake again. If you realize this, then you already know about character growth.

While we create, experience, and live with our characters, we may forget that with each impact, each mood swing, each reaction to the hits along the road to the character's goal, that character is changing. We also change as we react to life's lessons through our own personal disasters. With each problem, we change our perspective, our methods of coping, and we find new means to reach our goals. There isn't a time when we aren't constantly shifting to meet whatever specific goal we have set.

The same thing applies to your characters. A book is a slice of life, and real live characters react in the same way as real live people.

Many times, when a hopeful author finishes or nearly finishes a book, the vital point of character growth has been overlooked.

Keep in mind that your characters will never again be the same as they were at the beginning of the story. Their story lives will force them to change and grow.

Giving Your Characters Goals and Motivations

Just like you, if a character has a strong goal, she is strongly motivated to reach it.

Ask yourself these questions:

1. Are your main characters goal-oriented?

2. Do they have the inner strength, motivation, and persistence to fight for their goals?

Note: Perhaps at the beginning of the story, the two main characters have very different goals. But as they interact through conflict and disasters, they are drawn together and, in the end, achieve happiness with just a slight modification of their original goals—because of character growth.

3. Remembering that a reader doesn't want to read about weak, insipid characters, have you shown enough *present* strength and potential in your hero/heroine for them to grow and, through constant striving, achieve their goals?

4. As your characters progress and persist, are they taking honorable chances that will make them grow and try new things despite whatever obstacles they encounter?

5. Have you stayed away from the old and tired "victim of fate"? Remember, readers want ever-strengthening characters getting a handle on life while focusing on cherished goals.

Now, what are you supposed to do to keep your writing alive and well?

Read, Read, Read

Read everything and anything that piques your interest. Read fiction from the best-seller list. (*Whose* best-seller list is up to you. The order will be different, but all the lists will carry most of the same books.)

Read anything and everything from your general genre. Category romance? Read a couple from each category, then go back and read a couple more from each category. Get a good, overall flavor of the various lines and how they speak to different topics. This is one way to learn who you like most, what publisher you want to write for, and what the guidelines are that set up each line.

> *Write what you like to read most; it is what you will write best.*
>
> —Susan Kyle, aka Diana Palmer

Read nonfiction, any type you like: bios, poetry, narrative prose, do-it-yourself books, Westerns, spy stories, classics that weren't introduced to you in school . . . in other words, the entire gamut.

Read anything that will educate you on living. On becoming better at anything. On writing.

The most important research you can do is read. Read

everything, especially the category in which you want to write. Every writer I know is an avid reader. Reading is the first love; then writing comes naturally.

—Mary Tate, aka Tate McKenna

The point is that all books will be of some value to you and your writing. Maybe it won't benefit the book you're working on right this minute, but it might for the book that you do next, or the one after that, or the one after that. Every piece of information is something you'll use down the line.

Reading everything from cereal boxes to billboards will help you learn more about writing than anything else you can do for yourself. It will keep your mind active, keep you interested in writing, and help you learn to recognize and fix your mistakes.

And yes, you will make mistakes. Why? If you're not making mistakes, you're not writing. Just like life. It's as simple as that.

RITA CLAY ESTRADA is a founding member of the Romance Writers of America and has published more than thirty romance novels for Dell, Silhouette, Leisure and Harlequin. RITA GALLAGHER is a widely respected teacher of novel writing and writing workshops. They are the authors of *You Can Write a Romance* (Writer's Digest Books), from which this article was adapted.

The Marketplace

The Search Begins: Finding Agents and Editors

By Blythe Camenson and Marshall J. Cook

The majority of agents and major publishers are nestled within a few square miles of downtown New York City, but a trip to Manhattan is not a requirement; in fact, that wouldn't be a good idea at all. Agents and editors are very busy people with full schedules. Stopping to greet every new writer who decided to drop in would mean that no work would get done. Query letters wouldn't get answered; manuscripts wouldn't get requested and sent out; acceptances (and rejections) wouldn't get passed on.

"Every day we have people who call or drop by and want to meet with us on the spur of the moment," agent Frances Kuffel explains. "They don't realize how busy and scheduled our lives are. These people are often abrupt, demanding, and condescending. Don't they realize that the people concerned are going to weigh that in [when deciding] whether they're going to take a person on as a client [and] whether they're going to stick with someone when things get bad? It would be hilarious if it weren't such a trial."

A face-to-face meeting isn't a necessary step in the process, although at the appropriate time and place—at writers conferences, for example—it can be the best way to find an agent or editor.

Organize Your Search

Finding an agent and getting published is not a speedy process. It can take a year, often more, to land a contract. Marketing your work can feel like a full-time job—and it is. Writing the novel is only half the picture.

In the course of a year, you could contact dozens of agents and editors, sending out an equal number of query letters, synopses, and full and partial manuscripts. How embarrassing—and counterproductive—it would be to receive a rejection from Agent X in January and again in June, the latter including a note with a barely civil, "Didn't I turn this down before?"

Let's face it. Very few writers send out two or three query letters and land an agent or a book contract on their first mailing. With so many submissions circulating, it's important to keep accurate track of them.

Start by setting up a directory in your computer for submissions on each project. Make a file with a form or chart listing all of the agents and/or publishers you plan to contact. As you send your material out, note what you have sent next to each name, for example, query letter, chapters one through three, and synopsis, and the date you sent it. It is also a good idea to note where you found the particular agent or editor—at a conference or on page twenty-eight in a market guide, for example.

As material comes back—the rejection letters (and yes, those will come; it's part of the process) and requests for more material—note the response and when you received it.

With a tracking system set up, you are now ready to start your approach.

Four Ways to Approach Publishers
1. "Over the Transom"

Publishers still refer to an unsolicited manuscript as an over-the-transom submission, even though years ago, builders stopped

putting those little windows above the doors that supplied venti-
lation. (Did writers back then really throw their manuscripts
over the transom and then run?)

Big houses get one hundred or more over-the-transom manuscripts every week. The editors didn't ask for them. They
don't have time for them. They might not even have desk or shelf
space for them. And they certainly don't want to wade
through a thick manuscript to determine its market potential.

So they don't.

They might simply stuff it into the self-addressed stamped envelope (SASE) with a form rejection and wing it back unread.
If there's no SASE, such a submission will probably just hit the
recycle bin.

More likely, the editor will never see an unsolicited novel at
all. It will probably land on the "slush pile" of an over-
worked, underpaid editorial assistant, who must screen out all
but the rare project that might be worth the boss's attention.

No one knows how many unsolicited manuscripts publishers
receive. A few years back, *The New York Times* estimated the
odds against publication of such a project at fifteen thousand to
one, which would mean that only two or three unsolicited
manuscripts would actually make it to publication in a given year.

We hear about the occasional success story, of course. *Jonathan Livingston Seagull* began life on a slush pile, for example. But we hear about these stories because they're so rare, not
because they're the norm. We don't recommend making over-
the-transom submissions.

2. Direct Referral

Sure, a nice introductory letter from your pal Stephen King
wouldn't hurt your chances one bit. An endorsement from the
author you met at a writers conference or took a workshop from
might also help get your project onto the editor's desk, especially
if the editor knows and respects that writer's work. Folks go to

those conferences and workshops to learn their craft and to become savvy marketers. They also go to meet the right people.

But solid endorsements are hard to come by. And they aren't the only way to get your novel published.

3. Proposal

Instead of sending a manuscript, market-savvy writers send a proposal. The purpose of the proposal is to get the editor to ask for the rest of the manuscript. That way, when that manuscript arrives, it bypasses the deadly slush pile and goes directly to the editor for evaluation.

4. Agents

To work with the big New York publishers, having an agent is the best way to go. Read on and learn how to go about finding one and evaluating if he's the right one for you.

What to Look for in Agents and Publishers

To begin with, pinpoint agents or publishers who handle, specialize in, or publish the kind of book you've written. It sounds like an obvious guideline, but many new writers overlook it. The shotgun approach doesn't work here. Mistargeting your submissions is a waste of everyone's time and your postage. Sending fiction to a publisher who puts out only nonfiction or submitting your romance novel to an agent who handles anything but romance won't bring you any closer to your publication goals.

Agent George Nicholson of Sterling Lord Literistic says, "I'm bothered by writers who don't do their homework and writers who don't really know what an agent can and cannot do for them. I have to do a lot of homework to know where to submit manuscripts for the writer. Knowing the reputation of the agent or agency [and] what they require in the way of submissions is part of the homework a writer must do before even submitting to an agent. Too often the writer doesn't research who to submit to and very often sends material to the wrong people."

The Ideal Editor

John Cheever once said, "My definition of a good editor is a man I think charming who sends me large checks; praises my work, my physical beauty, and my sexual prowess; and who has a stranglehold on the publisher and the bank."

So much for wish lists. But there is one item on Cheever's list that merits serious consideration. Your editor (as well as your agent) should definitely believe in your book. While lavish praise might not always be forthcoming, tepid levels of enthusiasm won't generate many book sales—or future contracts—for you.

Your editor should also be someone with whom you can work. It's rare that a first-time novelist is handed a book contract and shortly thereafter, the book goes off to the printer. An editorial stage almost always comes in between. Editors make notes, and writers are expected to make revisions. An editor's insight into your work, ability to make constructive suggestions, and understanding of what sells and what doesn't coupled with your flexibility, talent, and belief in your editor's good judgment will make a winning team.

For that first novel, you might not feel you have a lot of room for argument or dissatisfaction. Let's just get that baby to print. If, once you have established yourself, you find you're butting heads with your editor on important issues, it might be time to take your work elsewhere.

The Ideal Agent

Best-selling author John Grisham says, "Having an agent is the difference between being published and not being published."

Insert the word *good* in front of the word *agent* because, actually, having no agent is better than having a bad agent.

What makes a good agent? In addition to handling the type of work you write and believing in your work, your agent must share your vision, understand your career goals, and be willing to support them.

Most agents (and editors) are not looking for one-book wonders. They want clients who are steady, serious writers who will produce a number of books over time.

It's important that you meet the agent's requirements, but it's equally important that the agent meets yours.

Ideally, your agent should be a member of the Association of Authors' Representatives (AAR). The AAR publishes a canon of ethics, and members are expected to adhere to them. One of their tenets is that AAR members are prohibited from charging reading fees. AAR members also don't charge excessive amounts for photocopying, faxing, and other administrative expenses. Legitimate agents make their money selling your work, not from fees they collect from hopeful writers.

If an agent isn't an AAR member, it doesn't mean she is unethical. Often new agents just starting out haven't applied for membership yet or haven't put in enough time or made enough sales to meet the AAR's requirements. And probably some are not joiners, just as some writers don't join writers associations.

To see a list of member agents and the AAR code of ethics, check out the Web page at http://aar-online.org.

Be sure to include an SASE—a no. 10 envelope with postage to cover up to two ounces. The AAR will not be able to provide you with information regarding the types of manuscripts different agents consider, nor will they be able to tell you which agents handle specific authors.

Here's a list of what to consider when making your choice of agent.

- The agent is an AAR member.

- The agent charges a standard 15 percent commission for domestic sales and does not have any hidden charges and fees.
- The agent has a sufficient track record, having sold books to established publishers.
- The agent's contract protects both parties' interests and has terms for a satisfactory dissolution of the relationship if that should become necessary.
- The agent will send your manuscript out to more than one publisher at a time.
- The agent is familiar and skilled with the auction process.
- The agent agrees to stay in touch with you on a regular basis and doesn't object to your calling.
- The agent will send you copies of all rejection letters.
- The agent will involve you in all phases of negotiations with a publisher and will not accept or reject any offers without consulting you.
- The agent's client list is not so huge that you will get lost in the crowd.
- The agent is equipped to handle subsidiary rights, such as movie options, book club deals, foreign rights, and electronic rights.

What Agents Do for You

Agents serve as the initial screen, filtering out inappropriate, inept, and near-miss projects. Good agents match projects with prospective publishers, saving the editors from having to wade through worthy submissions that just aren't right for their imprints.

Agents even know which editor at a given house is most likely to give you a receptive reading. When Marshall Cook's second agent, Marian Young, represented one of his novels, she decided to send it to Charles Scribner's Sons first. Why? The protagonist was a convert to Catholicism—and so was Charles Scribner, Jr. She figured he might give it a more sympathetic reading.

That's the sort of thing that good agents know.

"Look at the list of things an agent does," advises agent Lori Perkins, "and tell me you have the time, ability, or inclination to handle it all and won't make mistakes that may set back your career in ways you can't even imagine. Or let me put it to you another way: Only a fool has himself for a client."

Your agent will do a lot more for you than simply seek publication. Among the services a good agent performs, Perkins lists:

- sending your work to the right editors
- helping you choose the right publisher and editor
- negotiating the terms of your contract
- representing film, foreign, and subsidiary rights
- making sure the publisher keeps you informed on the book's progress
- helping prepare your next project for submission
- keeping on top of financial and legal aspects of your book after publication

Sure, but Perkins is an agent. Isn't her advice self-serving? Not at all. Good agents have no problem attracting good submissions. And book editors will tell you the same thing agents do.

"Find an agent first," says publishing director Marjorie Braman. "It takes much longer to have a manuscript looked at without an agent because we're inundated."

Agented submissions are often taken more seriously because an agent's job is to screen out inappropriate material. Agents, in essence, do the first round of selections for editors.

Not all large commercial publishers have closed the doors to proposals directly from authors. "An agent isn't necessary to approach St. Martin's Press," editor Anne Savarese told us, "but you should send your manuscript to a specific editor. Your

How to Recognize a Podunk Agent

Having what Bantam Books editor Wendy McCurdy calls an "absolutely lousy, podunk agent" can really hurt a writer. McCurdy says, "A podunk agent is somebody from the hinterlands who hardly handles anybody but is just doing this as a hobby. Some just hang out a shingle; there's no licensing, and anyone can call himself an agent and suddenly start deluging editors with faded photocopies and bad manuscripts. [Publishers] get a bunch of junk from them, and it's a shame if you're a good writer, because I'm going to have a lot of [negative] assumptions about that manuscript right away."

And if you're a beginning writer, you might find you can't trust the agent's opinion of your work. Usually, having an agent take you on validates you, tells you you're good enough to approach publishers. But what if you're not really at that point? A new writer might not have enough experience to judge her own work. It can be crushing to find out that your "agent" has ulterior motives.

"You're better off on your own than to have an agent who is not reputable," McCurdy says. "Warning signs are that no one's ever heard of him or her, or he doesn't have a list of published authors." (Don't be afraid to ask for that list.)

Something else you can do if you're in doubt is call the editors the agent gives you on that list. McCurdy says she's had a few calls from writers on that subject. "One agent had put my name on his list, and a writer called to see if I had, indeed, bought anything from him. He also asked me if I thought it was O.K. that the agent was charging him five hundred dollars. I had the opportunity to say, 'No, it's not O.K.' I might have bought something from him in the past, but I don't now. However, I haven't had

continued

a call from a writer about that particular agent for awhile. I must have been taken off the reference list.

"There are some reputable agents who charge reading fees, but, in general, people don't approve of that. You have to be suspicious, especially if it's exorbitant. No one should ever have to pay five or six hundred dollars to go through this process. I know there are agents who make all their money simply on charging large fees. They never publish anybody; they just make their money off of gullible people. They go through the motions, but they're not really agents."

Writers are not the only people who are hurt by shady agents. Editors find them a real nuisance, taking up their time with substandard or unprofessional manuscripts. "There's no rhyme or reason for what they're sending me," McCurdy says. "There are certain agents that if I get a submission from them, it goes right in the trash can. I don't even respond.

"There's a lot of word of mouth, and that's a good way to find a good agent. You should have heard about him and have no doubt as to his credibility. You should find other authors who have been represented by him or thanked him in the acknowledgments of their books, that sort of thing."

manuscript will get more consideration that way." Zebra Books is another house open to agentless submissions. "But do your homework," says editor John Scognamilglio. "Know what we are looking for . . . what kinds of books we publish."

Do you want to spend your time doing that kind of homework? Lori Perkins doesn't think you should. "Writers write," she says. "If you're spending the amount of time necessary to keep up with the publishing business, then you are either working for *Publishers Weekly* or you are not as serious about writing as you should be."

Good point. Okay, you're convinced. You need an agent if you want a shot at the big publishers. But can you get one?

The Truth About Agents

"You have to have an agent to get published," the saying goes, "but you have to be published to get an agent." Most of us confront this conundrum when we try to publish our novels. Unfortunately, too many believe it and stop trying.

You—yes, undiscovered, unpublished, unknown you—really have a chance. Editors have quotas for titles to develop and new writers to discover. They essentially get paid to say yes.

How about agents? Frances Kuffel, of the Jean V. Naggar Literary Agency, told us they're open to new clients. So did George Nicholson at Sterling Lord Literistic, and Jane Chelius, who heads her own agency.

What will induce an agent to take you on as a client? Jane Chelius looks for "wonderful writers whose work I feel personally very enthusiastic about."

Have you already started your search for an agent—without any luck? Here are three possible reasons why:

1. You are mistargeting, sending your proposal to the wrong agent.

2. The agent has a full load and isn't able to take on any more clients just now. (Having said that, if a query came in that was so compelling it knocked the agent's socks off, rest assured the agent would make room for that writer.)

And that leads us to point number three.

3. Your query isn't compelling enough. It's poorly written and/or the material it proposes seems flat and unoriginal.

Write with all the skill and passion you can muster. Then you will find someone to love your book as much as you do. It can be done. Nobody was issued an agent at birth, and every novelist was first an unpublished novelist.

BLYTHE CAMENSON is a full-time writer with numerous books and articles to her credit. She is director of Fiction Writer's Connection. MARSHALL J. COOK is the author of *Freeing Your Creativity*, *How to Write with the Skill of a Master and the Genius of a Child*, and *The Year of the Buffalo*. He teaches writing, editing, and creativity at the University of Wisconsin. Camenson and Cook are the authors of *Your Novel Proposal* (Writer's Digest Books), from which this article was excerpted.

Chapter 36

To Fee or Not to Fee

By John N. Frank

Take four atheists and put them in a room with four evangelical Christians. Now ask the assembled group to discuss one question: Is there a God?

What sort of exchange do you think you'd hear?

Animated? Without a doubt. Spirited and feisty? Most certainly. Vitriolic and dogmatic? Most likely.

The same type of dramatic debate ensues when you ask agents about charging reading fees. The two sides seem light years apart. Writer's Digest asked four non-fee agents and three fee-charging agents for their opinions on fees and other related topics.

Those who don't charge fees, including the more than three hundred members of the Association of Authors' Representatives, say such practices lead to abuse and so are bad, period. Those who charge fees say they're running a business and have a right to be compensated for their time and efforts.

A Meeting of the Minds?

Some non-fee agents say they understand that not all fee-chargers are out to bilk unsuspecting authors. And some fee-chargers say they can understand how the most successful agents can afford not to charge for their initial reviews of manuscripts.

Any chance for a middle ground between these two factions? It seems unlikely.

"We're a business," says Cindy Sterling, CEO of the Lee Shore Agency in Pittsburgh. "Would you come to my house and tutor my child for free?"

Donald Maass, who runs an agency bearing his name in New York City and is treasurer of AAR, says: "The top agents do not charge fees of any kind. We have to clearly separate the legitimate agents from those agents who are mostly about collecting fees."

"The average person who wants to write a book is not talented and those are the people who get taken advantage of," says Wendy Weil of New York's Wendy Weil Agency. Agents who charge fees are "in the business to write reports," she says.

"You definitely shouldn't pay a reading fee," says Betsy Amster with Betsy Amster Literary Enterprises, Los Angeles. "Agents are supposed to make their money on commissions."

Business Is Changing

Fee-chargers consider such thinking outdated. With fewer publishers printing fewer books and new authors getting smaller and smaller advances, agents have to do more work to break through a wall of publisher indifference to new writers, sometimes even performing the sort of in-depth editing once done by publishing house editors. Professional agents are entitled to charge professional fees, they believe.

"We don't purport to be the New York agents who scoop up John Grisham," jokes Donna McLean Nixon, a principal of McLean Literary Associates, which has offices in Washington State and California. Such agents can afford to live on commissions alone, she says. But 98 percent of the authors she works with are new writers, so the economics of doing business are different for her agency, which does charge a fee.

Nixon charges a $250 evaluation fee for most manuscripts

and $100 for children's book manuscripts. In return, she promises at least a three-page evaluation of a manuscript with suggestions for improving the work. "I think that's a service-for-fee value," she says. "You get to see what you're paying for." Some clients have come to her for the attention she gives authors, saying they've tried non-fee agents only to never hear from them. She gives clients monthly reports on efforts made to sell their works and allows clients to get out of a contract with a thirty-day notice.

One agent, who didn't want her name used, charges a $150 fee to defray expenses such as postage and copying. "Most people, when you tell them what it's for, either they accept it or they won't," she says. She doesn't promise to critique or edit a manuscript. Fees are becoming more and more a part of the business as publishing changes, she says.

Sterling agrees that the economics of publishing today necessitates fees. She sees authors getting advances of $3,000 to $5,000, of which she gets 15 percent. "That just barely covers postage," she says. She charges a $125 fee for which she promises to talk with an author for at least thirty minutes and to provide a written evaluation. "Not only do we evaluate, but we want to teach," she says of her agency. She does accept no-fee manuscripts, but those get no written or oral evaluation. "In my office, I have these big crates and the no-fee [manuscripts] go into these big crates," she says. Once a month, she'll read them looking for publishable works.

Aware of the criticism of those who charge fees, Sterling responds that her eleven years in business demonstrate the legitimacy of her operation. "If I were not responding to people paying me for a service, I think you would have heard that the first year I was in business."

Richard Curtis once worked for a fee-charging agency and even charged fees himself when he opened the New York agency that bears his name. But he decided to give up the practice and now adheres to the AAR position. "If fees could be charged in a way that would guarantee that agents could not take advantage of the vulnerability of authors" he would not object. "It seems a shame that agents can't be paid like lawyers. All agents that charge reading fees are not necessarily disreputable."

The Author's Responsibility

Curtis and others on both sides of the fee chasm agree that authors should be "very, very wary and ask a lot of questions" of any potential agent before agreeing to work with that person. However, just what the agent should be willing to share generates more debate.

Many agents balk at sending a complete client list in response to a query letter from an author with whom they've never worked. But many do supply brochures that list select clients and works published. Agents' Web sites also often contain such information.

Sterling will send a brochure listing clients who endorse her work and a list of books, but she doesn't give out client names lightly. "My authors are my authors and they do not want to be called at home," she says.

Amster recommends looking at lists of published works in such places as *Guide to Literary Agents*.

Maass says authors should ask agents about what types of material they handle. He suggests checking out agents by contacting groups that specialize in a particular genre, such as mystery or fantasy. He won't send out a client list to a new author "just as a doctor wouldn't ask the public to call all their patients." But if he begins seriously pursuing an author as a client, he will put that person in touch with existing clients.

Nixon, who has about one hundred clients, doesn't send out the entire list, but "I have no problem sending anyone a list of our sold titles. In fact, they're listed on our Web site (www.mcleanlit.com)."

The issue of recommending specific book doctors to authors brought general agreement from all the agents interviewed. Sterling won't recommend specific editorial services nor would Maass, again noting that AAR prohibits kickbacks from editors to agents. "We are not supposed to nor do we want to exploit" authors, he says. Nixon does some editing in-house and has some editors with whom she's worked, but adds, "I don't know why anyone would want a kickback" from book doctors. "I would shy away from agents who recommend book doctors," she says.

New York, New York

The other perennial issue of contention regarding agents is location, location, location. Can an agent based outside New York have the same clout and contacts as one who does business in the Big Apple? It's another polarizing question.

"The business, such as is left of it, is still in New York City," says New Yorker Curtis. "It's like breathing the air every day."

Maass says: "I also like being in the middle of the business," but isn't as strident about the need for other agents to be in New York. "I don't think an agent needs to be located in New York. Excellent agents are located all over the country today."

Technology is making that possible, says Pittsburgh-dweller Sterling. She asks: "Did anybody ever hear of phones, e-mails, and faxes?" Agents have to be in New York? "It's a ludicrous statement," she says. "We know how to fly" not only to visit publishers in New York, but to attend trade shows where publishers congregate. "Personal contact is always important," she says.

New Yorker Weil still makes such contacts at daily lunches with publishing types. "If it's the New York publishers you're really interested in, it's got to be someone who comes to New York," she says. "I think it's very useful for me to be in New York.

__Agent Spotting__

Looking for an agent? Check out these resources:

• *Guide to Literary Agents* (WD Books)—Lists literary agencies and information on fees (writersdigest.com)

• LiteraryAgent.com—Dedicated to connecting writers and agents

• WritersNet (writers.net)—A searchable database of agents

• The Association of Authors' Representatives, P.O. Box 237201, Ansonia Station, New York 10023 (http://aar-online.or g). Member list available online.

There's some people [in the business] that you know your whole life."

So what's the correct answer about where your agent should be? Like the fee issue, there seems no one answer every agent will agree upon. Such is the nature of working in an artistic profession. One person may see dross where another sees gold.

The only ultimate truth is the old maxim, "Let the buyer beware." Don't be lulled by faint praise and false promises. Take a hard look at whom you want representing you, what their capabilities and accomplishments are, and when you're comfortable paying them for their services—initially with fees that may not produce any income for you or down the road with commissions when your ship comes in.

Says Nixon of the fee debate: "I don't think there's ever going to be an agreement between the two factions. The writers are just going to have to go with their gut feeling." Adds Weil from the other side of the fee trenches: "If you've got a reputable agent, probably everything they do will be reputable." That's advice both camps should be able to agree on.

JOHN N. FRANK is Midwest correspondent for *PRWeek* magazine. He's also a freelance writer working on a fictionalized account about the immigration of his grandparents to America.

Chapter 37

"Study the Market!"

By Michael Seidman

You've heard the advice again and again, read it in every how-to book you've picked up: Read the publication you want to submit to, read recent books by the publisher you've chosen to send your proposal to, and make sure that what you've written is what they publish.

The problem with that old chestnut is that too many freelancers "read blind." They'll look at the *type* of material (mystery, science fiction, general nonfiction) being published, but won't pay attention to *how* the text is presented. I'm not talking about simple matters of format; I'm referring to language, taste, and myriad other things, including a book or magazine publisher's self-image.

Open Your Eyes

In the 1980s, I was editor of *The Armchair Detective*, a quarterly devoted to criticism, review, and commentary about crime fiction. Under my predecessors, the magazine had an academic tone; wherever possible, it seemed, contributors used foot- notes. Not to put too fine a point on it, I hate footnotes. I find them intrusive. I dislike seeing that superscripted number next to a comment and then having to turn to the end of the piece to see what it's all about. So when I took over the reins, I started editing pieces in inventory so as to incorporate the footnotes into the text. I made specific mention of this change of "style" in an editorial column and in the writer's guidelines sheet.

I made other changes as well, and a casual browsing should have made them clear to anyone. More columns were added, written by professional mystery writers. And rather than being in-depth studies of the development of a character in a particular series (such as the growth of Poirot), these were freewheeling commentaries about anything that in any way related to the fiction under consideration. Review columns were sometimes presented as dialogues between the reviewer and a friend. Living American writers and the things having impact on their lives, from the Mystery Writers of America to newspaper reviews to fan reactions at a convention, were all fair game. Rather than a specialized version of the *Journal of Popular Culture* then, *The Armchair Detective* became a magazine that anyone who enjoyed a mystery novel would be able to enjoy. As the editor, I chose to make the magazine one I would enjoy editing and reading. And footnotes were only a small part of what I didn't like.

In all fairness, it should be pointed out that my choices were not always popular and, while we didn't lose many subscribers, we did receive more than a few complaints. *The Armchair Detective* was well-enough established by that time that certain things were expected, and my kind of rabble-rousing was not among them. At any rate, articles continued arriving festooned with footnotes. After a year, I began rejecting anything that crossed my desk in that format. I also chose fewer submissions that I considered academic or pretentious. I still attempted to maintain a balance: I couldn't ignore the people who had helped build the magazine, but I did want other folks, the people like me, to feel welcome. If the writers had paid attention to what was being published, they would have not only understood what I was looking for, but submitted what I considered publishable.

An easily recognized difference between two similar magazines can be discovered by looking at issues of *National Geographic* and *Scientific American*. Both publications might cover the same story, but the voice in the former is much more informal. Most of its articles are first-person narratives, almost casual in nature. This doesn't mean that the information isn't there; it means that the approach feels like sitting down and having a drink with the authors while they regale you with tales of their discovery. In *Scientific American*, however, the articles are more scholarly in nature. For me, reading that magazine is like sitting in a lecture hall—after having missed the first half of the lecture.

The decisions made at these magazines are a result of the editors' understanding of their markets and needs. As a writer, you have to come to the same kind of understanding. Who are you writing for, and what does that person need? The answer to this question takes priority over what you perceive as *your* needs as a writer. If a publication does not address the audience you've chosen or if you're unable to write for its audience, it is the wrong publication for you. Expecting an editor to become so enamored of your prose's brilliance that he will forgo his own vision of his publication is authorial madness.

Differences Within Genres

I began with a discussion of nonfiction because, frankly, it's a whole heck of a lot easier to discuss—the issues are more obvious. When it comes to fiction, the nuances you must look for are no less important, but they may very well be a whole lot more diffuse.

First, you must realize that, within any category, each editor brings particular literary beliefs to the job. As a writer, though, how do you go about noticing such differences?

You do it by bringing a critical eye to your reading. What was going on in the last horror novel you read? Was it splatter-punk? Was a child at the heart of the story, either as the source of evil or the answer to it (or both)? Was the same theme driving other novels you read by the same publisher? Does that give you a hint?

Crime fiction brings the same issues to your decision-making process. Is every book from a particular publisher a hard-boiled P.I. story? A cozy? Is an editor doing mystery (in the sense that there's a puzzle built into the plot) as well as suspense? What about the levels of violence, gratuitous or otherwise? Do the criminals say *oh heck*, or do they use the kind of language criminals are like to use?

Questions about language, violence, and other aspects of the work being published by your target market have to be an-swered, by you, before your manuscript is put in the mail. The thing to remember, always, is that just because you're writing in a category doesn't mean that every publisher in that genre is, by definition, interested in *your* work.

Wait, It Gets Murkier . . .

The lines aren't always even *that* clear if one is interested in so-called "mainstream" or "literary" fiction. Especially when we consider book publishing. The first problem is defining those cate-gories—something, fortunately for my sanity, beyond the pur-view of this essay. If a publisher's list indicates strong support for some currently popular fiction mode—magic realism, post-modernism, deconstruction—and you're writing something that uses Cheever or Updike as a model, you're probably spinning your wheels if you submit there. (We're also assuming that you understand terms like *magic realism*. I don't. And I don't even

care to. Obviously, you wouldn't submit magic realism manuscripts to me.)

The same problems apply to magazines that publish fiction.
Reading magazines regularly is an urgent part of your job.
And read with an understanding of the business: When Kristine
Kathryn Rusch took over from Ed Ferman as editor of *The
Magazine of Fantasy and Science Fiction*, readers began talking
about the differences they claimed to discover in the first issue under
Rusch's guidance. The fact that was missed all too often was that
the stories in that first issue (and several after that) had actually
been acquired by Ferman. The lesson is simple. Never take anything for granted.

In the magazine market, the differences between literary fiction styles are a bit more clear-cut than they are in book
publishing. The stories in *The New Yorker* are not the same as
those in *Tri-Quarterly*. Some magazines encourage various
forms of experimentation in fiction; others define literary quality
as any story that doesn't have a point—vignettes taken from
life. (Yes, there's a certain cynicism on my part being revealed
here. But a perceptive writer will make himself aware of that
kind of feeling on the part of an editor; it helps determine what
he'll buy!) Again and again, read the publisher's products
looking for an understanding of what is driving the selections,
digging for the philosophies that guide the editorial staff.

Some specifics: Is the language rich and lush, or is it plain?
Does the editor show a preference for complex constructions
as opposed to simple declarative sentences?

While considerations like those may seem beside the point—
after all, you've written a wonderful piece and isn't that all
that counts?—the reality is that editorial taste goes far beyond
simply choosing a story that fulfills a particuilar guideline. It
is a function of the editor's "literary" beliefs and understanding
of what makes a good piece of writing, be it fiction or nonfiction. There is no way to argue with those feelings; all you can

do is try to figure them out and, most vitally, appeal to them.

Once you begin to do that, you'll have come to learn what the editor is *really* looking for: a manuscript that fulfills *all* the expectations we have when we open your envelope.

MICHAEL SEIDMAN is an editorial consultant, serving publishers and individual writers. He is the author of four books for writers, most recently *The Complete Guide to Editing Your Fiction* (Writer's Digest Books) and *Fiction: The Art and Craft of Writing and Getting Published* (Pomegranate Press). He can be contacted at mseidman@aol.com.

Chapter 38

Commanding Book Proposals: The Rejection Slip's Greatest Enemy

By Don Prues

Many writers attempting to find an agent to represent their books perceive themselves to be a diminutive David staring down a monstrous Goliath. Even worse, they think no weapon exists to slay the giant and prove their book is worth publishing. Such folks are wrong. An effective weapon does exist: It's called a book proposal. The hitch, however, is that writers must build this weapon themselves.

And therein lies the problem: Most writers don't know which materials to use nor how to put the pieces together to stand a fighting chance. That's where this chapter comes in. We'll show you what you need to include in your proposal and how to assemble it, ultimately equipping you with the necessary weaponry to conquer even the most colossal rejection pile.

Before we get into the specifics about composing and organizing your proposal, we need to get one fact out of the way: The proposal you create depends upon what the agent wants. And the most nonintrusive way to know what she wants is to follow the submission specifications to a tee. Do nothing more, nothing less. Remember, you must play by each agent's rules if you want that agent to represent you.

The Novel Proposal

The golden rule in publishing fiction is your novel must be completed before you solicit an agent. Will you be permitted to send your entire novel upon initial contact? Probably not. Unsolicited manuscripts are ignored, returned, and sometimes even thrown away when sent to an agent who does not accept them. That's the catch with fiction: You need to have your novel finished before soliciting an agent, but rarely are you allowed to send the complete manuscript. Don't waste your time, energy, paper, and postage sending material to an agent who doesn't care about it.

Many agents prefer to receive a one-page query letter first, and only ask for the proposal or the manuscript after having their interest piqued by the query letter. Check the agents' guidelines to see what they accept—rarely will it be a complete manuscript, but often it will be a novel proposal.

Novel proposals are easy to put together. You can anticipate sending a cover letter, a synopsis, three consecutive sample chapters (almost always your first three chapters) or the first fifty pages, possibly an author biography, and an endorsements page. These are by far the most important—and most requested—parts of your proposal. Some agents require only a cover letter and three sample chapters because, with fiction, the writing itself (your sample chapters) matters most. Again, what you send is determined by what the agent demands.

The Components
Cover Letters

The type of cover letter you compose depends on whether you're sending a blind ("unsolicited") proposal or a requested ("solicited") proposal.

If the agent accepts or even prefers a blind proposal upon initial contact (instead of a query letter), you'll need to tailor a sharp cover letter to hook the agent and encourage her to dive eagerly into the rest of your proposal. A cover letter accompanying a blind proposal submission is like a tightened version of a query letter. Similar to the query letter, your cover letter lets the agent know who you are *and* what you have to offer. You don't need to spend much time arguing that your proposal is worthwhile because what you have to offer (the proposal) is actually enclosed.

If you've already sent the agent a query letter and she has requested a full proposal, keep the cover letter short—just a paragraph or two will do. Simply let the agent know what material you've enclosed, and mention whether any other agents are considering the same proposal.

Cover/Title Page

Although the title is but a small part of a large book, a telling and catchy title can be so important. The difference between an adequate title and a superb title can mean the difference between mediocre book sales and gargantuan ones. Think about some of the successful titles you know—most are under five words (excluding the subtitle) and emit something unique about the book.

For fiction proposals, the cover page, or "title page," follows your cover letter. When formatting the cover page, be sure to put the book's title in all caps about a third of the way down the page. Include your contact information (name, address, phone number, fax, e-mail) with the date in the bottom right corner. Put the word count in the top right corner.

Table of Contents

Your contents page lets the agent know precisely what's in your proposal package, and lends order and organization to all the disparate proposal elements. Be sure to list every item you're sending and the corresponding page numbers in the order they appear in your proposal. You obviously need to make your contents page neat and easy on the eyes. It should be double spaced and organized according to its sections. The contents pages should *not* be numbered.

The Synopsis

A synopsis is a brief, general overview of your novel, sometimes referred to as a "short summary." The goal of your synopsis is to tell what your novel is about without making the agent read the novel in its entirety. You need to supply key information about the primary elements in your novel (plot, theme, characters, setting), then show how all these aspects work together to make your novel worthy of publication. The trick with the synopsis, however, is doing all of the above quickly.

How quickly? Well, that depends on the person you're soliciting. There are no hard-and-fast rules about the synopsis. Some agents look at it as a one-page sales pitch, while others expect it to be a comprehensive summary of the entire novel. Not surprisingly, there's conflicting advice about the typical length of a synopsis. Over the years, I've contacted numerous agents to get their take on just how long it should be, and nearly all agents prefer a short synopsis that runs from one to two single-spaced pages, or three to five double-spaced pages. Because every novel is different—with its own number of important characters, plot twists, subplots, and so on—there is obviously some disagreement among agents about the specific length of a typical synopsis. Nevertheless, every agent agrees there's one truism about a synopsis: "The shorter, the better." That's why one to five pages is generally the preferred length for a novel synopsis.

That said, some plot-heavy fiction, such as thrillers and mysteries, might need more space, and can run from ten to twenty-five double-spaced pages, depending on the length of the manuscript and the number of plot shifts. If you do opt to compose a longer synopsis, aim for a length of one synopsis page for every twenty-five manuscript pages (a 250-page manuscript should get a ten-page synopsis), but attempt to keep it as short as possible.

A few other important aspects of your synopsis:

- Write in third person (even if your novel is written in first person).
- Write in present tense (even if your novel is written in past tense).
- Only focus on the essential parts of your story, and try not to include sections of dialogue unless you think they are absolutely necessary.
- Make your story seem complete. Keep events in the same order as they occur in the novel (but don't break them down into individual chapters), and be sure your synopsis has a beginning, a middle, and an ending. And yes, you *must* tell how the novel ends.

Chapter-by-Chapter Outline

An outline describes each chapter as its own entity; the descriptions range from a few paragraphs to two pages per chapter. In short, you're expanding and specifying what you've generally written in the synopsis.

Few agents want chapter-by-chapter outlines with fiction (most just request a cover letter, a short synopsis, and a few sample chapters). Therefore, you should never submit an outline for your novel proposal unless an agent specifically asks for it. Chapter-by-chapter outlines will be requested occasionally with genre fiction, which often has numerous plot shifts. When possible, limit the novel outline to one paragraph per chapter.

Author Biography

If you think aspects of your life are important and relevant to the salability of your book, then include an author biography. The goal of your author bio is to sell yourself in ways that com-

The components of a novel proposal:

- Cover letter
- Cover/title page
- Contents page
- Synopsis
- Chapter-by-chapter outline (rarely requested)
- Author biography
- First three sample chapters (or about fifty pages)
- Endorsements (if possible)

plement the proposal. Don't include information that doesn't directly help the pitch. Do tell about your profession, particularly if it's pertinent to your book, and always highlight noteworthy publishing credits if you have any. Try to keep the author bio to one page.

Endorsements Page

An endorsements page is not essential, but having one can improve the salability of your manuscript. Your endorsements must come from noteworthy people, typically prominent industry insiders (well-known authors, agents, experts on the topic) who've read your manuscript and commented favorably on it. Unless you have contacts, though, it is difficult to obtain a quote from someone noteworthy. But don't fret if your proposal doesn't have an endorsements page—few authors include one.

A Reply Postcard

If you're a bit paranoid about whether or not your material actually makes it to the agent or publisher, you may send a reply postcard with your proposal package. Having it signed by the agent or someone on the staff and sent back to you will alleviate any worries that the package didn't make it to its destination. Two caveats: (1) Not all agents are gracious enough to send your reply postcards back, but most do. (2) Just because you receive a postcard reply, you cannot assume your proposal has been read or will be read in the next few weeks. Your reply postcard's only function is to let you know your package has been received.

Now you have all you need to know to craft a powerful proposal. Just be smart, target the right agent, honestly acknowledge the commercial viability of your proposal, and *send the agent what the agent wants to receive.* Sound doable? Good. Go do it—Goliath is waiting.

DON PRUES, former editor of *Guide to Literary Agents*, now freelance writes and edits from home. With Jack Neff, he co-authored *Formatting and Submitting Your Manuscript* and with Jack Heffron, he co-authored *The Writer's Guide to Places* (both Writer's Digest Books).

Chapter 39

Producing a Knockout Novel Synopsis

By Evan Marshall

Your novel is finished and ready to be mailed to an agent or editor. You shoot off a query letter. The agent or editor asks to see your manuscript, *or* she asks to see a proposal: three chapters and a synopsis, or one chapter and a synopsis, or just a synopsis.

A *what*? A synopsis—a brief narrative summary of your novel. It's a vital marketing tool for a novelist, because it often has to do the entire job of enticing an agent or editor enough to want to read your novel. Think of the synopsis as a sales pitch for your book.

A synopsis has other uses, too. Later, when you sell your novel, your editor may ask you for a synopsis to be used as the basis for jacket or cover copy for your book. Other departments in the publishing house, such as art or sales or publicity, may want to read your synopsis to get a quick idea of your story.

Even later, when it's time to sell your next novel, you may be able to secure a contract solely on the basis of a synopsis and a few chapters, or just a synopsis. As you can see, the synopsis performs a number of important functions. It therefore deserves as careful attention as you've given the novel itself.

Synopsis Mechanics

The synopsis is formatted much like your manuscript. Use courier type; double-space all text; set your left, right, and bottom margins at 1¼″ (3.2cm), your top margin at ½″ (1.3cm). Justify the left margin only.

On every page except the first, type against the top and left margins a slugline consisting of your last name, a slash, your novel's title in capital letters, another slash, and the word *Synopsis*, like this: Price/UNDERSUSPICION/Synopsis. Number the pages consecutively in the upper right-hand corner of the page, against the top and right margins. The first line of text on each page should be about ¾″ (1.9cm) below the slugline and page number.

On the first page of your synopsis, against the top and left margins, type single-spaced your name, address, and telephone number. Against the top and right margins, type single-spaced your novel's genre, its word count, and the word *Synopsis*. (The first page of the synopsis is not numbered, though it is page one.)

Double-space twice, center your novel's title in capital letters, double-space twice again, and begin the text of your synopsis.

Synopsis Basics

Before we get to the subtleties of writing the synopsis, be aware of a few basic rules.

1. The synopsis is always written in the present tense (called the historical present tense).

2. The synopsis tells your novel's *entire* story. It doesn't leave out what's covered by the sample chapters submitted with it. Nor does it withhold the end of the story—for example, "who done it" in a murder mystery—in order to entice an agent or editor to want to see more. The synopsis is a miniature representation of your novel; to leave anything out is to defeat the purpose of the synopsis.

3. The synopsis should not run too long. An overlong synopsis also defeats in purpose. My rule is to aim for one page of synopsis for every twenty-five pages of manuscript. Thus, a four hundred-page manuscript calls for a sixteen-page synopsis. If you run a page or two over or under, don't worry.

4. To achieve this conciseness, write as clean and tight as you can. Cut extra adverbs and adjectives. Focus on your story's essential details. Let's say, for example, you have a section in which your lead meets another character for dinner at a chic French bistro to try to convince her to lend him some money. We don't need to know where they had dinner or what they ate or even exactly what was said. We need something on the order of "Ray meets Lenore for dinner and tries to convince her to lend him the money. Lenore refuses." Actual dialogue is rarely, if ever, needed in the synopsis.

5. Don't divide your synopsis by chapters; write one unified account of your story. You can use paragraphing to indicate a chapter or section break.

How to Make Your Synopsis Sizzle

Now, keeping all of the above in mind, translate your manuscript into synopsis. Begin with your lead and her crisis as the hook of your synopsis. Then tell how your lead intends to solve the crisis (what is her story goal?). For example:

> BARBARA DANFORTH has never been especially fond of her brother-in-law, GRAHAM, but she would never have murdered him. Yet all the clues point to her as Graham's killer. She'll have to prove her innocence if she doesn't want to end up as dead as Graham.

PATRICK WARMAN, founder and director of Philadelphia's Friendship Street Shelter for runaway children, has always been careful to maintain a professional distance from the young people he helps. That's why he is especially horrified to realize he has fallen in love with PEARL, a teenage girl in his care. If he can't come to terms with these forbidden feelings, he'll lose everything he's worked for. Yet he can't bear to lose sixteen-year-old Pearl.

RITA RAYMOND is delighted when an employment agency sends her to work as a companion to a man recovering from an accident. She would never have accepted the job if she had known the man was her ex-husband, AARON. And damn if she isn't falling in love with him again. Yet Aaron was the cause of everything wrong in her life.

Soon after your problem hook, give the vital details about your lead: age, occupation, marital status (if you haven't already), as well as details of time (the present? the past?) and place.

Barbara, single at thirty-eight, has lived quietly in Rosemont, Texas, working as a stenographer and generally minding her own business. When her sister TRISH invited her to a party to celebrate the tenth anniversary of Trish's marriage to Graham, Barbara balked. She'd never liked Graham. But she accepted—her first mistake. Agreeing to let Graham take her for a moonlit walk around the couple's lavish estate was her second. . . .

Patrick, twenty-eight, has been married to MARI-

ANNE for nine years, but although she helps at the shelter, their marriage is in name only. . . .

At twenty-nine, Rita has made peace with her life as a divorcée. She earns enough money as a high-school teacher to support herself and her seven-year-old daughter, ALLEGRA, though Allegra's severe asthma has been an emotional and financial strain. Even so, life these past five years without Aaron has been better than life was *with* him. . . .

Now continue telling your story, keeping to the main story points. Remember that the synopsis is not necessarily meant to convey the circumstances of *how* something happens; the happenings themselves are the concern here.

Most important, remember that *motivation and emotion are things that happen*; they are plot points, as important as any physical action a character might perform. Some of the worst synopses I've seen from would-be clients are dry and lifeless because these aspects have been left out.

Don't just tell us that Brandon tells Carla he's accepted the job in Sydney and that the next morning Carla has coffee at her friend Tanya's house and tells her the news. Tell us that when Brandon tells Carla he's accepted the job in Sydney, Carla sees her happy life collapsing around her. Devastated, the next morning over coffee she pours her heart out to Tanya.

Don't just tell us that Jake Hammond stomps into the bank and dumps a sack of money on the president's desk, announcing he's repaying his loan. Tell us that Jake, full of angry self-righteousness at how the bank has treated his sister, stomps into the bank and dumps the money on the president's desk.

The agents and editors who will read and evaluate your synopsis are looking for the same things as your eventual readers:

emotion and human drama. Bear down on these life-breathing aspects of your story and you can't go wrong.

Indicate other characters' story lines in your synopsis by beginning a new paragraph and describing the character's actions. Sometimes transitions such as "Meanwhile" or "Simultaneously" or "At the hotel" can help ground the reader in time and place.

As you write the synopsis, think of it as your novel in condensed form, and present events in the same order that they occur in the novel itself. Also, reveal information at the same points you do so in your novel.

Stay "invisible" in your synopsis; by this I mean several things. First, don't use devices that emphasize the mechanics of storytelling. One of these is the use of such headings as "Background," "Setting," and "Time" at the beginning of your synopsis. All of these elements should be smoothly woven into the narrative. Another such device is the use of character sketches or descriptions at the beginning or end of the synopsis. All of these elements should be smoothly woven into the narrative. Second, they make it difficult for the agent or editor to follow your story: If he reads the synopsis first, it's meaningless because he has no information about the characters. If he reads the character sketches first, they are equally meaningless because the characters are not presented in the context of the story. Characters and story do not exist independently of each other. Give any important facts or background when you introduce a character.

In the text, type a character's name in capital letters the first time you use it—a technique borrowed from film treatments. Also, to avoid confusion, always refer to a character the same way through the synopsis (not "Dr. Martin" in one place, "the doctor" somewhere else, and "Martin" somewhere else).

Another way to stay invisible is to avoid referring to the structural underpinnings of your story. When I was a kid, we used

---

Keys to a Knockout Synopsis

- A well-written synopsis is a vital marketing tool for your novel, both before and after it's sold.
- Follow correct manuscript format.
- Write the synopsis in the present tense.
- Tell the entire story, with events in the same order as in the novel.
- Aim for a length of one synopsis page for every twenty-five manuscript pages.
- Focus on story essentials.
- Start with a problem-and-story-goal hook.
- Include characters' motivations and emotions.
- Don't let story mechanics show.

---

to go to an amusement park with a scary jungle ride that went through a dark tunnel where a native jumped out and scared us silly. One day as we floated through the tunnel and the native jumped out, I noticed that the figure of the native had come loose from its metal support. I could see ugly gray metal and a tangle of electrical wires. The ride was never the same after that.

That's how I feel when I can see the scaffolding of a synopsis, for example, "In a flashback, Myron. . . ." Better to simply say "Myron remembers. . . ." Don't write "At the darkest moment of her Point of Hopelessness . . ."; just tell what happens. Avoid "As the story begins . . ." or "As the story ends . . ."; just tell the story.

As you near the end of the synopsis and your story's resolution, quicken the pace by using shorter paragraphs and shorter sentences. A staccato effect increases the suspense.

Above all, never review your story in your synopsis, such as "In a nerve-jangling confrontation . . ." or "In a heart-wrenching confession. . . ." This kind of self-praise is amateurish and inappropriate in a synopsis, which presents "just the (story) facts, ma'am." Let your story's attributes speak for themselves.

Once your synopsis is finished, polish, polish, polish! In many cases, your synopsis will be your foot in the door, and many agents and editors will judge your storytelling and writing style from this selling piece alone. When I receive a synopsis containing misspellings, poor grammar, and sloppy presentation, I do not ask to see the manuscript. I assume it will contain the same kinds of errors.

Writing the synopsis is an art you should become proficient in. A masterful synopsis starts telling your novel to an agent or editor before she even looks at your manuscript. In fact, a few times during my career, I have read a synopsis so well-crafted that later I felt I had read the book! That's real magic.

EVAN MARSHALL is the president of The Evan Marshall Agency, a leading literary agency that specializes in representing fiction writers. He is the author of the Writer's Digest titles *The Marshall Plan for Novel Writing*, from which this article was adapted, and *The Marshall Plan Workbook*. He is also the author of a mystery series that features literary agent Jane Stuart and her cat Winky. The latest book is *Stabbing Stephanie*.

Chapter 40

Marketing Your Novel: The Ten Commandments

By E.L. Wyrick

I keep them taped on the wall behind my computer—a page of notes to myself. It's a habit I began as a student teacher twenty years ago: Write down everything you learn and keep staring at the adages until they're hammered in your brain.

The page behind my computer contains ten main admonishments with a lot of scribbling beneath each one. My own Ten Commandments for getting published.

I'm constantly amazed at how many new writers—would-be published writers—don't know the commandments. They can be found in many references over and over again. But they tend to be presented singly or in pairs. That's how I found them. So let me put them all in one place.

I. Thou Shalt Write

This is an easy one. Everybody knows that you can't get published until you write something, for goodness sake.

So, if it's so obvious, why do I keep encountering new writers who have such a hard time with it? The principles of behavioral contingency management provide the answer.

To ensure that a behavior continues, it should be rewarded. Punishment stops behavior. New writers are seldom rewarded (that is, published) and are often punished (by rejection letters). No wonder they don't want to find the time to write.

But it's a fact that even slugs can be trained to behave in certain ways. So can writers. With slugs, scientists use electric shock. For you and me, it takes some cognitive restructuring—although a red-hot poker would probably be useful at times.

The first step is to determine a goal and make a commitment. Imagine a long-distance runner who thinks, " I'm going to run twenty miles . . . unless I get tired. Then I'll quit." He'll never get there. Never. The writer must say, "I'm going to finish this by July" or "I'll write five pages a day, no matter what," and then do it. Hey, a page a day—a single page a day— makes a novel in a year.

Treat your writing as a second job, not a hobby. Imagine telling your boss, "Yo, I'm just too tired to work today. Think I'll watch the soaps instead." When you write, you're your own boss.

Accept the fact that you must give up leisure time. I haven't gone to a movie since the first *Batman*. But my second novel is now on the shelves. You must decide what you want.

And after you've sent a story off, get back to work.

II. Thou Shalt Learn to Write Well

On June 4, 1989, I wrote my first line of fiction. As a former English teacher who'd written many academic pieces, I assumed I could already write well.

Donna Wenzel lived across the street. She edited scientific magazines and volunteered to look at some chapters.

Poor Donna, I thought, when she returned them. Surely she'd cut herself badly and bled on my papers. You've guessed, of course, that the red covering those pages was ink, not blood. This former English teacher learned that he had much to learn about writing standard English.

But isn't that what editors are for? No. Big time *no*.

C. Michael Curtis, fiction editor of *The Atlantic Monthly*, looks at 12,000 short story submissions each year. According to him, roughly 90 percent of the stories can be rejected quickly because of grammatical errors in the first sentence or paragraph, poor technical execution, and stories that are far too long or way too short. When you simply write well, the competition goes from 12,000 to 1,200. Still long odds, but much better.

Most new writers are obsessed with plot. While the story line is important, it's the easiest part. Major plot flaws can often be fixed with a few well-placed sentences. You must focus on making your manuscripts technically perfect. Don't expect an editor to love your plot and "fix" your writing. It won't happen.

The only way to learn to write well is through sweat equity. Read and reread handbooks on standard English usage, so that the conventions are fixed in your mind. (William Strunk and E.B. White's *The Elements of Style* remains at the top of the stack.) Attend community classes on writing. Find a good proofreader.

Be certain that your writing is easy to follow. For example, be sure that all pronouns have a clear antecedent. Also, when characters haven't been seen for awhile, provide a short clue to remind the reader who they are.

Do not provide exposition in big chunks. Drop it in throughout the action.

Pay attention to the physical structure of your story. For popular novels, use short chapters with hooks at the end of each one. People who read for pleasure often do so late at night. As their eyes droop, they look ahead to see how much longer until the end of the chapter. Ah, two pages, they think, and read on. Then you hook 'em at the end of the chapter and they have to keep reading. Agents and editors to whom you're submitting read the same way, only they're on the subway as they peruse the slush pile. This is just one example of the things you must think about when learning to write well.

Do not be seduced by the praise that comes from family, friends, and your writers' group. Enjoy the plaudits you'll surely receive, but ask specifically for what they don't like. That's what you need to know.

III. Thou Shalt Learn About the Publishing Business

My experience suggests that most writers aren't terribly interested in being business people. (Quick quiz: Do you read *Publishers Weekly*? Uh-huh.) But to become published, it's important to realize publishing is a business. Then you must find some way to demonstrate your understanding of this to agents and editors.

For example, my first novel was a mystery. After reading books and trade magazines, it was clear that mystery publishers want to see a series. That's how they make money on mysteries, and making money is why they're in business. In my query, I wrote that my goal was to write a series and, to prove it, I included three chapters of the next Tammi Randall mystery with the manuscript of the first.

It's an axiom that to make money, you must spend money. That's true with writing, too. I've got a credit card devoted to my writing business. The payment sometimes exceeds twenty dollars, but every submitted manuscript is fresh, and my shelves are filled with magazines and books about writing and the business of writing.

It's an investment that has paid off.

IV. Thou Shalt Not Write Nor Submit Based on N-of-One Stories

In the social sciences, an *n-of-one* study occurs when the investigator closely observes a single person, group, or incident, and then attempts to extrapolate truths that can be applied to all of us. Works fine for them. Seldom works for writers. Yet, I often meet writers who try to build a career on the principle of the *n-of-one*.

A woman had a sublimely written short story. She was complaining because a very well-known literary magazine had turned it down. "Ten thousand words is a little long," I suggested. "The journal's guidelines have that as an outer limit."

"But," she replied, " I saw one that long in it once. I counted every word."

I'd bet the farm the story she saw was written by a well-known author. But even if it was written by a newcomer, it doesn't matter. I'm not a gambler. I like the odds of writing stories that fall somewhere near the midpoint of a magazine's word count. Maybe even on the short side, since an editor can buy more short than long pieces. Same with query letters. Even if you hear of a writer who wrote one that took up three pages and received a positive response, don't write one like it. Keep your query to the universally preferred one page.

The bottom line is that when you read over and over what to do and not to do, follow the advice, no matter the rare exceptions that you hear about.

V. Thou Shalt Learn to Revise Happily

After writing three chapters of my first novel, I started reading everything I could find on how to sell it. The consistent advice was to revise, revise, revise—examine and reexamine each paragraph, each line, each word of your book carefully before sending it off. Early on, that task seemed impossible to me.

It's not. It's what you must do.

Once again, it's time to do some cognitive restructuring. I've heard new writers complain time and again about how they enjoy the creative aspect of writing, not the polishing. Rethink that.

After the first draft is completed, the writer's creativity can truly be released. You're free of the burden and stress that comes from making up a plot and getting the story out; you can look deeply into each character. Dialogue can be sharpened to nudge it from being merely adequate to being ear-on splendid. The story can be restructured with a solidity that can only take form once it's on the pages.

Even if you love a scene that you've written, trash it willingly if it doesn't advance the story. After you let the manuscript rest, those scenes will jump out at you. Excise and save them for another story.

Fight the impulse to send your work out quickly. After you write the first draft, set it aside for a day, a week. After the second draft, store it again. And so on.

VI. Thou Shalt Seek Agents and Editors Knowledgeably

Shortly after beginning my first novel, a friend told me he'd heard that a lot of books are sold on the basis of the first three chapters. Wow! I stopped writing the book and wrote a query letter. I'd read enough to know to keep it to one page. Cleverly, I did that by using tiny print and quarter-inch margins all around. The content of that letter is too embarrassing to mention here. I mailed that letter to agents and editors by starting at the beginning of the alphabet in the guides.

Don't do it that way. It doesn't work.

First, complete your book and make it as good as you can. On rare occasions, unknown writers sell on the basis of partials. People win the lottery, too, but the odds are way long.

Do not submit a query to "Dear Trade Editor" or "Dear Agent." Find the names of specific agents or editors who handle writing like yours. *Guide to Literary Agents* and similar directories are good places to start, but there's more work to be done. Look at the acknowledgments pages of books like yours to see if an agent or editor is mentioned. Publishers' catalogs often list who's handling the foreign and film rights for the books they publish. Usually, that's the author's agent. Or, call the publishing house's publicity office and ask which agent and editor handled the book. In short, be a detective.

Work as hard on the query letter as you do on your manuscript. The query is your one shot to be noticed. Make it perfect. Be businesslike and avoid cuteness. Use a professional letterhead that includes your name, address, daytime phone number, and, perhaps, your e-mail address. That's enough. Personalize the letter by including a line regarding books the agent or editor has handled. Include only information that is relevant to your book. Be able to categorize your book without equivocation. (Don't write, "This is a mystery that is more than a mystery. It's also a romance with a touch of science fiction.") Read everything you can on how to write a query letter and follow the advice.

If the listings say to query first, do so. Don't send a manuscript unless that's the stated preference.

When writing a synopsis or outline, include the ending. I am amazed by the number of new authors who don't want to do that. Two reasons agents and editors request a synopsis/outline is to see if the story is complete and if it works. They can't do either without an ending.

Always include a self-addressed stamped envelope (SASE).

With agents, be a careful consumer. While the vast majority of them are honest, the fact is that anybody can claim to be an agent. And unfortunately, there are some who troll the waters for suckerfish. Before spending any money, ask for specific names of recent books that the agent has handled. Ask for referrals. Run from an agent who refuses to provide such information.

VII. Thou Shalt Learn to Use Rejection

Rejection is negative reinforcement, a punisher, and punishment is used to stop behavior. Realize that and overcome the natural tendency.

Transform rejection into a motivator. Tell yourself, *Oh yeah? Well, I'll show you.* That can be effective if you go back to work instead of sitting around whining.

Take what little information the rejection offers and use it. If you're receiving nothing but poorly copied rejection letters of various sizes, that's a big-time clue to look at your technical writing skills. Agents and editors encourage good writers, even if they aren't enamored with a particular story.

When an agent or editor takes the time to make some comments regarding your story, don't reject them out of hand. Even a seemingly off-base remark can lead to further thought that can make a story better. And write them a short thank-you note.

Having a sense of humor is good. I once submitted manuscripts to two agents simultaneously (with permission). The rejection letters arrived on the same day. One had written, "The emotional content is too abstract—it didn't get right down to appealing to my feelings." The other said, "There's a lot of strong feelings, but. . . ." I held them up and laughed. What else was there to do?

VIII. Thou Shalt Not Irritate Agents Nor Editors

The agent finished a conference presentation and was finally able to extricate herself from the crowd of authors who wanted to talk to her. The guy had waited anxiously until she was alone. He approached, shoved a manuscript into her hand, and said, "Read this. You'll love it." The agent, being a nice person, didn't hit him over the head with the manuscript, but her eyes shot daggers as he walked away. The manuscript became a part of the conference site's landfill. Who wants to work with a jerk?

Agents and editors work long and hard hours. While searching for new material, they must follow contracted projects through the process of becoming published; they must make contacts and maintain relationships. They don't need phone calls from unknown authors asking, "Has my manuscript arrived yet?" If the promised response time has passed, write and enclose another SASE.

In short, be considerate. If your writing is rotten, that won't matter. If it's good, your tact might put you ahead of an equally gifted writer who's a jerk.

IX. Thou Shalt Learn How to Wait

The publishing business operates far slower than the average human being expects. If you don't realize this going in, you're in store for a lot of frustration.

I finished the first draft of *A Strange and Bitter Crop* in May 1991. Editor Ruth Cavin asked to see the entire manuscript in December 1992. It was published in July 1994. I submitted *Power in the Blood* in May 1994. It wasn't published until April 1996. That's the way it works.

Don't sit on the porch brooding and looking for the mailman. Once you've submitted, get back to work. If your primary goal is to have been published, find some other way to spend your time other than writing. You will be miserable if you don't enjoy writing and learning the craft of writing for its own sake.

X. Thou Shalt Restrain Yourself Until the Published Work Is in Hand

I opened the letter from an agent that said, "We will be happy to represent you." The whole neighborhood heard my joyful shout. "I've got an agent," I screamed.

Six months later, I learned it was a scam.

Writing is hard. Waiting is hard. Rejection is hard. But there's nothing harder and more demoralizing than dashed high expectations.

As hard as it may be, keep an even keel until the check and the author's copies of your published work arrive.

That's when you jump for joy and pop the champagne. Because *that's* when you'll be published.

E.L. WYRICK is the author of *A Strange and Bitter Crop* and *Power in the Blood.*

Chapter 41

Understanding the Digital Revolution in Five Easy Steps

By Richard Curtis and William Thomas Quick

One: The Digital Revolution in a Nutshell

In its purest sense, electronic publishing is in full swing today. Every time you visit a Web site to read an author's chatty newsletter or download a short story or even a book, you are taking advantage of electronic publication. Every time you put your own work on a Web site or allow it to be downloaded by somebody else, you are acting as an electronic publisher. Every time you put a CD or DVD game, book, video, or music disk into your computer, you are consuming an electronically published product. Every time you burn a CD-ROM, you are "publishing" electronically.

The essence of electronic publishing is *the presentation of content in digital form*. It doesn't matter what that content is; sound, video, pictures, or writing can all be reduced to bits and bytes and then packaged, published, transmitted, viewed, and passed on to the millions of machines (and not just personal computers) able to interpret those bits and bytes.

Writers must understand this definition of electronic publishing because it is so far-reaching and it affects everything about their literary creations, including distribution, marketing, sales, and even the most basic concepts of intellectual property itself.

Two: Revolutionary Formats

Until the advent of digital electronic formats, the presentation of intellectual property—a legal term for an artist's creative work—was either entirely ephemeral (the songs heard round the campfire) or based on some real-world medium like print-on-paper, disks, or tapes (or papyrus scrolls, chiseled stones, or illuminated sheepskins). In order to permanently transfer the content, it was necessary to transfer some physical item—a book, a record, a videotape. This model, which has held sway for most of human history, had both advantages and disadvantages for the author. It allowed for a high degree of security. That is, one had to purchase a physical book in order to read it (or at least borrow it from a friend or library that had purchased it). However, in order to widely distribute books, the author had to give away most of his potential profit to huge companies who had the capability to make, distribute, and sell the book.

The ability to digitize intellectual content has destroyed that model. The reason is simple: Digital formats have entirely erased the notion of scarcity. Here's how that works.

Three: Scarcity—What It Means and Why It's Important

Until recently, in order to distribute a book widely, the book had to be printed. No matter how large the print run was, there was still a finite number of physical books created. If you wanted a copy, you had to buy one or borrow it from somebody else. Nor was it easy, if you wanted a second copy of the book, to make one yourself. Oh, you could tear the book apart and stick each page into a photocopier, but you would end up with a less appealing (though accurate) copy of the content. Further, the cost of your time to do this would be considerably greater than just buying another copy.

Until now, all of publishing has been based on the idea that books could only be produced in a finite and, therefore, scarce number of copies. Further, in order to make and market any large number of copies, a big industrial operation was required. Digital formats do away with all that. What is a book anyway? Is it the physical book itself or the content presented therein? Think about it. When an author writes a book, he transcribes his thoughts into words that others can read and sets those words down on some medium that others can read— generally print on paper.

Is there any difference between a hardcover book and a paperback? How about a book on audiotape? They are certainly different physical items, but is the book itself different? Not at all. The book is the *content*, not the presentation of that content.

Digitization deals directly with the content itself, not the way it is presented. Once the content of a book has been rendered into bits and bytes as a computer file, it has the potential to be produced in almost any format. The file, for instance, can be fed into a computer-automated printing press and produced as a physical book printed on paper. Or it can be transferred into a sound file and distributed on a CD or an audiotape. It can reside on a computer hard drive and be viewed with a text editor or word processor. But most important, the file can be *copied*. And it can be copied infinitely.

Four: Infinite Copies

The ability to copy a book with such ease is the most revolutionary aspect of the digital age, and it threatens to change or destroy everything we've ever known about how books are created and published.

Here's an illustration: Let's say you've written a book. It sits on your computer hard drive as a digital file. You have a mailing list of ten friends to whom you want to send this book. You e-mail the file to each of those friends. What has really happened? Did you send the file that originally was on your hard drive? Nope. You sent each friend a *copy* of that file. You still have the original.

There is no real difference between mailing that file to ten friends or a million. Once the original content has been created in digital format, the number of copies that can be made is infinite. Further, each person who receives that file has the same ability to make as many copies as they wish and to do whatever they would like with them. This ability to make unlimited copies of a digitized version of your book's content is at the heart of the digital revolution we now have entered, and it presents authors with both opportunities and problems that have never been seen before. Digital content has opened a Pandora's box of technology, and we have no idea what sort of good fairies or bad demons may yet come flying out.

E-publishing is one such spirit. Many regard it as a good fairy, but many others see it as the most evil of demons. For authors, a lot depends on your perspective: How do you, as a writer, see your work? What are your goals for it? What are your goals for yourself?

Do you, for instance, simply wish to place your work before as wide an audience as possible, with no thought to whether you get paid for it? Or do you only want readers who pay for the privilege to read your work? Maybe you would be willing to accept some combination of the two.

And what about issues of control? While it is exciting to think of millions of people reading your book, remember anything that can be copied can also be *changed*. How would you feel if one of those friends to whom you sent your novel opened it up in his word processor and wrote a new ending to the book, one he liked better than yours? Or added sections of ribald commentary? And then (remember, any digital format can be endlessly copied) sent your original work with his changes to his own list of a thousand friends?

Infinite copying means infinite loss of control. You may become unable to control what is done with your own intellectual property once you've distributed it in digital format to even one other person.

Five: Acts of Creation—Copyright Enforcement in a Digital Age

Which brings us to the question of content itself. You, as a writer, perform an *act of creation*, and the result of that act is content—the specific rendering of your ideas into a novel, a nonfiction book, or a collection of stories, essays, or poems that can be read by others. But can they legally change your work? Under copyright laws, *ideas* cannot be copyrighted, only the specific *rendering* of ideas. You could take the idea, "boy meets girl, boy loses girl, boy regains girl in the end," and write innumerable specific variations of that general idea. Each story would be different. Each *story* based on that idea could be copyrighted, but the original idea itself cannot.

But what does digital format do to the idea of copyright? After all, copyright law is basically nothing more than law that governs the *right* to make *copies*. Up until very recently, laws like this were more or less enforceable. An author would "rent" the right to copy his original work to a publisher. The publisher would make lots of physical copies (books) and then distribute and sell them. If another publisher made a copy of the original book and then printed and sold any appreciable number of them, it was immediately obvious that the author's right to copy had been infringed.

But law is not written on stone, immutable and unchanging forever. Law responds to reality. As we noted earlier, the *ability* to make copies was never erased by law, only the legal right to do so. As a practical matter, making physical copies on a small scale was always possible, but it was constrained, not only by legal issues but also by relative difficulty. As mentioned earlier, it was simpler and cheaper to buy a new copy than to make one for yourself. The law and the real world worked together, one reinforcing the other.

What does the fact that it is now possible to make a million copies of a work with the click of a mouse button do to the whole notion of copyright law? There is no longer any practical restraint on making copies. Since making a copy of a digital format is now both effortless and free, how can copyright be enforced?

The answer is, it cannot. At least not yet, not in any way we have yet devised, though this is not to say that technology may not come up with something practical in the future. Unfortunately, that future has not yet arrived.

The implications are enormous. They affect not just writers, but all creators of intellectual property, from musicians, to filmmakers, to software programmers. And those implications inform every aspect of this wonderful—and frightening—new world of electronic publishing.

Bet you didn't think much about *this* when you posted your diary—or first chapters of your novel—on your Web site, did you?

RICHARD CURTIS is the founder of e-reads and president of Richard Curtis Associates, Inc., a leading New York literary agency. He is the author of *How to Be Your Own Literary Agent, Beyond the Bestseller, Mastering the Business of Writing,* and *This Business of Publishing.* WILLIAM THOMAS QUICK is a science fiction author of more than thirty books, a screenwriter, and the owner of Iceberg SOHO Systems, a small business network consulting firm. Curtis and Quick are the authors of *How to Get Your E-Book Published* (Writer's Digest Books), from which this article was adapted.

Part Six **6**

The Interviews

Chapter 42

Margaret Atwood: "As a Writer, You Must Do What Beckons to You"

By Katie Struckel Brogan

Who would have thought that when Margaret Atwood published seven of her poems on a small-bed letterpress at the age of twenty-one, she'd emerge as one of the most respected artists of this century? Canadian-based Atwood is the author of over fifty titles, including *The Handmaid's Tale*, *Alias Grace*, and her most recent novel, *The Blind Assassin*. Named by *Writer's Digest* as one of the one hundred Best Writers of the Century, Atwood has made a place for herself in all walks of literature.

Being proficient at writing in a variety of forms is one of Atwood's strengths. She has written everything from fiction to poetry and most recently opera, simply because no one told her not to. "I think if I had gone to creative writing school, they probably would have said, 'Pick one or the other,' " she says. "But since there were hardly any creative writing schools at that time, I didn't see any reason why I shouldn't do what struck me."

Atwood began her writing career while still in high school, where she wrote for the school newspaper and contributed pieces to the yearbook literary section. In college she wrote for both school literary magazines and nonschool publications. It was at this time that she published her poems.

"I published seven poems and made them into a little book, which cost fifty cents," she says. "I wish I had kept a lot of them." Atwood took the two hundred books to local bookstores and "low and behold, some of them agreed to take those little things." Most likely those same bookstores stock Atwood's titles today.

Here Atwood takes time to share her views on the novel form, the fundamentals of writing, and the socio-political impact the writer has on society.

You've said that novels aren't sociological texts or political tracts. How would you characterize novels?
Well, novels are stories; they don't purport to be factual relations of events that have actually happened. In other words, they're not like stories in a newspaper in that you kind of hope they might be true. The idea with a novel is that it's true in a different way. It's true about human nature, but it's not true about somebody called "John Smith," whose name is also John Smith in the novel. You're telling stories about the kinds of things that happen and you're telling "what if" stories, but you're not telling, "On June the 5th, year 2000, Katie phoned Margaret and had the following conversation."

However, that's not to say that the novel has nothing to do with society. Of course it does, because you're telling "what if" stories and "this is the kind of thing that happens" stories about us, who we are, where we are, where we've been, and all of those kinds of things. Sometimes you're telling them about Mary Queen of Scots, but they're still about human nature.

So then, overall, you're saying a novel is about human nature and that's really the role it plays in society—to reflect our humanity.
Well, you can't help that, because human beings write them. And they write them either well or badly. But with the good ones, the reaction the reader has is "that's right," or "that's the way it is," or "that's what would have happened," or "I'm surprised to hear that, but now that you tell me, it all fits." And sometimes you say, "I don't believe that in a minute." In that case, the novel's gone off the track.

How important are the fundamentals of writing?

When I was about seventeen, I announced to my parents, who were quite horrified, that I was going to be a writer. My mother said, "Well, in that case, you better learn to spell." And I said, "Other people will do that for me." And you know, they do. I'm not that bad, but I would never win a spelling bee. I'm like a lot of writers in that respect—we tend to spell a little bit by ear.

As for punctuation, it's the single big argument issue when we're editing a book. The editor always wants to stick to a house style. I feel that punctuation is simply like the flats and sharps on a musical score, that punctuation has to do with the ear. The editors feel that it has to do with the rule book. So we always fight over that. I win. The buck stops with the author. The author is the one who is accountable, not the editor. So I don't want to be accountable for punctuation I don't like. My second novel, *Surfacing*, has a lot of run-on sentences in it because it's stream of consciousness in places. The galleys were edited by someone who had never edited a book of fiction before, and he took out all my punctuation and put in proper punctuation. I had to go through it with a magnifying glass and put it all back in.

How much do you allow your political activism to manifest itself in your writing?

I gave a whole lecture on this subject at Cambridge quite recently. I think that people have duties as citizens and those have nothing to do with writing. Everyone should be taking those kinds of interests in the place where they live. And, if everybody did, it would be quite a different sort of place. But writers often get shoved into the forefront, partly because they're articulate, partly because they often do have opinions. Also partly because they don't have jobs—nobody can fire them. Therefore, they find themselves being spokespersons for people who might think the same thing but would be afraid to say it. That's just a kind of job hazard.

When you look at writing in general there have been many writers, such as Charles Dickens, who have done what we might call political or social things in their novels, and there have been lots who haven't. It doesn't necessarily go with the territory. As a writer, you have to do what beckons to you as a writer. In other words, falsely straining yourself to put something like that into a book where it doesn't really belong is not doing anybody any favors. And the reader can tell. You can tell when you're being preached to and you can tell when you're being told a story—there is a difference.

I asked about your activism and its role because most of your novels tend to have a very feminist feel to them.
That's because they have women in them. Just because something has a woman in it doesn't mean it's feminist. You can call James Joyce's *Ulysses* a feminist novel and it would be. But what kind of world are we living in where half the human race is women, and if you put some of them in your book, you're a feminist? It's weird.

You put a strong woman in there and all of a sudden . . .
Then you put a weak woman in it, what is it then? You have to be either antifeminist or a feminist, you can't just be talking about human nature. Well, too bad, I don't agree with that.

You always have highly developed, multifaceted, strong female characters in your fiction. Have you, or will you, ever create a strong male role?
I already have. It's just that people tend not to notice them because I'm a woman writer, so they're biased to begin with. Similarly with men who write strong women—they're often either not noticed or they're taken as some kind of criticism. You know, we could discuss Jane Austen and say, "What kind of a person is Mr. Darcy?" Where does that leave us with Jane Austen as a feminist or not a feminist? She probably wasn't even thinking about it. She had opinions about women and men, there's no doubt about that, but she was of her time and her place.

A lot of writers tend to project themselves through their characters. How do you view yourself in relation to your work?
My characters can express themselves, mostly. As for the rest of it, I don't really consider that I am putting myself into it. I mean, I don't consider it. If I wanted to write something called *This Is the Story of My Life*, that's what I'd do.

In many of your novels, the endings are very open and ambiguous so people can form their own opinions. Is there any particular reason why you don't provide absolute, concrete endings?
Partly because I live in the twenty-first century and we don't have total faith anymore in, "This is the happy ending, this is the only happy ending, and this is the only way the story can possibly end." We tend to consider alternatives. We also know that when the bride and groom walk down the aisle, that's not an ending—it's a beginning. It may not even be the first time they've done it, and it may not be the last time they're going to do it. We don't get closure in our society as much as we used to. Things are just more open-ended.

And the other reason is that I like the reader to feel that *the reader* can participate in the active imagination that is the novel.

KATIE STRUCKEL BROGAN is the editor for *Writer's Market* and former associate editor of *Writer's Digest.*

Chapter 43

Seven Questions With Maeve Binchy

by Dawn Simonds Ramirez

Maeve Binchy proved as gracious and charming as her characters when she spoke about her book, *Tara Road*.

What's a typical writing day like?
We live in a very small place in Ireland called Dockey, where I grew up. I'm married to a writer, Gordon Snell, and we regard writing like a job. We race up the stairs at eight in the morning when we have to be at our desks. We rush around the place and say "Gosh, we'll be late!" I work from eight until two five days a week.

How do you get started?
I regard my work as storytelling. People want to know what happens next, so I spend a lot of time plotting: by the end of chapter one, this has to happen, and then this must happen by the end of chapter two.

I think about a feeling first, or an emotion—friendship or betrayal or hypocrisy. *Tara Road* is about the shock of a betrayal and the strength that comes from friendship. And I always have to advance these things. I try to imagine what would happen if it happened to me or my friends. I try to believe in characters as people, and I imagine what I would do if this happened to me, how would I react.

This is a great writer's tool: "What would I feel like if this would happen to me?" It helps you flesh out the book a bit.

You have to live in your mind or imagination in your writing, more than you do in your real life. I'm a matronly, mumsy woman, and if it was all about me and my cats, it would be boring for the readers, and that's not the way novels are made—there's no tension or drama.

Tell us about *Tara Road*.

I hope people like it because there are two very strong women who do a home exchange, one in Connecticut and one in Ireland, and it's really about coping and surviving. There's something very strange and intimate about living with someone else's possessions. When I did a home exchange, I felt very protective about her, the woman who owned the house. . . . It's an intimate relationship. I knew all about this woman, and I had never met her.

What's the most difficult aspect of writing for you?

I have a frightful temptation to use a cast of thousands and to deal with the details of all the neighbors and friends, a huge wide tapestry. I have to remind myself, keep it focused. If you spend too much time on the small characters, we have a hard time remembering who the biggest characters are.

Do you revise?

Hardly at all. I've been two things that helped me with writing: a journalist and a teacher. A journalist is used to being edited and that's good training to be a novelist. I say, if you think it's too wordy, then cut it. I believe in my editor and agent. I think writers should be prepared to listen to the professionals.

Any advice for future novelists?

You have to keep at it and refuse to be upset by rejection. We all have rejection. I was rejected five times before I started, and there must be five publishers now who are sick and regretting that!

And the other thing is to write as you speak. . . . I write as I speak and it's very quick and breathless. And it worked. I thought it would only work in Ireland, but it works everywhere. You know when people put on an accent, it's annoying. When someone speaks like themselves, it's much nicer and you want to be friends with them. That's what makes it good.

What's coming up next?

I write a big book every two years. I've been doing that for the last eighteen years. I've started to think about the book after this. But if you talk about it, you think you've written it and you haven't and then the publisher's coming looking.

DAWN SIMONDS RAMIREZ is a freelance writer. She has worked for *Writer's Digest* and *Fiction Writer*.

Chapter 44

A Conversation With Tom Clancy

By Katie Struckel Brogan

When asked how he was discovered, Tom Clancy says, "I was discovered on April 12, 1947, at Franklin Square Hospital in Baltimore." He says he doesn't remember the name of the doctor, "but I imagine he slapped me on the ass, and I probably let out the requisite noise."

In high school, Clancy, the best-selling author of the Jack Ryan books *The Hunt for Red October*, *Patriot Games*, and *The Bear and the Dragon*, knew that one day he'd see his name on a book cover. He says it took him twenty years to finally see that, "but I managed to get that dream accomplished, and then I got very lucky."

While running his own independent insurance agency, Clancy wrote *The Hunt for Red October*. A member of the U.S. Naval Institute, Clancy learned the Institute was about to enter the fiction business as Naval Institute Press. So he drove the book to Annapolis and drove home. "A few weeks later, the publisher expressed interest and so I've never had a rejection slip."

The Hunt for Red October was published in October 1984. Soon after, Gerry O'Leary, an editor with *The Washington Times*, asked Nancy Clark Reynolds, a member of the President's Commission on White House Fellowships, to take a copy of the book to the American Ambassador to Argentina in Buenos Aires. "It's a long flight to Buenos Aires," Clancy says. "And Nancy Clark Reynolds read the book on the flight."

He says Reynolds liked the book so much that she bought a case and handed them out as Christmas gifts, one of which was given to President Reagan. "It's not widely known that President Reagan was a voracious reader. He devoured *Red October.*"

On March 24, 1985, *Red October* came in at number ten on *The New York Times* best-seller list. After catapulting up the list, Clancy continued to write more books about Jack Ryan, reinventing the wheel nearly every time. "Whenever Jack finds himself in a new situation, it exposes parts of his character that the reader hasn't seen yet."

The same is true in *The Bear and the Dragon*, which took him "fully six endless months" to write. Readers can expect the "latest installment in the continuing life of Jack Patrick Ryan." But that's all he'll say about the book, except, "If you want more, buy it."

What was the biggest challenge you faced while writing *The Bear and the Dragon*?

Writing a book is an endurance contest and a war fought against yourself, because writing is beastly hard work which one would just as soon not do. It's also a job, however, and if you want to get paid, you have to work. Life is cruel that way.

How do you create intricate plots while still managing to build a sharp element of suspense?

I'm probably the wrong person to ask, because I really do not think in these terms. I'm just trying to tell a story. I pace the story in the same way that the story unfolds in my mind, and so you could say that I do the important parts instinctively, or at least with a minimum of conscious thought. The virtue of my writing, therefore, is that I do not overintellectualize the production process. I try to keep it simple: Tell the damned story.

What are the most important parts in your books?

The important parts are the prime plot elements. . . . The peripheral elements spinoff of those, sometimes affecting things directly, sometimes not, but you play them out because they are useful.

Do you think readers could understand your novels without technical details?
I think it's necessary to describe the tools my characters use to lend verisimilitude to my work, which is why I include it. . . . Verisimilitude provides texture that adds to the richness and plausibility of the story.

How do you maintain reader identification with Jack Ryan?
Obviously, most people perceive themselves to be "regular" people, and they're more likely to identify with a normal person than with Batman or Julius Caesar. So, you take an ordinary sort of guy and drop him into a serious situation. It's the same technique Hitchcock used, though he always seemed to use Cary Grant or Jimmy Stewart as his "regular guy." I would go so far as to say that the way I tell my stories largely results from a ninety-minute show I once saw on PBS about Hitchcock and his films. Suspense is achieved by information control. What you know. What the reader knows. What the characters know. You balance that properly, and you can really get the reader wound up.

What's your advice to aspiring writers?
Keep at it! The one talent that's indispensable to a writer is persistence. You must write the book, else there is no book. It will not finish itself. Do not try to commit art. Just tell the damned story. If it is entertaining, people will read it, and the objective of writing is to be read, in case the critics never told you that. . . . But fundamentally, writing a novel is telling a story.

Chapter 45

Interview With Elizabeth George

by David A. Fryxell

If Elizabeth George were a character in one of her psychological mystery novels, figuring out her "core need" would be a snap. The core need is part of how George defines her characters, a step in a rigorous process that the self-confessed "left-brained" writer uses to unleash her creative right brain.

"My core need is that I'm dominated by the need to be really competent at what I do," says George, whose resumé includes a master's degree in counseling/psychology as well as eleven published novels.

So, in her nightmares, she's back teaching English at El Toro High School in Orange County, California, running late or not prepared for class.

Not likely. George's success has taken her far from the blackboard. Her books sell a million copies and get translated into twenty languages. Her latest novel, *A Traitor to Memory*, spent last summer on *The New York Times* best-seller list. Late this year, Bantam will publish her first collection of short stories, *I, Richard*. She's been nominated for an Edgar award and has won the Agatha, the Anthony, and France's Le Grand Prix de Literature Policiere. And when *Mystery* airs an adaptation of her first novel, *A Great Deliverance*, she'll become the first American writer ever featured on the popular PBS-TV series.

"I knew from the age of seven that I was meant to be a writer," she says. Born in Warren, Ohio, and raised in the San Francisco Bay area, George used to scan *The San Francisco Examiner* for true-crime fodder. She wrote her first novel—"Nancy Drewlike," she describes it—at the age of twelve, and collected rejection slips on five books before getting published in 1988.

Two of those rejected books starred the cerebral forensic scientist Simon Allcourt-St. James, a supporting player in her subsequent novels. It was only when George decided to see if the New Scotland Yard detectives who helped St. James—the aristocratic Thomas Lynley and his frumpy partner, Barbara Havers—could solve a case on their own that she broke through with *A Great Deliverance*.

"I wish that I had known back then that a mastery of process would lead to a product," she reflects. "Then I probably wouldn't have found it so frightening to write."

George's process for novel writing today is complex but ultimately as clear as her plots. "I have to know the killer, the victim, and the motive when I begin. Then I start to create the characters and see how the novel takes shape based on what these people are like."

Besides a core need and the rest of a psychological profile, each character gets a physical description, a family history, and what George calls a "pathology," which she defines as "a particular psychological maneuver that he engages in when he's under stress." Much of this material, written in stream-of-consciousness form, never makes it into the actual novel, but it helps George discover the truth about her characters. When she gets it, George says, she feels something right in her solar plexus.

"Creating the characters is the most creative part of the novel except for the language itself. There I am, sitting in front of my computer in right-brain mode, typing the things that come to mind, which become the seeds of plot. It's scary, though," she adds, "because I always wonder: Is it going to be there this time?"

George's plotting process is equally detailed. "I outline the plot beginning with the primary event that gets the ball rolling. Then I'll list the potentials that are causally related to what's gone before.

"I continue to open the story and not close the story, putting in dramatic questions. Any time the story stalls out on me, I know I've done something wrong—generally, I played my hand too soon, answered a dramatic question in a scene without asking a new one."

Her running plot outline might cover up to the next fifteen scenes. "The plot outline doesn't forbid the inspiration of the moment, but it does prevent a wild hare, something out of character that drags the story off in a wrong area."

For each scene, the outline notes what George calls her "THAD," short for "Talking Head Avoidance Device." The THAD that animates each scene, George says, springs from her prep work getting to know her characters.

The outline also notes the point of view for each scene. Unlike many mystery writers, George shifts her point of view among multiple characters—rather than, say, sticking with the detective's viewpoint. "In any given scene, I ask, 'Whose story is being advanced here?'" she explains. "I can usually tell the point of view by which character's part in the narrative I've gotten to."

Sometimes that's the killer. "I wanted the challenge of writing from the killer's viewpoint after the killing's taken place. The killer is thinking about the killing, but the reader never knows that's what the person is really thinking about.

"I wanted to write books that bore a second reading," George goes on. "Books that play fair with the reader but sometimes would be the kind of book where the reader wouldn't realize I'd been fair to them until a second reading. The reader is always in possession of vastly more knowledge than the investigators are."

As George has set herself more daunting writing challenges, her novels have grown longer and more time-consuming to write. She wrote *A Great Deliverance* in three and a half weeks; her latest took eighteen months. "The books are vastly more complicated now. I'm more interested in subplot, how subplots could unify the novel and reinforce the theme."

Research takes time, too, especially since all her novels are set in England, half a world away from her home in Huntington Beach, California. The most common question she gets is: Why write about England when you're an American? George can't understand why people find that so surprising. Her stock response: "It worked for Henry James."

But it does mean spending weeks at a time in England, which George first visited and fell in love with on a summer Shakespeare course in 1966. She keeps a flat in South Kensington, London, home base for research excursions armed with camera and tape recorder. For *Well-Schooled in Murder*, for example, she visited a half-dozen schools and created architectural plans and a brochure for her fictional British school setting.

"I want to ground myself in specifics, not generics. I want to force myself to deal in details. I can't make these up, that's not my talent."

Writers who want to follow in George's footsteps often complain that they don't have the time to write. George has little patience with that excuse: "Evaluate how you're using your free time every day for a week—talking on the phone, reading the newspaper, watching TV, listening to the radio. All these things are bleeding away from your writing time, thinking time, preparation time. You have to structure your life to allow yourself to write.

"Writing is 10 percent inspiration and 90 percent endeavor," she adds. "It's a job and has to be approached as a job. Writers write—they don't wait for it to be fun."

Clearly writing is more than just a job to George. Yes, she allows, it helps fulfill that core need at the foundation of her character.

"Only when I write," she says, "do I feel whole and at peace."

DAVID A. FRYXELL is editor-in-chief of Writer's Digest and Writer's Digest Books, and is the author of *How to Write Fast (While Writing Well)* and *Elements of Article Writing: Structure and Flow.*

Chapter 46

Eight Questions With David Guterson

By Dawn Simonds Ramirez

David Guterson's first novel, *Snow Falling on Cedars*, sold more than two million copies and won the PEN/Faulkner and the ABBY. We talked with the highly successful first novelist to find out what writing novel number two—the eagerly awaited *East of the Mountains*—was like.

The second novel has a reputation for being an obstacle. How do you feel now that *East of the Mountains* is done?
I've heard about that before as well, you know, the second novel curse, and I've always felt that the inherent difficulties of writing a novel are deep enough without worrying whether it's your first or your second or your third book. I think I have enough difficulty just dealing with the page in front of me, the sentence in front of me, without worrying about the second novel curse.

What are some of those difficulties?
In terms of language, I'm asking myself whether the words I'm using are actually expressing what I mean. That can be a protractive process—you're constantly asking yourself whether in fact there is not only a better word, but a better way of combining words, to get at the meanings you intend. And always that has to be colored by larger concerns—the sweep of the story—so you may get bogged

down in a sentence that's descriptive detail about landscape, spend a lot of time on it, then realize that the entire paragraph, maybe the entire page, maybe the two or three pages of descriptive detail are doing nothing . . . and it's time to remove them. But there's a lot of satisfaction in tearing away, and allowing something really clear to emerge as a result.

Do you read poetry?
I think [poetry is] . . . generally a great benefit to any human being, and because it enhances you as a person, it enhances you as a writer. People respond strongly to beautiful prose, prose with a poetic dimension, and I think it makes the reading experience itself so much more enjoyable when the words are like music. There's some exquisite pleasure simply in the sound of the words. This is a large part of what the reading experience is about for people, and they respond powerfully when it happens.

Is there a music to writing?
Oh definitely. Any writer hears the music of their prose in their inner ear as they work. That's why it's so interesting to go to readings and to hear the particular music that a writer will bring to his or her own prose; it's sometimes unexpected because the reader might bring a different music to it.

There's been a certain evolution to the music of my prose, and I think my early work was a much more conventional kind of music. The rhythms were much more predictable, and I think that as I've gone on, I've achieved a much more refined sound and a leaner, more spartan music.

When you're writing and revising, are you looking for the pronunciation of words for any kind of rhythm?
It has to do in part with stresses, in the same way that you might analyze poetry for its stresses. Iambic pentameter is a rhythm I sometimes pick up in my prose. I also look at combinations of vowel

sounds, the harshness or softness of relative consonant sounds in combination, the length of sentences and how they transmit mood, and variety in sentence length and sentence type. All of those things contribute to the music of one's prose.

I've read that the theme of *East of the Mountains* is the relationship between love and work. What is the connection between love and work?

The new book explores how love supports work, and how the best work is done out of love and that work is an expression of love on a number of levels. So in those regards, the book explores the connection between the two. We experience the paradox of work—love and toil—simultaneously on a daily basis. I know that's true for me in my writing—it's definitely toil, but I wonder what I would do without it.

What in writing is the most toilsome for you?

Well, I think it's extraordinarily fun to write, and I look forward to it every day, but that doesn't mean I think it's easy. There's a difference between the two. It's fun in the way all worthwhile things are fun—there's difficulty attached to it. I think that a writer has to accept a certain amount of frustration. It's inherent in the task, and you have to simply persevere. It's part of the definition of the work.

Writers shouldn't underestimate the difficulty of what they're doing, and they should treat it with great seriousness. You're doing something that really matters, you're telling stories that have an impact on other people and on the culture. You should tell the best stories you can possibly tell and put everything you've got into it.

In a new AWA book, Charles Johnson mentioned you as a writer who has an incredible propensity for research.

Yes, it's true. I do more research than most writers. I think that if you want a place to be palpable, you should be able to describe the place in complete detail, and to do that you need to know what its history is and how people make a living, what the cultural and social terrain is of a particular place. That, of course, involves research. I can't imagine writing just from the well of my own imagination; it seems so limiting. My imagination is so fully enhanced by research, that gives my imagination so much more range, so much more material.

Chapter 47

Gish Jen: "You Never Get Bored"

By Anne Bowling

Gish Jen doesn't believe in suffering for her art. And although she has been quoted as saying her favorite part of writing is "when it's done," still Jen admits that for her, the work is play. "Someone was saying at a party the other day that you get to a certain age, and you realize that you're just going to do the same thing over and over again for the rest of your life," she says. "And even though part of me felt terrible for it, I couldn't help but say writing is totally not like that. It's endlessly fresh. You never get bored."

Jen's enthusiasm comes through clearly in her prose. The daughter of Chinese immigrants, her approach to the subjects of ethnicity and cultures-within-cultures is marked with humor and warmth, in a way that sets her apart from the majority of authors working with the subject matter today. Jen projects her stories through a prism of humor for an effect the *Los Angeles Times* has called "a shining example of multicultural message," and a voice so fresh it nearly bounces off the page.

In the title story of her short story collection *Who's Irish?*, Jen tells her story through the voice of an irascible Chinese grandmother, here observing her Chinese-Irish-American granddaughter: "Sophie is three years old American age, but already I see her nice Chinese side swallowed up by her wild Shea side," the narrator says in her pidgin English. And when Sophie takes aim at her with a shovel of playground sand, "I am not exaggerate: millions of children in China, not one act like this."

A thread of humor has run through nearly all Jen's published works, which have appeared in such periodicals as *Atlantic Monthly*, *The New Republic*, and *The New Yorker*, and in collections of *The Best American Short Stories*. Her "Birthmates" was selected to run alongside the works of Hemingway and Barthelme in *The Best American Short Stories of the Century*. Her first novel, *Typical American*, was a *New York Times* Notable Book of the Year, and a finalist for the National Book Critics Circle award. Jen followed that novel with *Mona in the Promised Land*, which drew praise from the likes of Grace Paley and Amy Tan, and was honored among the best books of the year by both *The New York Times* and the *Los Angeles Times*.

Perhaps Jen's gentle satire and incisive wit spring from her feeling that writing is fun. And perhaps it was guilt over the pleasure she took in writing that caused Jen to wait until she was nearly thirty to commit herself to the identity of "writer." Even now, married with children, "I still struggle with the question, 'Is it selfish?'" she says in a 1999 *Publishers Weekly* interview. "It's hard on the people around me, it's hard on my children. Is it worth it? I was programmed to be selfless, and I go through periods where I wonder."

As a girl growing up in the affluent New York suburb of Scarsdale, Jen struggled with a cultural mindset that valued scholarship, but did not regard fiction writing as scholarship. She attended Harvard as an undergraduate, and although it was there she first connected with expression through poetry and "immediately fell in love with it," she says in an online interview, "I didn't even for a moment consider becoming a poet." She tried premed and prelaw, attended business school at Stanford, and considered careers in architecture, contracting, and antiques before permitting herself to pursue fiction writing.

With all her options, why fiction? "When I thought about other professions, the one thing I realized was that I would be interested in the process of mastery, but then I would be bored. And one of the attractions of writing is that the process is unending," she says. "Also, there is a way in which because you see more, it makes you live more deeply, and I love that about writing. And it gives you permission to be interested in anything. It's all work: You can talk to people about an architectural landmark on the wharf, or whatever, and it's all legitimate because it's all work—you're doing your job."

Here, Jen shares the details of her writing process, her relationships with her characters, and how she leaves her audiences both moved and amused.

You said at one point that pursuing writing was something that you "just had to do." Would you elaborate?

It was the only thing that I loved. Theoretically, I could have done all kinds of things. People would say, "You could definitely get into law school, you could definitely become a doctor." It was kind of confusing. So I kept on trying out all of these professions, only to discover that while I could do them, I just didn't love them.

I did a lot of reading as a child, and I had a ton of books. I think there's a way in which I wanted to be in dialogue with those books. It's funny, though—I was very, very late in thinking I could write. I was much more interested in reading all those years. It took me a long time to understand that this impulse to write was real, that I wasn't going to grow out of it, that it wasn't going to go away.

So you chose to commit yourself to the craft?

Because I had tried all these professions on, at one level or another, by the time I came to writing, it was do or die. And that was a good thing, because going to graduate school is fine, but after you get out of graduate school, it's hard to be a writer. About three years out, when people are still struggling, a lot of them start talking about going to law school. But I thought, I can't go to law school. I've already been through this decision. I did manage, in a highly creative manner, to come up with another six or seven or eight options for myself anyway. But in the end I realized I had to try, that it was my deepest self. Writing was my home.

In some ways, it sounds as though you're self-taught.
I'm not self-taught because I went to Iowa, and I've read all the craft books. But it is true that I work in a very intuitive manner, and I'm often playing around. I garden in the same way.

So you're not a plan-ahead gardener, who says "here will be an oval bed with four-foot perennials, bordered by variegated annuals in alternating colors. . . ."
I'll have a mix of plants already in the garden. And then I'll be walking down the aisle in the gardening store, and on impulse I'll back up and pick out some lemon thyme. And although when I bought it I didn't realize it was so lime green, suddenly the color will strike me, while when I bought it, it was only a scent. One thing leads to another.

Can writers be taught to write with wit and humor, or is it more an outgrowth of a writer's sensibility, a natural impulse?
There are many ways of skinning the cat. For some people, maybe it's learned. For me, it's mostly natural. When you're writing, you feel, feel, feel, and then you back up, and for me, that's when the humor comes out. It's the dual perspective, the being in and being out of the situation at the same time that produces this poignant humor.

Also, the distance between the character in your mind and the words on the page. By the time you've put it into words, you've created a distance which is potentially funny. The words themselves are so funny, and the comic potential in the words draws attention to itself. That's to say that the words are not transparent to me. I see the words and hear them as I'm writing, and that brings out my tendency to be funny.

You have a great deal of fun with your characters, but there's a warmth and compassion under it; the sense that, as one critic put it, they are "lovingly imagined." Does your humor and empathy sweeten what could otherwise be fairly bitter, painful subject matter?

Of course, and I try not to shy away from painful subject matter. Where there's pain, there's often something big. You cannot shy away from anything that's painful—quite the contrary. And yet for me, there's a mix. It is in my character to always see the painful, the funny, all at once, and I don't know why that is.

The humor is never mean—I am in the situations with my characters, and I always love my characters. To me, you've got to live with these characters year in and year out, so you'd better pick characters that you like. Yes, they're deeply flawed, but if they weren't deeply flawed, you wouldn't have anything to write about.

As you were wrapping up *Typical American*, your ideas for *Mona in the Promised Land* started to flow. I think that a lot of writers work that way, and I wondered what hazards does that pose? Is there a cost to the writing itself if you have what are almost distractions?

There can be. There was a very interesting review that John Updike wrote of one of Philip Roth's books, in which he said the book read as though it had been too long in the writing, and little side interests had sprung up. I thought that was really true. People often say, "If your novel takes eight years to write, oh well." But as a practitioner, I think that's entirely too sanguine.

There are certain activities that are meant to take a certain amount of time, and if the time is not there, the outcome suffers. We can all think of many things—sleeping, screwing—that have their own timetable. You cannot say "I'll stretch this out to twelve hours." Novel writing is similar. There's a period of time during which you are passionate and completely engaged, and if it goes on for too long, little distractions like little side-shoots start to come up.

It's nice to be able to pluck the shoots and turn them into a story, and get rid of them so you can go back to your work. But if I were in the middle of a novel, and that that was happening pretty regularly, I would worry about the book. That would tell me I wasn't enthralled. If you're not enthralled, how are your readers going to be? If you're not interested, you have fallen out of love in some important way, and that's not good news for the book.

With your novels and short stories, you're critically batting 1.000. Are you surprised by the positive and sustained critical reaction to your work?

I couldn't be more surprised. And I feel like it can't go on. But what a happy position to be in. Many people have ideas about what the critics' function is, but I don't think it has hurt me to have this positive criticism. Some critics think that's a terrible thing for a writer, but it's difficult to write, even if you love to play. It's very hard to reconcile with real life, with raising kids, and how nice to have a little wind at your back.

The far greater danger, at least among the women writers I know, is that they stop writing. It seems to me that many of them fall into silence. From what I've seen, it's very hard to continue working, especially if you have a family. I don't think the critics need to worry that they're spoiling you.

Would you share a few details of your writing on a really bad day? Do you ever sort of pack it up and say, "Okay, not happening today"?

No, I don't. It might have been Isaac Asimov who said being professional means you don't have bad days. Partly because I am a mother, and my time is so precious, and it's so hard getting to my desk, I don't have writer's block anymore. I sit down, I look at my watch, I start typing. I don't have a choice.

Don't get me wrong—some days what comes out is better than other days, but you have to accept that. It's just part of the process.

Maybe because it's provisional, and I expect to change it, I don't get bent out of shape every time I write a bad line. I accept that it's there now, but can be gone in seconds.

You have this feeling early on that you're not going to have that many words, or that many ideas. You're going to run out, or you're going to write yourself out. And then you realize the world is endless, and therefore your words are endless. You're not going to write yourself out; there's just going to be more and more, so you don't have to get too panicked if this particular word, this particular sentence, this particular paragraph, this particular character, this particular story, is not very good. You make it the best you can and go on.

You've received a number of awards for your work, but I wondered whether inclusion in *The Best American Short Stories of the Century*, with so many distinguished masters of the form, might have been a particular honor.

An unbelievable honor. And on days that it's hard to clear your life, and put your baby with a sitter, that helps you get to your desk. And when the writing is so much fun it seems self-indulgent, and you wonder as you manage to make a living fooling around whether that's fair to your family and the people around you, things like that make you believe that it is a worthwhile thing to do. It's very affirming.

ANNE BOWLING is editor of *Novel & Short Story Writer's Market,* and a columnist on children's and young adult literature for *Pages* and *BookStreet USA.*

Chapter 48

Jerry B. Jenkins: Left Behind Series

By Chantelle Bentley

With more than twenty-five million copies sold, the apocalyptic thriller Left Behind series has made *The New York Times* best-seller list and become the best-selling evangelical fiction series of all time. But co-authors Jerry B. Jenkins and Tim LaHaye also are hearing individual stories of rekindled or new faith from their readers.

"Dr. LaHaye and I have heard from more than two thousand people in person, via e-mail, snail mail, or phone who say they have become believers in Christ through reading these books," Jenkins says.

The ninth book in the adult series, *Desecration*, is almost certain to carry on the series' success. But Jenkins's writing resumé includes more than the Left Behind series. He has more than one hundred other books to his credit, including biographies of Hank Aaron, Orel Hershiser, Nolan Ryan, and Brett Butler. Jenkins also assisted Billy Graham with his best-selling memoir *Just as I Am*. In addition, Jenkins writes on the topics of marriage and family life, and has written numerous fiction titles for both children and adults. He has worked as the sports editor of a daily newspaper, the managing editor of a periodical, executive editor of a magazine, and, finally, as editor of *Moody Magazine*.

While reviewing your list of published titles, I was amazed by the volume of books you've written in the past twenty years. How do

you maintain such a hectic pace while also writing on such a wide variety of subjects?

I don't sing or dance or preach. This is all I do. I don't find it hectic if I maintain my family priorities. I have never written while my kids were at home and awake, which allowed me to write—when I did have the time—without guilt. Until 1990, I wrote only from nine in the evening to midnight. Now I write during the day when my high schooler is at school.

How has your editing experience affected your writing ability and how you promote your work?

When I arrived at the Moody Institute in October of 1974, I had already published eight or nine books. But because of all my editing experience, I've become a better rewriter and editor of my own work, having done that kind of thing to other people's writing all day.

As far as the ability to sell my work, I suppose my visibility didn't hurt, and I may have gotten the benefit of the doubt. But I had already been fairly fortunate in that regard, having learned to sell on the basis of queries and proposals. I have always been able to sell my stuff. I have been turned down on ideas, but not on written work, having learned to write only after getting a green light.

Which genre is most challenging to write and why?

Most challenging is writing for kids, because naturally you must use a limited vocabulary. As-told-to autobiographies are tricky, but I've learned to catch the subject's voice and write as he would if he were a writer, rather than as I would if I were him.

What kind of research do you do for the books that make up the Left Behind series?

The idea for fictionalizing an account of the Rapture and the Tribulation was Dr. LaHaye's, and he has been studying prophecy and theology since before I was born. I have become, in essence, his protégé and now own everything he has written or read on these subjects. He provides a chronology of biblical events, and I get the fun part of making up the stories and writing the novels.

After connecting with Tim LaHaye through literary agent Rick Christian and deciding to write Left Behind, how did you find a publisher for the series?
I wrote and Rick shopped an early version of chapter one (which did not even include Buck, the second protagonist) among several publishers. We got solid offers from five, top offers from two, and eventually selected Tyndale.

Was the entire series proposed to potential publishers or was the first book sold and then interest in a series developed from there?
After contracting with Tyndale, I wrote half of the first (and only, at that time) title, realizing that I had covered only one week of the seven-year period. Tyndale agreed to a trilogy. In the middle of book two, I told them it would likely take six books, and they agreed. Then we decided on seven.

When book four took us only to the two-and-one-half year mark, the publisher asked if I really thought I could finish the series in just three more books. I said I could but that it would become plot-driven rather than character-driven. He said, how many if you stay at the same pace? I said twelve. That's where we stand now. Book six took us to the halfway point. Six more should finish it. The story is told at the same pace, but I'm writing two a year now, rather than one.

Does Tyndale House have much input over what goes into each book?
They have that right, but Dr. LaHaye is considered the leading evangelical scholar on these matters, and the fiction seems to have worked, so they're thrilled and trust us. Of course, we count on them for their part of the editing process too.

How does publishing the Left Behind series compare with finding a publisher for some of your own work?
It's the same. We pitch ideas, get a contract, and I write.

With the publicity and attention brought to you through the success of the Left Behind series, do you have a more difficult time finding that space within yourself that is required to write?

Yes. I always thought writing full-time would give me unlimited blocks of time to write. But the business of writing (media, and so on) has become my new full-time job, and I still must carve out the time to write.

Do you feel the quality of the writing in the later books in the series has been affected by the speed at which you have to write them?

I never rush the writing. I write at the same speed as always, but of course I have less down time between finishing each book. The people closest to the project (Tyndale, an agent, my first readers, and so on) feel each book is better than the last. I want each to be better and work hard at that.

Do you have any advice for other Christian writers who struggle to sell their work in the secular publishing market?

A Christian publisher, two Christian authors, and a story as overtly evangelical as it can be combined to produce the biggest Christian crossover success ever. The lesson is apparently to not hold back or try to soft sell the message. Readers tell us they have fallen in love with the characters and loved to keep turning the pages, so clearly the fundamentals of fiction still apply.

Do you believe that Christian writers are at a greater disadvantage when it comes to publishing and selling their work?

The general market seems thrilled with anything that entertains and sells, so where there might have seemed to be a prejudice against Christian themes, that has been dispelled by several best-sellers (not just our own).

CHANTELLE BENTLEY is the former editor of *Poet's Market*.

A Conversation With Tony Hillerman

By Brad Crawford

Tony Hillerman is best known for his Jim Chee and Joe Leaphorn mysteries set in the Southwest, but his résumé includes thirty years as a newspaper reporter and editor, plus a post as the head of the journalism program at the University of New Mexico. He continues to write fiction, essays, articles, and nonfiction of all kinds. His latest work is *Seldom Disappointed*, a memoir.

Your mysteries tend to emphasis setting, description, and culture. Do you consider yourself to be a "pure" mystery writer?
I feel my first priority as a writer is to entertain the audience. But I'm also fascinated by the cultures we have [in the Southwest], and I think people ought to know about them. My second priority is to develop plots that will force the reader to attend a Native ceremony or get involved in the religious tradition in order to follow the plot. Sometimes it works better than others.

Are you a visual writer?
I have to go to the reservation, to the spot I'll be writing about to get comfortable with it. If something's going to happen in the late evening, I want to be there at twilight and listen to what's going on. Are the coyotes out there? Even if I never use a lot of this stuff, I like to feel at home in my mind with the spot I have on the page.

Maybe I don't put in the creosote bush and what it smells like when rainwater hits it, but I want to know.

Are there visual clues that you include to entwine that setting with the story?

I've been out hiking with a Navajo before and noticed that he wouldn't step in the water when crossing a ravine. "It shows respect for the water," he said, which makes sense in a dry country. I try to remember those elements later on and use them as clues in stories. They might not tell a city cop anything, but they'll tell Joe Leaphorn something.

How have you gone about researching for novels set outside the Southwest?

In *Finding Moon*, for example, I had planned to go to Laos to do research, but I couldn't get a visa at the time. I could only get as far as Manila, so I modified the plot and went to Palawan Island [between Borneo and the Philippines] and moved a lot of the action there and to Manila. I have sons who are the right age to know a lot of Vietnam veterans, and I imposed on some of them who were in the so-called "Brownwater Navy" [which patrolled the Mekong in these little-bitty boats] and picked their brains. And, I did plenty of reading and sifted through *National Geographic* photos to get a sense of the setting and atmosphere.

You're known for not liking to use outlines for your fiction.

I would do it if I could, but I can't ever think that far ahead. When I decided I wanted to [write fiction], I analyzed what I had going for me. I've been a journalist for years and years. I knew what I was good at—narrative and description. I had no idea if I could develop characters or a plot. That led me to a place where the setting is important, both in the landscape and the culture. Already being interested in Navajo culture, I decided the Southwest was a good place to do this.

Hunting Badger, though, has less Navajo culture in it. It involves a southern Ute legend, but it also involves a problem cops have, especially tribal cops—dealing with the FBI. A couple of years ago, we had a hellacious manhunt in the Four Corners area. A policeman was machine-gunned to death by three guys. . . . *Hunting Badger* chronicles a similar crime that takes place and the fear that spreads through the Four Corners area because people are remembering what happened with this last manhunt. This story turns on the local cops' work. [Joe Leaphorn] connects this crime with a legendary southern Ute hero who used to kill Navajos. That's how the crime is solved, with the local cops knowing the area and the peculiarities of the culture.

You've had to scrap a large number of first chapters. Have you since found a way to avoid that?
Not yet. That happens when I've got the chronology wrong. I like a book to cover a relatively short period of time. Usually, when that happens, I'm starting the book too early in the event sequence, or it's going to take too long for the principal character to appear. If I start the chapter at that point, I'll leave the main character hanging so long that it will lose significance for the reader.

BRAD CRAWFORD is an editor at Betterway Books and works on photography, genealogy, and writing titles.

Chapter 50

Terry McMillan: "Everything I Write Is About Empowerment"

By Anne Bowling

Terry McMillan is content to leave the pulse-pounding plots to Tom Clancy and John Grisham; it's the characters who drive her novels. The women McMillan crafts draw readers by the millions. These characters seem familiar enough to walk through your apartment door, drop a Coach bag on the coffee table, and flop down on the couch for a chat.

And although her characters are primarily middle-class African-American women, the issues they confront are universal enough to draw readers from across race, class, and even gender lines. Her cast of women invite readers in for an intimate look at the struggle to balance homemaking and careers, follow their ambitions, hold together extended families, manage their men, and wear the hell out of "bad" dresses.

As McMillan puts it: "The grocery store where I shop is predominantly white, and I get stopped by these little old ladies and they're like, 'Workin' on another book? I loved all the others.' And it's this little old lady with a cane—it's just amazing."

"Amazing" could also describe McMillan's rise in publishing. After just six weeks, her first novel, *Mama*, was already in its third printing. *Disappearing Acts* earned her critical acclaim for her first-person handling of her male lead character, Franklin Swift. The paperback rights for *Waiting to Exhale* brought $2.64 million, one of the largest deals of its kind in publishing history. And those who missed the books are catching the movies—*Waiting to Exhale* was one of 1996's most popular films, and the film version of *How Stella Got Her Groove Back* came out in 1998.

"I never dreamed in a million years that this would have happened," McMillan says. "I had no expectations. All I ever wanted was a decent audience, and for people to appreciate my stories."

McMillan came to writing in the mid seventies through a fiction class at the University of California, Berkeley, after a middle-class upbringing in Port Huron, Michigan. "I don't even know what made me take my first fiction writing class, but I had heard of Ishmael Reed," McMillan said. "I ended up writing a story for his class, and he said my voice was just amazing. I didn't know what he was talking about. I have a deep voice, so when I talk a lot of times people think I'm a guy. Until he explained what 'voice' meant, I didn't even know what he was talking about."

After her first short story publication in Reed's magazine *Yardbird*, the going got rougher. She took *Mama* with her to the Harlem Writer's Guild, where they encouraged her to work what was then a short story into a novel.

Brief stays at the McDowell Colony and Yaddo yielded four hundred pages of a novel and a previously written collection of short stories she was determined to sell. The response from Houghton Mifflin a year later was that her short-story collection might be difficult to sell, but would she send along her novel?

Houghton Mifflin published *Mama* in 1987, but it was McMillan who sold the book. "As soon a I found out the publicity department wasn't going to do any publicity other than send out the standard releases, and that I wasn't going on a book tour, I said 'What is going on here?' " McMillan wrote bookstores, colleges, and universities, setting up readings and promoting the book, and sent her publicist her itinerary. She ended up selling about ten thousand books.

After stumping for *Mama*, McMillan has continued coming on

to her readers like a country preacher, with a steady stream of readings, book signings, and television appearances on national programs such as *The Oprah Winfrey Show* and *Today*. She became as familiar as her characters, available and comfortable, sitting on the couch.

McMillan explains: "People read these books, and they're moved by them, and you don't want them to deify you," she says. "You want them to know you're just an everyday person who happens to write books. And that's why I will sign everybody's book who walks in that room and stands in a line.

"I mean, I have a built-in audience; I don't have to go on book tours anymore," she says. "But a lot of times I'll take readings where I read stuff in progress. I don't mind if it's kind of tacky. I'll tell an audience in the opening some of this stuff isn't finished, but I'll try it out on you guys."

I caught up with McMillan as she was putting the finishing touches on her next novel. And like the characters in her books, McMillan proved to be candid, funny, and gracious.

Why do you think your characters are so compelling, and why do they connect with such a wide range of readers?
There's a saying that you'll never understand a person until you write his or her story, and I don't write about characters unless I don't fully understand why they do what they do. And it's sort of like the only way, even if that person is confused and flawed, like most of us are, you get a chance to connect with them. A lot of times when I do that in first person, it gives me a chance to forgive myself for my own weaknesses because I realize that I'm not alone. Sometimes it's the characters you like the least that you end up liking the most, and I think that it's those kind of decisions that end up making your work come alive. That's what it is for me.

Also, I let my characters do the talking, simple as that. And I don't try to put words in their mouths. I let them talk. And that's why there's profanity in my work—even though I do use profanity,

I don't use it the way a lot of them do. I give them a voice, and I'm dedicated to that voice, simple as that. A lot of times, once I know my characters, I sort of know the words that are going to come out of their mouths in a certain situation, and that's the fun of it.

A *New York Times* article published shortly after the release of *Waiting to Exhale* described your novels as focusing on the lives of essentially conventional, middle-class blacks. How do you explain their crossover appeal? Is it feminism at its core?
Everything I write is about empowerment, regardless of what kind it is. It's always about a woman standing up for herself and her rights and her own beliefs, and not worrying about what other people think. But one of the things I think fiction should not do is be didactic. I'm not here to preach. I'm not trying to be Gloria Steinem in disguise. I would prefer that you be affected, that by reading something you get a sense of empowerment, and hopefully if it's subtle enough, you won't even know it happened.

Your characters have gotten you into trouble. You were sued for defamation over the character of Franklin Swift, from *Disappearing Acts*, by a former lover who claimed you used him as a model. Although the New York Supreme Court ruled in your favor, did this affect the way you draw your characters?
I wasn't worried so much for myself. My fear was the effect it could have on other writers who use real people as a pool from which to get material.

That was when I started doing character profiles; that's when I created Franklin and gave him those nuances. Yes, he was my boyfriend and yes, he worked construction, that much I kept. But there were like two scenes in that entire book I could say sort of actually happened, and even the way I handled it was different. The bottom line is I have a right. I have a right to do what I want to do with information and my life experiences. I have a right, and I'm not going to be bullied.

How do your character profiles work?
I'd go to places and act like I wanted a job, and get these employment applications and then I'd retype them on my computer like a form, and then I'd add to it: What is your biggest secret? Do you pay your taxes on time? Do you lie? What is it that really gets on your nerves about other people? What do you think your strengths and weaknesses are? How do you see yourself? What are your hobbies? What foods do you eat? What are you allergic to? What shoe size do you wear? Are you overweight? I'd do that for all my characters.

I'd end up with this profile, even if it's stuff I don't ever use. My favorites are strengths and weaknesses, what pisses them off, and what the biggest obstacle in their lives are right now. And they answer that for themselves or I give it to them, and that determines what sort of situations I will put them in, so that they will have to deal with it. I test them, but you've got to know them first.

Have you created characters who've ended up edited out? Who just didn't work?
In *Waiting to Exhale*, I created a character who was part black and part Chinese. Somebody published the chapter as a short story. It worked as a short story, but I was trying too hard, with the Chinese part of it, to show these mixed cultures.

Your style is very engaging—there's nothing formal or practiced about it—which may have a lot to do with your characters' appeal. Who were your stylistic influences?
I think I was influenced by Ring Lardner, just the real conversational tone. And I'd have to say J.D. Salinger and *The Catcher in the Rye*— that whole stream of consciousness thing. It's just the fact that you can weave this whole monologue with things and make a story out of it, and it's as if you're talking to someone. That is really quite effective. Also, just before *Mama* was published, I began reading Zora Neale Hurston, which was hard for me at the time because it was in dialect, but it became easier.

When you first started writing, were you bothered by the relative lack of African-American women novelists?
At the time, I didn't really think of it in those terms. I still think that good writing is good writing, no matter who writes it. Back then I read Katherine Anne Porter and Jane Austen and Virginia Woolf— those writers I really found powerful. Katherine Anne Porter in particular is one of my favorite writers. What she could do with a short story just blew me away. Back then you don't know what's affecting your work, you just know what moves you, and their work moved me.

At that time, Toni Morrison and Alice Walker were just coming to the forefront, and I was barely in college. Prior to being in college, I hadn't done a whole lot of reading of literature by African-Americans because I didn't know it existed and because I didn't think, hey, why don't black people write books? I wasn't there yet.

Later I moved to L.A. and they had a class on African-American literature, and I thought, what is this? And they had a whole ocean of writing by black people, male and female alike.

Your first writing experiences must have come later in life.
It was 1971 or 1972. I was living in L.A., and I wrote a poem. I think it was my first experience with heartbreak. I started writing more poetry after that because it seemed like it was gratifying, it felt good to be able to express how you felt, and it was a way to react to things, and you could keep it to yourself. That's how it started, and it just kind of evolved.

Having spent time writing *Mama* at McDowell Colony and Yaddo, what's your opinion of writers' groups?
They're dangerous. In some groups, nobody knows what they're doing, it's not led by someone who is knowledgeable about the craft itself. I don't know that someone leading the workshop has to be published, but it wouldn't hurt to have someone who at least has a clue about structure and the rules of fiction, and advice about what

would make a greater character, as opposed to just responding to what you think you would like.

Someone once said you should never stay in a writers' group longer than a year because there are people who've been in these groups for years and it's just comfortable, [they lose focus on] the product.

As an instructor, you've been known to caution writers not to put the publishing cart before the writing horse.
A lot of young writers, all they think about is being published. That's their priority—how much money can I make, how many books can I sell, can I make it on the best-seller list? You don't know how many books I see, and it's written all over them. It's kind of sad. For some of these young writers out here, it's like prostitution.

A lot of people don't see writing as an act of self-discovery, and I think that's a very big danger. A lot of them are more interested in telling you what they know, or what they think they know. They've already figured it out. If they've already figured it out, what is the point?

Each book is a different kind of challenge. *How Stella Got Her Groove Back* was sort of like my reaction to what happened to me, and I was trying to question it. So I wrote that book in like three weeks. It started out as a poem, and then I decided to establish some distance in which to create this woman. So it was going to be a little story, and then it was going to be a novella, and then it was going to be a little short novel, just so I could get it off my chest. Next thing I know, my agent says, "Terry, shut up and just write it, okay?"

It wasn't planned at all, but what it ultimately ended up doing was freeing me to make some other decisions in my life; you don't owe anybody any fucking apologies or explanations for your behavior. And in some ways, I think a lot of other women feel the same way, not so much about being with a young man, but being in a job you hate, or doing things that make you feel good.

So you don't have a road map when you start on a novel? They change as you work?

I'm working now on a novel I'd started a few years back, and I'm about eighty pages into it, and there are these adult children—it's a family—and the mother was in first person and the kids were all in third person. The first chapter is somewhat of a monologue. It takes place in this hospital, and you get the mother's take on everybody else, on her kids and her husband. Then you meet her husband, and his character is in first person, and you get his take on her. Then you meet the son. Originally, I'd written the son and three daughters all in third person and I realized that it wasn't going to be as effective once I got the structure down. I had this chapter sitting here, an old chapter, and it worked perfectly fine in third person, but it was . . . it was so easy to do, and you can't go emotionally where you want to go. I mean, there's a way to do it, but it's the safer way. And by doing it in first person, it's not as safe, it takes more energy.

My old editor said the other day, "You don't have to do it in first person." I know I don't have to, but the story dictates the structure. Just before you called, I read the whole thing in first person and it's right. It's right. Now if you ever see it published and it's in third person, you'll know I changed my mind.

Is the market healthy for young writers aspiring for their first publication?

I'd say for young writers who take the craft seriously, who aren't worried about stardom, the climate is still very good. Because editors are always looking for a good story, with really compelling characters and writers who use their own voice. Not Terry McMillan's voice, not Anne Tyler's voice, their own voice. Unfortunately, there are a lot of young writers who are scared, and they don't trust their own instincts. That's what they need to do. And they need to stop having these visions of grandeur, and just be honest and write a good story.

Chapter 51

Find Identity With Joyce Carol Oates

By Katie Struckel Brogan

As a little girl, novelist and short story writer Joyce Carol Oates used to tell stories and then illustrate them. "That's very typical of children to be extremely creative," she says. "Children are creative without any purpose other than to express their imaginations." Oates, the author of the novels *Blonde* and *Wonderland* and, most recently, of *Faithless: Tales of Transgression*, a collection of short stories, has come a long way from that little girl "without any purpose."

Oates has won the National Book Award, the PEN/Malamud Award for Achievement in the Short Story, and various other awards. Known best for her short stories, many of which have been anthologized in *The Pushcart Prize* and *The Best American Short Stories of the Century*, Oates still manages to bridge the natural gap that exists between novel and short story writing. That's a feat that she acknowledges is not an easy task.

"A novel is so much more difficult than a short story. If you run, it's almost like you can think through your whole short story as you ran. Say you ran forty minutes or an hour, you can think through the whole story and have it very finite and controlled. With a novel, it's almost impossible to do that."

But that's not to say that Oates doesn't enjoy writing novels. "A novel is much more challenging, and it's also very rewarding because you stay with it for so long, you get to love your characters. I feel very close, emotionally engaged with most of my main characters."

Two Different Spaces to Write In

Like many writers, Oates has a specific space in which she crafts her stories and novels; however, she is unusual in that she has two spaces to write in—a generalized space and a physical space. "I write on airplanes and I write in my head a lot. I do a lot of running and walking, and I compose in my imagination. So, that's kind of generalized space."

The physical space, on the other hand, the space that she literally writes in, is in a study "with a lot of glass" and a skylight.

While in her study, Oates writes first in longhand and then on a typewriter, a somewhat ancient tool given current technology standards. "I don't have a computer. I had a computer for two years and I got very tired of looking at that little screen for so many hours.

"I didn't really want to spend the rest of my life staring at a little electronic thing. I made a conscious decision just to get rid of it."

Given that one of her writing spaces is always with her, it's no wonder that Oates has emerged as the writer she is today.

Two Names to Write By

But there is one thing that some may not know about Oates— she also writes suspense, thrillers, and mystery novels as Rosamond Smith.

"I wanted to write under a pseudonym because I really wanted to have a separate identity for those novels—suspense, mystery, thrillers. They tend to be leaner and shorter than my other novels. They don't have as much sociological or political detail; they're more cinematic."

However, Oates never intended for readers to know that she was the person behind Rosamond Smith, and she still doesn't really know how the information actually got out.

"It's very hard to keep a secret today because of copyright and income tax, and certain things in our society make it difficult to have that kind of privacy that people had in the past."

Oates illustrates her point by citing that Jonathan Swift and Voltaire wrote under pseudonyms and they were never tracked down the way that she was. Still, she continues writing under the name Rosamond Smith and, in fact, has had a couple of books published that said, "Joyce Carol Oates writing as Rosamond Smith."

Oates says that writing under a pseudonym has helped her develop a separate identity, but that it has also allowed her the freedom to write "novels that were faster and leaner, more like movies." In fact, she has a unit in her writing workshop at Princeton University, where she has been a professor since 1978, in which she focuses on the process of writing under a pseudonym.

"I suggest to my students that they write under a pseudonym for one week. . . . That allows young men to write as women, and women as men. It allows them a lot of freedom they don't have ordinarily."

Oates believes that writing under a pseudonym has its good and bad points, especially in relation to her role as a female writer.

"I think it's still difficult for women to be taken very seriously as writers—that there's some resistance—even though things have changed wonderfully for the better. It's very hard to be an experimental woman writer."

She says that *Blonde* was an experimental novel and almost nobody talks about that, but had she been a male writer, it would be accepted as such.

"If I had been writing under a pseudonym, just initials, I might have a different reputation, but then I couldn't be myself either.

"I think everything in life has compensation. We may do one thing and then because of that there are advantages and also disadvantages."

Chapter 52

Finding Creativity With James Patterson

By Katie Struckel Brogan

Creativity comes in different ways to each author. For James Patterson, it comes from a folder. "I have a big folder of ideas and when it comes time for me to write a new book, I'll pull it out and go over everything that's in there."

Patterson, creator of the Alex Cross mystery/thriller series featuring *Along Came a Spider*, *Kiss the Girls*, *Jack & Jill*, *Cat & Mouse*, and *Pop Goes the Weasel*, says that he takes five or six ideas from the folder, puts them on paper, and then narrows them down to one or two. Then, "maybe write a page or two on each to begin to see if there's a story I like."

Finding the creativity to write the story has been a key element in Patterson's career. Patterson, the author of seven consecutive hardcover best-sellers, won the prestigious Edgar Award for his first novel, *The Thomas Berryman Number*. Recently, he has further developed his career by testing the literary waters with two dramatically different new books.

The first book, *1st to Die*, is Patterson's most recent mystery/suspense novel and the first in a new series surrounding four women known as the "Women's Murder Club."

"Two of the large challenges were one, writing in a woman's tone of voice, and two, . . . the notion of introducing four heroines, a villain, and a love interest while keeping the action moving very crisply," he says.

On the other end of the spectrum is *Suzanne's Diary for Nicholas*, a love story about families, love, and hope. The idea for this untraditional Patterson novel came from Patterson's own family.

"I have a three-year-old, Jack, but before I had Jack, I always thought it would be a cool thing for parents to do to sit down once a year and videotape themselves," he says. "Talk about what they believed, what they felt, what the joy in their lives was at that particular time, and how they felt about their kids."

Then, Patterson says the parents would give the tapes to their children when they are older, so that the children could gain an understanding of their parents and what they were like during a given time period.

Interestingly enough, after his son was born, Patterson's wife began keeping a factual diary about what Jack did on a given day, what he ate, what he said, and so on.

So Patterson decided to combine his initial idea and his wife's diary in book form. He approached his publisher, pitched the idea, and said, "I have to try and put this down on paper and see if it can be affecting for people." And that's what he did.

With two new books on the market, it seems very easy for a commercially successful author to become formulaic, but not Patterson. He says that he goes with the flow and just tries to write different kinds of books.

"What I'm doing and what I enjoy is writing books that a lot of people sit down [to read], can't put down, and at the end of the reading, they're glad that they picked it up in the first place."

Patterson says that it's only natural for readers to see certain patterns in an author's work. "There's nobody that I can think of where I couldn't sit there and go, 'I see patterns continuing in their stuff'— from John Updike to Stephen King, so some of that is just in there."

However, if Patterson does notice a pattern developing in his writing, like in his novel *Cat & Mouse*, he throws a big challenge into the book.

"In the middle of the book, I changed first-person narration and went from Alex [Cross] to another character. From the reader's point of view, it seemed that Alex was dead."

But throwing in such a big challenge is actually a challenge for Patterson. "I knew that that was a big challenge for me—to hold interest and to keep down disappointment."

Once Patterson has opened his file of ideas, found his creativity, and battled the threat of becoming formulaic, he writes and tells the story. For Patterson, the physical writing of the story is completed in five to eight drafts, all written in longhand.

"I have somebody who types for me, and once there's one draft, then I get back triple-spaced manuscripts and I write between the lines," he says.

Beyond the physical task of putting the words down on paper lies the storytelling process, which Patterson says can easily get "hairy."

"We all know how to tell stories . . . but if we try to tell a story and we worry about the first sentence, it gets a little hairy because sentences are hard, stories are easy."

Patterson believes that at times, sentences can get in the way of crafting and telling a good story. He says that he has read a lot of stories where the authors are good stylists, but very bad storytellers.

"I think sometimes we give people a lot of credit just because they're writing nice sentences even if it isn't adding up to much."

For Patterson, being a good storyteller is key to his career and the driving force behind the kind of books that he writes. "I enjoy building roller coasters for people to have a good time on," he says. "If you went on tour with me, you would meet a lot of happy people."

Chapter 53

A Journey With Anne Rivers Siddons

By Katie Struckel Brogan

Anne Rivers Siddons is the embodiment of Southern sophistication. She takes her love of the South and transforms it into best-selling novels that look at the South from a historical, social, feminist, and romantic perspective. Her novel, *Nora, Nora*, continues this keen tradition in a story set in the small-town South during 1961, where she explores a time of great cultural upheaval and transition.

Are there any specific writing devices you like to focus on when writing a new novel?
Always the place. The actual, physical land gets to be so important to me . . . what it looks like, what plants grow where, how light would look in different seasons. . . . The place is the thing that's such a strong force and is probably the first thing in every book that I try to make clear to people.

The way you present the Southern atmosphere in your novels seems very hypnotic, almost fairy tale-like.
Well, in a way, it is. You have to realize that the cities, Atlanta and cities like that, have long been just any generic city anywhere. But when you get out into the smaller towns, the suburbs, you see everything through a kind of shimmer that's made up half of heat haze and half of just that so little has changed. It's like all those years,

people and events dance a little "squim" in front of your eyes and you see everything through that.

Many reviewers categorize your work as "gothic." Why do you think they classify it that way?

I think what they mean is that there's a darkness to some of it. It's always been hard for me to pin down what they are talking about, but I think it's sort of a Southern thing. A kind of darkness of character rather than the plot because most of the things I write about could happen anywhere.

Most of your characters are highly developed. Is there any particular device you use to develop them?

I think that the ideas of some people are always suggested by people I know or know of, but quite quickly they become their own people. I am always curious as to how people get to where they are, and in order to understand my people, I have to go back and figure that out about them.

You've said that you write about women who are in transition and are unfinished.

Women who have, at some point in their lives, discovered that they needed to take a really sharp, new direction in their lives, are just more interesting to me. They're courageous women, they're brave, frightened, often badly hurt women, and of course, that's the stuff of drama in fiction. Women especially are almost, by definition, going to have to take a journey some times in their lives, usually around the middle of them, when they change from one thing to another. . . . That's the journey I'm interested in, that interior journey.

You took your own journey in your battle with depression. Is there any advice you can offer others on the same journey?

There's no moral payoff to going through something like that. Sometimes all you can do is put your head down and hang on. If you can do that, the person will almost always lift. . . . I found that I didn't necessarily need to write about the experience, but that the writing I did seemed to come from a different place. It went a little deeper, it was broader. I was a different writer when I came through it. I think in a way, [for] creative people, it's like a dust of fertilizer—if you can wait it out. It's just the act of surviving it.

Chapter 54

Updike: Still More to Say

By Kelly Nickell

Since the release of his first novel, *The Poorhouse Fair*, in 1959, John Updike has published fifty books, written a barrage of essays, reviews, and short stories for the likes of *The New Yorker* and *The New York Times*, and received two Pulitzers—not bad for someone who says he "only meant to be a magazine writer."

With such an astounding body of work, one can't help but wonder: Does it get easier to sit down with a blank page and turn whiteness to words of power and resilience?

"No, it never gets easier. But I've written enough now that I wonder if I'm not in danger of having said my say and of repeating myself," he says. "You can't be too worried about that if you're going to be a creative writer—a creative spirit—but yeah, you do, as they say in pitching, lose a little of your fastball."

From poetry and book reviews to short stories, novels, and even a play, there's not much the sixty-nine-year-old author hasn't tried his hand at over the years. And each form has presented its own distinct creative satisfaction.

"I must say, when I reread myself, it's the poetry I tend to look at. It's the most exciting to write, and it's over the quickest," he says. "But they all have their pleasures. The book reviews are perhaps the most lowly of the bunch, but even they have an occasional creative thrill. I like short stories. I'm sorry that I haven't been doing so many lately, but they're very satisfying."

Whatever the form, Updike's made an art of turning life's lost and tormented souls into literary everymen by not only honing their voices, but by anchoring their societal influences and surroundings so aptly with modern thought. And as Updike wrote in *The Handbook of Short Story Writing, Volume II*:

> No soul or locale is too humble to be the site of entertaining and instructive fiction. Indeed, all other things being equal, the rich and glamorous are less fertile ground than the poor and plain, and the dusty corners of the world more interesting than its glittering, already sufficiently publicized centers.

He proves this ideology with a four-book series that includes *Rabbit, Run*; *Rabbit Redux*; *Rabbit Is Rich*; and *Rabbit at Rest* (the latter two received Pulitzers and National Book Critics' Circle awards). Using protagonist Harry "Rabbit" Angstrom, Updike offers a running commentary on middle-class America. Written between 1960 and 1990, the books explore everything from racial tension and sexual freedom to drugs and middle age. And with Rabbit, Updike illustrates that even the flawed and ordinary can become legends given the proper landscape.

"We're past the age of heroes and hero kings," he says. "If we can't make up stories about ordinary people, who can we make them up about? But on the other hand, that's just a theory, and as in America, of course, there's a democracy that's especially tied to that assumption.

"Most of our lives are basically mundane and dull, and it's up to the writer to find ways to make them interesting. It's a rare life so dull that no crisis ever intrude."

Despite saying the Rabbit series was complete with 1990's *Rabbit at Rest*, Updike couldn't resist returning to the story line one last time in *Rabbit Remembered*, a novella appearing along with several short stories in 2000's *Licks of Love*.

"It was like coming home every ten years and paying a visit," he says. "It was easy because I was at home in that world, and it was a world that I had lived through as a child, and then it was a world that I had made."

The real world Updike created for himself didn't come without a few risks. After graduating from Harvard in 1954, he went on to join the staff of *The New Yorker*. Two years later, with no other job prospects, he left the magazine and moved with his family to Ipswich, Massachusetts, to pursue freelancing full time.

"I didn't quite know what I was getting into," he says. "It's possible I might have had to find employment. But I was willing to do journalism and *The New Yorker*'s kind of journalism—I was able to carry some of it with me when I came to New England. It was a gamble, but I was young and that was the time to make it . . . when I was young and full of what I had to say."

What felt like a gamble more than forty years ago now seems an admirable tale of bravery—one man's pursuit of his dream. But even Updike recognizes that in these changing times, his literary start is one not likely duplicated by today's young writers.

"My generation was maybe the last in which you could set up shop as a writer and hope to make a living at it," he says. "I began when print was a lot more glamorous medium than it is now. A beginning fiction writer—Kurt Vonnegut comes to mind—could support himself and a family by selling to magazines. I'm not sure you could do that now."

With the consolidation of major publishing houses and fewer magazines embracing short fiction, up-and-coming authors may find publication even more of a challenge.

"It's harder to make a splash nowadays," he says. "When I was beginning, we weren't getting rock star-type attention, but I think now the buzz seems softer. Publishers are looking for blockbusters—all the world loves a mega-seller. And, there's less readership for fiction that isn't purely escapist."

In 1999, Updike served as editor of *The Best American Short Stories of the Century,* a compilation of stories selected from the annual volumes of *The Best American Short Stories.* While the book honors a form in which—and about which—Updike has long written, he says there seems to be less of a readership for such work.

"That kind of audience is being trained at universities, but general readers want to sink into longer works, not the stop and start of short stories."

Keeping to his frenetic pace—though he says, "I don't mean to be too overproductive"—the author is currently at work on another novel. But, as he writes away the mornings and early afternoons in his Massachusetts home, even Updike is tempted by the same distractions that plague so many others.

"I work at home, upstairs, so it's unfortunately handy to any number of little chores that seem to have attached themselves to the writer's trade . . . answering mail or reading proofs."

Despite the fact that it may not get any easier to start each new book, Updike's long and diverse career now enables him to draw on a wealth of insight inherited from the various forms he's perfected throughout the years.

"Poetry makes you a little more sensitive to the word-by-word interest of prose, and book reviews make you a little more erudite in some regards. . . . Probably had I not written so many reviews, I wouldn't have tackled something like *Gertrude and Claudius,* which is a sort of bookish inspiration," he says.

"I'm generally sort of more cautious in the way I write now than I used to be, though. I write slower, try to think a little more."

And to the legions of struggling writers waiting in the wings to make a "splash" of their own, it's perseverance and dedication that Updike advises:

"It's never been easy. Books are still produced and sold, and it might as well be you. Try to develop steady work habits, maybe a more modest quota, but keep to it. Don't be thin-skinned or easily discouraged because it's an odds long proposition; all of the arts are.

"Many are called, few are chosen, but it might be you."

KELLY NICKELL is the features editor for *Writer's Digest* magazine.

Chapter 55

"Whatever Works, Works": Kurt Vonnegut on Flouting the Rules of Fiction

By Kelly Nickell

Kurt Vonnegut has witnessed the evolution of fiction—and in some ways, propelled it, perhaps. From the decreasing popularity of literary magazines and the increasing price of books, to his own evolving status as a "cult figure" and "popular author," Vonnegut has been a constant observer of—and a steady contributor to—the literary world for nearly half a century. And the oft-quoted literary giant remains a vocal commentator on the changing publishing industry.

A published author of everything from novels and short stories to essays and plays, Vonnegut says fiction is an art form unto its own. "All of fiction is a practical joke—making people care, laugh, cry, or be nauseated or whatever by something which absolutely is not going on at all. It's like saying, 'Hey, your pants are on fire.' "

And with his characteristic biting wit and humor, Vonnegut often combines social satire, autobiographical experiences, and bits of historical fact to create a new form of literary fiction, as in *Slaughterhouse-Five*, which became a number one *New York Times* best-seller when it was published in 1969.

Alternating between linear and circular structures and differing points of view, Vonnegut has spent much of his life testing literary boundaries. And it's become a Vonnegut axiom that writing rules apply only to the extent that they strengthen the effect of the final piece. "You want to involve the reader," he says. "For example,

Mother Night was a first-person confessional—the narrator ruined his life and he needn't have. But there's no way you can put together a manual about when to use first person and when to use third person.

"James Joyce broke all the rules. He's a writer like no other, and he got away with it. You have to get away with it. When I was teaching, if I gave a basic rule, it was 'whatever works, works.' I experiment, and my waste baskets are always very full of failed experiments," he says. "Can I get away with this? No. The trick is getting the reader to buy it."

It's fairly safe to assume that readers do indeed "buy it." Among his numerous honors and awards, Vonnegut has received a Guggenheim Fellowship and a National Institute of Arts and Letters grant, served as the vice president for the PEN American Center, and lectured in creative writing at Harvard University and the University of Iowa.

Remember Your Reader

"When I teach, what I'm teaching is sociability more than anything else because that's what most beginning writers, being young, aren't doing," Vonnegut says. "I try to teach how to be a good date on a blind date and to keep the reader in mind all the time. Young writers will dump everything they want to say on some poor reader, not caring whether the reader has a good time or not."

Vonnegut's early experience in journalism—he was editor of the college newspaper in 1941 while studying biochemistry at Cornell University, and later a police reporter with the Chicago City News Bureau in 1947—clearly has influenced his style. Staying true to the basic elements of journalism, Vonnegut says he tries to give readers as much information as he can, as soon as he can—a writing trait he's also tried to teach others.

"I hate a story where on page seventeen you find out, 'My

God, this person is blind.' Or that this happened one hundred years ago or one hundred years in the future. I tell students, 'Don't withhold information from your readers, for God's sake. Tell 'em everything that's going on, so in case you die, the reader can finish the story.' "

Another Vonnegut specialty is weaving bits of factual information into his fiction's lining, to draw in readers on an emotional level. "The facts are often useful to the reader, if they're historical events. You can expect the reader to be emotionally involved. And to make the reader believe and say, 'Oh Jesus, I guess that's right.' "

Vonnegut used both historical facts and his personal experience as a World War II prisoner of war in Dresden to create *Slaughterhouse-Five*. He says the latitude used when combining fact with fiction depends on how much the writer is willing to claim as fact: "The viewpoint character in *Slaughterhouse-Five* was Bill Pilgrim, and he was actually a real guy from Rochester," Vonnegut says. "He never should have been in the army, and he died in Dresden and was buried over there. He just simply allowed himself to starve to death. You can do that if you're a prisoner, you can just decide not eat. He decided he didn't understand any of it, and he was right, 'cause there was nothing to understand, so he died.

"I didn't have him die in the book, but had him come home and go to optometry school. So I didn't tell the truth about his life, but I never said it was his life in the first place."

"Write What You Write"

What's the best piece of advice Vonnegut's ever received? "Quit," he says. "It's such a relief." But he didn't. "No, I didn't quit— I'm still pooping along."

Yet there were times early in his career—when he was working as a freelancer, receiving little pay, and trying to raise a family—

that the notion of quitting wasn't unthinkable. Fortunately, the author chose to follow the advice of agent Kenneth Littauer.

"I was working as a freelancer—it's a harrowing way to make a living—and I would talk to Ken about how to make more money and he said, 'Don't trim your sails to every wind, just go ahead and write and see what happens. Don't look at the market. Don't look at the best-seller list to see what's selling.' That wouldn't help anyway. You have to write what you write, or get out of the business."

Vonnegut's battle with depression following publication of *Slaughterhouse-Five* almost did get him out of the business. He even vowed never to write again. And not until 1973 did he publish another book, *Breakfast of Champions*. Subtitled *Goodbye Blue Monday*, the book certainly didn't skirt the issue of depression, but Vonnegut says he's still not sure how the whole experience influenced his work: "There used to be a theory that tuberculosis helped to make someone a genius because they ran higher temperatures. It's now believed, and I guess it's a clinical fact, that most writers are troubled by depression. And I don't know whether it helps or not, but it sure doesn't feel good."

Whether it's his seemingly natural ability to create strong characters or his remarkable modesty ("I certainly didn't expect to succeed to the extent I have. I didn't expect to amount to much"), generations of writers continue to attempt to follow in Vonnegut's legendary footsteps. And to these many aspiring writers, Vonnegut offers some simple advice: "Don't worry about getting into the profession—write anyway to make your soul grow. That's what the practice of any art is. It isn't to make a living, it's to make your soul grow."

On the Changing Fiction Market

"Books don't matter as much as they used to, and they cost too much," Vonnegut says of the current state of publishing. "But publishers have to sell books to stay in business. Before television, publishers would admit that what paid the freight for everything else they published, all the serious fiction, poetry, and so forth, were cookbooks, garden books, and sex books. They had to publish those or they'd go out of business."

While many of his recent books, including *Bagombo Snuff Box*, *Fates Worse Than Death: An Autobiographical Collage of the 1980s*, and *God Bless You, Dr. Kevorkian* showcase the shorter form—most have been collections of essays, interviews, and speeches—Vonnegut says short stories seem to be losing their allure as fewer and fewer prominent magazines publish high-quality pieces.

"This country used to be crazy about short stories," he says. "New short stories would appear every week in the *Saturday Evening Post* or in *The New Yorker*, and every middle-class literate person would be talking about it: 'Hey, did you read that story by Salinger?' or 'Hey, did you read that story by Ray Bradbury?'

"But that no longer happens. No short story can cause a sensation anymore because there are too many other forms of entertainment. People can still go through old collections of short stories on their own and be absolutely wowed. But it's a private experience now."

Vonnegut in the Twenty-First Century

At what readers may hope is only a short break during a very prolific writing period, what is Vonnegut planning next? "Well, as I'm sitting around right now, I'm trying to think of what would be a neat idea. Most people do other things with their time. But writers, we'll sit around and think up neat stuff. Not something just anybody could do."

Index